# GMAT*

# SECRETS

## Study Guide
Your Key to Exam Success

GMAT Exam Review for the
**Graduate Management Admission Test**

*Navneet*

**Published by**

# Mometrix Media LLC
GMAT Exam Secrets Test Prep Team

*ISBN-10: 1609718518*
*ISBN-13: 978-1-60971-851-0*

# MOMETRIX
## TEST PREPARATION
*The World's Most Comprehensive Test Preparation Company*

Dear Friend,

Thank you for ordering Mometrix products!

We take very seriously that you are entrusting your test preparation needs to us and we have meticulously prepared these materials to ensure we are offering you the most concise, relevant study aid possible. There are many resources available for your exam and we sincerely appreciate you choosing ours to help you attain the highest score within your ability to achieve. With this purchase, you are helping to provide for the many families that make up our company and in turn we hope to help you attain the results you need in order to achieve your dreams.

You are about to experience an incredible transformation. Over the next few hours, days, weeks or months of studying, you will transition from your current level of preparedness to an understanding of the exam content that you never thought possible. You hold in your hands the information you most need to know in order to succeed on your exam. Regardless of whether this is your first time to take the exam or your fifth time, our goal is to give you exactly what you need to maximize your score so you can go where you most want to go and be what you most want to be.

In addition to the products you have ordered from us, we have included a few bonuses that will help in your preparation. Be on the lookout for a special bonus website included in each product that offers additional tips and insights. In response to the test anxiety many people experience, I have also developed a free report to help you overcome this obstacle that you can access by visiting: www.mometrix.com/testanxiety.

From my family to yours, I sincerely thank you and wish you the best on your exam and every journey life has in store for you.

If you have any questions or suggestions as to how we can improve our products or service, please contact us at 800-673-8175 or support@mometrix.com.

Sincerely,

Jay Willis
Vice President of Sales
Mometrix Media LLC

*P.S. - We would greatly appreciate you recommending our products to your friends and colleagues!*

Dear Future Exam Success Story:

Congratulations on your purchase of our study guide. Our goal in writing our study guide was to cover the content on the test, as well as provide insight into typical test taking mistakes and how to overcome them.

Standardized tests are a key component of being successful, which only increases the importance of doing well in the high-pressure high-stakes environment of test day. How well you do on this test will have a significant impact on your future- and we have the research and practical advice to help you execute on test day.

The product you're reading now is designed to exploit weaknesses in the test itself, and help you avoid the most common errors test takers frequently make.

## How to use this study guide

We don't want to waste your time. Our study guide is fast-paced and fluff-free. We suggest going through it a number of times, as repetition is an important part of learning new information and concepts.

First, read through the study guide completely to get a feel for the content and organization. Read the general success strategies first, and then proceed to the content sections. Each tip has been carefully selected for its effectiveness.

Second, read through the study guide again, and take notes in the margins and highlight those sections where you may have a particular weakness.

Finally, bring the manual with you on test day and study it before the exam begins.

## Your success is our success

We would be delighted to hear about your success. Send us an email and tell us your story. Thanks for your business and we wish you continued success-

Sincerely,

Mometrix Test Preparation Team

**Need more help? Check out our flashcards at:**
**http://MometrixFlashcards.com/GMAT**

# TABLE OF CONTENTS

# Secret Key #1 – Time is Your Greatest Enemy

To succeed on the GMAT, you must use your time wisely.  Most students do not finish at least one section.  The time limits are presented in the table below:

| SECTION | Total amount of time allotted | Number of questions | Time to answer each question |
|---------|------------------------------|---------------------|------------------------------|
| Analytical Writing I Issue Analysis | 30 min | 1 Topic | 30 min |
| Analytical Writing II Argument Analysis | 30 min | 1 Topic | 30 min |
| Rest Break (optional) | Up to 15 min | N/A | N/A |
| Quantitative | 75 min | 37 | 2 min, 1 sec |
| Rest Break (optional) | Up to 15 min | N/A | N/A |
| Verbal | 75 min | 41 | 1 min, 49 sec |

As you can see, the time constraints are brutal.  To succeed, you must ration your time properly.  If you run out of time on any passage, the questions that you do not answer will hurt your score far more than earlier questions that you spent extra time on and feel certain are correct.

## Success Strategy #1

## *Pace Yourself*

Wear a watch to the GMAT Test.  At the beginning of the test, check the time (or start a chronometer on your watch to count the minutes), and check the time after each passage or every few questions to make sure you are "on schedule."  An onscreen clock display will keep track of your remaining time, but it may be easier for you to monitor your pace based on how many minutes have been used, rather than how many minutes remain.

Remember that on the quantitative section you have slightly more than two minutes per question, and on the verbal section you have slightly more than 1 ¾ minutes per question, which makes it easy to keep track of your time.

If you find that you are falling behind time during the test, you must speed up. What makes this difficult is that you cannot return to skipped questions. After making your answer selection, you will be asked to confirm your answer. Once you confirm the answer, that is it. You cannot return to the question. Yet even though a rushed answer is more likely to be incorrect, it is better to miss a couple of questions by being rushed, than to completely miss later questions by not having enough time. It is better to end with more time than you need than to run out of time.

If you are forced to speed up, do it efficiently. Usually one or more answer choices can be eliminated without too much difficulty. Above all, don't panic. Don't speed up and just begin guessing at random choices. By pacing yourself, and continually monitoring your progress against the clock or your watch, you will always know exactly how far ahead or behind you are with your available time. If you find that you are two minutes behind on the quantitative section, don't skip one question without spending any time on it, just to catch back up. Spend perhaps 1 ½ minutes on the question and after four questions, you will have caught back up more gradually. Once you catch back up, you can continue working each problem at your normal pace.

Furthermore, don't dwell on the problems that you were rushed on. If a problem was taking up too much time and you made a hurried guess, it must have been difficult. The difficult questions are the ones you are most likely to miss anyway, so it isn't a big loss.

GMAT is a computer-adaptive test (CAT), which means that your questions are selected while taking the test, and are not predetermined beforehand. This allows each student to take a test that is custom tailored to their abilities. The first question in each section is of medium difficulty. If that question is answered correctly, the next question will be of increased difficulty. If it is answered incorrectly, an easier question will be provided next.

This means that most of the questions that you are asked will not be too easy or too hard for you, and should help you maintain a good pace throughout the test. Thus, because guessing increases your chances of getting a question incorrect, and if you are behind on your time and are forced to guess and guess wrong, then the questions will become easier, making it easier to speed up your pace and catch back up on your time. However, do not intentionally guess wrong in order to make the questions easier. Easier questions are factored into your final score calculations, so it does not help you.

Lastly, sometimes it is beneficial to slow down if you are constantly getting ahead of time. You are always more likely to catch a careless mistake by working more slowly than quickly, and among very high-scoring students (those who are likely to have lots of time left over), careless errors affect the score more than mastery of material.

## Estimation

For some quantitative problems, estimate. Calculation takes time, and you should avoid it whenever possible. You can usually eliminate three obviously wrong choices quite easily. For example, suppose a graph shows that an object has traveled 48 meters in 11 seconds, and you are asked to find its speed. You are given these choices:

  a. 250 m/s
  b. 42 m/s
  c. 4.4 m/s
  d. 1.2 m/s

You know that 48 divided by 11 will be a little over 4, so you can pick out C as the answer without ever doing the calculation.

## Scanning

For Verbal sections, don't waste time reading, enjoying, and completely understanding the passage. Simply scan the passage to get a rough idea of what it is about. You will return to the passage for each question, so there is no need to memorize it. Only spend as much time scanning as is necessary to get a vague impression of its overall subject content.

# Secret Key #2 – Guessing is not guesswork.

Most students do not understand the impact that proper guessing can have on their score. Unless you score above 600 or so, guessing will contribute about 60-80 points to your final score.

## Monkeys Take the GMAT

If you have five answer choices, then you have approximately a 20% chance of getting it correct. What most students don't realize is that to ensure a 20% chance, you have to guess randomly. If you put 20 monkeys in a room to take the GMAT, assuming they answered once per question and behaved themselves, on average they would get 20% of the questions correct. Put 20 college students in the room, and the average will be much lower among guessed questions. Why?

1. GMAT intentionally writes deceptive answer choices that "look" right. A student has no idea about a question, so picks the "best looking" answer, which is often wrong. The monkey has no idea what looks good and what doesn't, so will consistently be lucky about 20% of the time.
2. Students will eliminate answer choices from the guessing pool based on a hunch or intuition. Simple but correct answers often get excluded, leaving a 0% chance of being correct. The monkey has no clue, and often gets lucky with the best choice.

This is why the process of elimination endorsed by most test courses is flawed and detrimental to your performance: students don't guess, they make an ignorant stab in the dark that is usually worse than random.

# Success Strategy #2

Let me introduce one of the most valuable ideas of this course: the $5 challenge:

*You only mark your "best guess" if you are willing to bet $5 on it.*
*You only eliminate choices from guessing if you are willing to bet $5 on it.*

Why $5? Five dollars is an amount of money that is small yet not insignificant, and can really add up fast (20 questions could cost you $100). Likewise, each answer choice on one question of the GMAT will have a small impact on your overall score, but it can really add up to a lot of points in the end.

The process of elimination IS valuable. The following shows your chance of guessing it right:

| If you eliminate this many choices: | 0 | 1 | 2 | 3 | 4 |
|---|---|---|---|---|---|
| Chance of getting it correct | 20% | 25% | 33% | 50% | 100% |

If you accidentally eliminate the right answer or go on a hunch for an incorrect answer, your chances drop dramatically to 0%. By guessing among all the answer choices, you are GUARANTEED to have a shot at the right answer.

That's why the $5 test is so valuable: if you give up the advantage and safety of a pure guess, it had better be worth the risk.

What we still haven't covered is how to be sure that whatever guess you make is truly random. Here's the easiest way:

*Always pick the first answer choice among those remaining.*
Such a technique means that you have decided, **before you see a single test question**, exactly how you are going to guess. And since the order of choices tells you nothing about which one is correct, this guessing technique is perfectly random.

Let's try an example:

A student encounters the following problem on a Quantitative section:

What is the cosine of an angle in a right triangle that is 3 meters on the adjacent side, 5 meters on the hypotenuse, and 4 meters on the opposite side?

   A.  1
   B.  0.6
   C.  0.8
   D.  0.75
   E.  1.25

The student has a small idea about this question. He is pretty sure that cosine is opposite over hypotenuse, but he wouldn't bet $5 on it. He knows that cosine is "something" over hypotenuse, and since the hypotenuse is the largest number, he is willing to bet $5 on both choices A and E not being correct. So he is down to B, C, and D. At this point, he guesses B, since B is the first choice remaining.

The student is correct by choosing B, since cosine is adjacent over hypotenuse. He only eliminated those choices he was willing to bet money on, AND he did not let his stale memories (often things not known definitely will get mixed up in the exact opposite arrangement in one's head) about the formula for cosine influence his guess. He blindly chose the first remaining choice, and was rewarded with the fruits of a random guess.

This section is not meant to scare you away from making educated guesses or eliminating choices- you just need to define when a choice is worth eliminating. The $5 test, along with a pre-defined random guessing strategy, is the best way to make sure you reap all of the benefits of guessing.

# Specific Guessing Techniques

## *Slang*

Scientific sounding answers are better than slang ones. In the answer choices below, choice B is much less scientific and is incorrect, while choice A is a scientific analytical choice and is correct. Example:

A. To compare the outcomes of the two different kinds of treatment.

B. Because some subjects insisted on getting one or the other of the treatments.

## *Extreme Statements*

Avoid wild answers that throw out highly controversial ideas that are proclaimed as established fact. Choice A is a radical idea and is incorrect. Choice B is a calm rational statement. Notice that Choice B does not make a definitive, uncompromising stance, using a hedge word "if" to provide wiggle room. Example:

A. Bypass surgery should be discontinued completely.

B. Medication should be used instead of surgery for patients who have not had a heart attack if they suffer from mild chest pain and mild coronary artery blockage.

## *Similar Answer Choices*

When you have two answer choices that are direct opposites, one of them is usually the correct answer. Example:

A. Passage 1 described the author's reasoning about the influence of his childhood on his adult life.

B. Passage 2 described the author's reasoning about the influence of his childhood on his adult life.

These two answer choices are very similar and fall into the same family of answer choices. A family of answer choices is when two or three answer choices are very similar. Often two will be opposites and one may show an equality. Example:

A. Operation I or Operation II can be conducted at equal cost

B. Operation I would be less expensive than Operation II

C. Operation II would be less expensive than Operation I

D. Neither Operation I nor Operation II would be effective at preventing the spread of cancer.

Note how the first three choices are all related. They all ask about a cost comparison. Beware of immediately recognizing choices B and C as opposites and choosing one of those two. Choice A is in the same family of questions and should be considered as well. However, choice D is not in the same family of questions. It has nothing to do with cost and can be discounted in most cases.

## Hedging

When asked for a conclusion that may be drawn, look for critical "hedge" phrases, such as likely, may, can, will often, sometimes, etc, often, almost, mostly, usually, generally, rarely, sometimes. Question writers insert these hedge phrases to cover every possibility. Often an answer will be wrong simply because it leaves no room for exception. Avoid answer choices that have definitive words like "exactly," and "always".

## Summary of Guessing Techniques

1. Eliminate as many choices as you can by using the $5 test. Use the common guessing strategies to help in the elimination process, but only eliminate choices that pass the $5 test.

2. Among the remaining choices, only pick your "best guess" if it passes the $5 test. If you eliminated one or more choices with the $5 test in step 1, then guess randomly by picking the first remaining choice. Otherwise, pick the first answer choice.

# Secret Key #3 – Practice Smarter, Not Harder

Many students delay the test preparation process because they dread the awful amounts of practice time they think necessary to succeed on the test. We have refined an effective method that will take you only a fraction of the time.

There are a number of "obstacles" in your way on the GMAT. Among these are answering questions, finishing in time, and mastering test-taking strategies. All must be executed on the day of the test at peak performance, or your score will suffer. The GMAT is a mental marathon that has a large impact on your future.

Just like a marathon runner, it is important to work your way up to the full challenge. So first you just worry about questions, and then time, and finally strategy:

## Success Strategy #3

1. Find a good source for GMAT practice tests.
2. If you are willing to make a larger time investment, consider using more than one study guide. Often the different approaches of multiple authors will help you "get" difficult concepts.
3. Take a practice test with no time constraints, with all study helps "open book." Take your time with questions and focus on applying the strategies.
4. Take another test, this time with time constraints, with all guides "open book."
5. Take a final practice test without study material and with time limits.

If you have time to take more practice tests, just repeat step 5. By gradually exposing yourself to the full rigors of the test environment, you will condition your mind to the stress of test day and maximize your success.

# Secret Key #4 – Prepare, Don't Procrastinate

Let me state an obvious fact: if you take the GMAT three times, you will get three different scores. This is due to the way you feel on test day, the level of preparedness you have, and, despite GMAT's claims to the contrary, some tests WILL be easier for you than others, especially on the Verbal - Reading Comprehension passages.

Since your acceptance and qualification for scholarships will largely depend on your score, you should maximize your chances of success. On most standardized tests, that means you can take the test multiple times and only report your best score for an application for admission. The GMAT works differently.

Immediately after you have completed taking the GMAT, and while you are still in the testing room, you have the opportunity to cancel sending out your scores. Note: This is before you have ever even seen your unofficial Quantitative, Verbal and Total scores.

If you decide to cancel your scores, you will not be able to view your scores. If you do not decide to cancel your scores, then and there, the opportunity has passed. You will not be able to cancel them after that point. Therefore, prepare for this moment in advance. You know your abilities and can probably base a good guess as to what you might expect based on other standardized tests and percentile rankings that you have scored in the past.

By checking with your university of choice, you can determine what score you will need to be accepted or to receive a scholarship. This will give you an idea of how difficult it will be for you to meet your targeted goal. After you have taken the test, if you feel that you have met that goal, go ahead and accept your scores. You should only cancel your scores if you:

A. expect that you will definitely have the time, money, and desire to take the GMAT again

B. are confident that you did not meet the score that you needed to get into your school of choice

C. would not be satisfied at another school with a lower standard of admission

Note: Once a score is cancelled, it cannot be reinstated.

Even if you do decide to cancel your scores, your record will still bear evidence of your test. In the future when you take another test and submit those scores, that recent score, as well as the last two GMAT scores you have taken will also be submitted. If you had canceled a prior score, it will show that a score was canceled, though the score itself will not be revealed.

If you have taken the GMAT more than once, the most recent three scores will be submitted simultaneously to the schools of your choice. Most schools will simply average your three most recently reported sets of scores. Some schools have a different approach and will disregard any score that is significantly lower than another score, so that the low score will not unfairly distort the student's true ability. A few schools will even take your highest score in each section.

Note: If you plan to take the GMAT multiple times, check with your schools of choice and determine their policy on multiple GMAT scores. That may help in your decision to retake the test.

Also, remember that you can only take the GMAT once per calendar month. This applies even if you took the test and canceled the scores earlier that month.

## Success Strategy #4

Since repeatedly taking the GMAT usually offers only marginal improvements and older scores are still reported along with newer scores, make sure that you are adequately prepared the first time. Even though you can cancel your score, that cancellation will still be reported in the future.

Don't take the GMAT as a "practice" test. Feel free to take sample tests on your own, but when you go to take the GMAT, be prepared, be focused, and do your best the first time! Determine in advance whether or not you have the time and resources to take the GMAT multiple times. Don't make a hasty emotional decision after taking your test. You will feel drained after taking such an intense test and should think through your options ahead of time.

If all else fails, you can always take the test three additional times. Since only the last THREE scores are reported, by taking the test four total times, your first score report will be dropped from the report sent out to your selected schools of choice.

## Secret Key #5 - Test Yourself

Everyone knows that time is money. There is no need to spend too much of your time or too little of your time preparing for the test. You should only spend as much of your precious time preparing as is necessary for you to get the score you need.

Once you have taken a practice test under real conditions of time constraints, then you will know if you are ready for the test or not. If you have scored extremely high the first time that you take the practice test, then there is not much point in spending countless hours studying. You are already there.

Benchmark your abilities by retaking practice tests and seeing how much you have improved. Once you score high enough to guarantee success, then you are ready.

If you have scored well below where you need, then knuckle down and begin studying in earnest. Check your improvement regularly through the use of practice tests under real conditions. Above all, don't worry, panic, or give up. The key is perseverance!

Then, when you go to take the test, remain confident and remember how well you did on the practice tests. If you can score high enough on a practice test, then you can do the same on the real thing.

# Top 20 Test Taking Tips

1. Carefully follow all the test registration procedures
2. Know the test directions, duration, topics, question types, how many questions
3. Setup a flexible study schedule at least 3-4 weeks before test day
4. Study during the time of day you are most alert, relaxed, and stress free
5. Maximize your learning style; visual learner use visual study aids, auditory learner use auditory study aids
6. Focus on your weakest knowledge base
7. Find a study partner to review with and help clarify questions
8. Practice, practice, practice
9. Get a good night's sleep; don't try to cram the night before the test
10. Eat a well balanced meal
11. Know the exact physical location of the testing site; drive the route to the site prior to test day
12. Bring a set of ear plugs; the testing center could be noisy
13. Wear comfortable, loose fitting, layered clothing to the testing center; prepare for it to be either cold or hot during the test
14. Bring at least 2 current forms of ID to the testing center
15. Arrive to the test early; be prepared to wait and be patient
16. Eliminate the obviously wrong answer choices, then guess the first remaining choice
17. Pace yourself; don't rush, but keep working and move on if you get stuck
18. Maintain a positive attitude even if the test is going poorly
19. Keep your first answer unless you are positive it is wrong
20. Check your work, don't make a careless mistake

# General Strategies

The most important thing you can do is to ignore your fears and jump into the test immediately. Do not be overwhelmed by any strange-sounding terms. You have to jump into the test like jumping into a pool: all at once is the easiest way.

## Make Predictions

As you read and understand the question, try to guess what the answer will be. Remember that several of the answer choices are wrong, and once you begin reading them, your mind will immediately become cluttered with answer choices designed to throw you off. Your mind is typically the most focused immediately after you have read the question and digested its contents. If you can, try to predict what the correct answer will be. You may be surprised at what you can predict.

Quickly scan the choices and see if your prediction is in the listed answer choices. If it is, then you can be quite confident that you have the right answer. It still won't hurt to check the other answer choices, but most of the time, you've got it!

## Answer the Question

It may seem obvious to only pick answer choices that answer the question, but the test writers can create some excellent answer choices that are wrong. Don't pick an answer just because it sounds right, or you believe it to be true. It MUST answer the question. Once you've made your selection, always go back and check it against the question and make sure that you didn't misread the question, and the answer choice does answer the question posed.

## Benchmark

After you read the first answer choice, decide if you think it sounds correct or not. If it doesn't, move on to the next answer choice. If it does, mentally mark that answer choice.

This doesn't mean that you've definitely selected it as your answer choice, it just means that it's the best you've seen thus far. Go ahead and read the next choice. If the next choice is worse than the one you've already selected, keep going to the next answer choice. If the next choice is better than the choice you've already selected, mentally mark the new answer choice as your best guess.

The first answer choice that you select becomes your standard. Every other answer choice must be benchmarked against that standard. That choice is correct until proven otherwise by another answer choice beating it out. Once you've decided that no other answer choice seems as good, do one final check to ensure that your answer choice answers the question posed.

## Valid Information

Don't discount any of the information provided in the question. Every piece of information may be necessary to determine the correct answer. None of the information in the question is there to throw you off (while the answer choices will certainly have information to throw you off). If two seemingly unrelated topics are discussed, don't ignore either. You can be confident there is a relationship, or it wouldn't be included in the question, and you are probably going to have to determine what is that relationship to find the answer.

## Avoid "Fact Traps"

Don't get distracted by a choice that is factually true. Your search is for the answer that answers the question. Stay focused and don't fall for an answer that is true but incorrect. Always go back to the question and make sure you're choosing an answer that actually answers the question and is not just a true statement. An answer can be factually correct, but it MUST answer the question asked. Additionally, two answers can both be seemingly correct, so be sure to read all of the answer choices, and make sure that you get the one that BEST answers the question.

## Milk the Question

Some of the questions may throw you completely off. They might deal with a subject you have not been exposed to, or one that you haven't reviewed in years. While your lack of knowledge about the subject will be a hindrance, the question itself can give you many clues that will help you find the correct answer. Read the question carefully and look for clues. Watch particularly for adjectives and nouns describing difficult terms or words that you don't recognize. Regardless of if you completely understand a word or not, replacing it with a synonym either provided or one you more familiar with may help you to understand what the questions are asking. Rather than wracking your mind about specific detailed information concerning a difficult term or word, try to use mental substitutes that are easier to understand.

## The Trap of Familiarity

Don't just choose a word because you recognize it. On difficult questions, you may not recognize a number of words in the answer choices. The test writers don't put "make-believe" words on the test; so don't think that just because you only recognize all the words in one answer choice means that answer choice must be correct. If you only recognize words in one answer choice, then focus on that one. Is it correct? Try your best to determine if it is correct. If it is, that is great, but if it doesn't, eliminate it. Each word and answer choice you eliminate increases your chances of getting the question correct, even if you then have to guess among the unfamiliar choices.

## Eliminate Answers

Eliminate choices as soon as you realize they are wrong. But be careful! Make sure you consider all of the possible answer choices. Just because one appears right, doesn't mean that the next one won't be even better! The test writers will usually put more than one good answer choice for every question, so read all of them. Don't worry if you are stuck between two that seem right. By getting down to just two remaining possible choices, your odds are now 50/50. Rather than wasting too much time, play the odds. You are guessing, but guessing wisely, because you've been able to knock out some of the answer choices that you know are wrong. If you are eliminating choices and realize that the last answer choice you are left with is also obviously wrong, don't panic. Start over and consider each choice again. There may easily be something that you missed the first time and will realize on the second pass.

## Tough Questions

If you are stumped on a problem or it appears too hard or too difficult, don't waste time. Move on! Remember though, if you can quickly check for obviously incorrect answer choices, your chances of guessing correctly are greatly improved. Before you completely give up, at least try to knock out a couple of possible answers. Eliminate what you can and then guess at the remaining answer choices before moving on.

## Brainstorm

If you get stuck on a difficult question, spend a few seconds quickly brainstorming. Run through the complete list of possible answer choices. Look at each choice and ask yourself, "Could this answer the question satisfactorily?" Go through each answer choice and consider it independently of the other. By systematically going through all possibilities, you may find something that you would otherwise overlook. Remember that when you get stuck, it's important to try to keep moving.

## Read Carefully

Understand the problem. Read the question and answer choices carefully. Don't miss the question because you misread the terms. You have plenty of time to read each question thoroughly and make sure you understand what is being asked. Yet a happy medium must be attained, so don't waste too much time. You must read carefully, but efficiently.

## Face Value

When in doubt, use common sense. Always accept the situation in the problem at face value. Don't read too much into it. These problems will not require you to make huge leaps of logic. The test writers aren't trying to throw you off with a cheap trick. If you have to go beyond creativity and make a leap of logic in order to have an answer choice answer the question, then you should look at the other answer choices. Don't overcomplicate the problem by creating theoretical relationships or explanations that will warp time or space. These are normal problems rooted in reality. It's just that the applicable relationship or explanation may not be readily apparent and you have to figure things out. Use your common sense to interpret anything that isn't clear.

## Prefixes

If you're having trouble with a word in the question or answer choices, try dissecting it. Take advantage of every clue that the word might include. Prefixes and suffixes can be a huge help. Usually they allow you to determine a basic meaning. Pre- means before, post- means after, pro- is positive, de- is negative. From these prefixes and suffixes, you can get an idea of the general meaning of the word and try to put it into context. Beware though of any traps. Just because con is the opposite of pro, doesn't necessarily mean congress is the opposite of progress!

## Hedge Phrases

Watch out for critical "hedge" phrases, such as likely, may, can, will often, sometimes, often, almost, mostly, usually, generally, rarely, sometimes. Question writers insert these hedge phrases to cover every possibility. Often an answer choice will be wrong simply because it leaves no room for exception. Avoid answer choices that have definitive words like "exactly," and "always".

## Switchback Words

Stay alert for "switchbacks". These are the words and phrases frequently used to alert you to shifts in thought. The most common switchback word is "but". Others include although, however, nevertheless, on the other hand, even though, while, in spite of, despite, regardless of.

## New Information

Correct answer choices will rarely have completely new information included. Answer choices typically are straightforward reflections of the material asked about and will directly relate to the question. If a new piece of information is included in an answer choice that doesn't even seem to relate to the topic being asked about, then that answer choice is likely incorrect. All of the information needed to answer the question is usually provided for you, and so you should not have to make guesses that are unsupported or choose answer choices that require unknown information that cannot be reasoned on its own.

## Time Management

On technical questions, don't get lost on the technical terms. Don't spend too much time on any one question. If you don't know what a term means, then since you don't have a dictionary, odds are you aren't going to get much further. You should immediately recognize terms as whether or not you know them. If you don't, work with the other clues that you have, the other answer choices and terms provided, but don't waste too much time trying to figure out a difficult term.

## Contextual Clues

Look for contextual clues. An answer can be right but not correct. The contextual clues will help you find the answer that is most right and is correct. Understand the context in which a phrase or statement is made. This will help you make important distinctions.

## Don't Panic

Panicking will not answer any questions for you. Therefore, it isn't helpful. When you first see the question, if your mind goes blank, take a deep breath. Force yourself to mechanically go through the steps of solving the problem and using the strategies you've learned.

## Pace Yourself

Don't get clock fever. It's easy to be overwhelmed when you're looking at a page full of questions, your mind is full of random thoughts and feeling confused, and the clock is ticking down faster than you would like. Calm down and maintain the pace that you have set for yourself. As long as you are on track by monitoring your pace, you are guaranteed to have enough time for yourself. When you get to the last few minutes of the test, it may seem like you won't have enough time left, but if you only have as many questions as you should have left at that point, then you're right on track!

## Answer Selection

The best way to pick an answer choice is to eliminate all of those that are wrong, until only one is left and confirm that is the correct answer. Sometimes though, an answer choice may immediately look right. Be careful! Take a second to make sure that the other choices are not equally obvious. Don't make a hasty mistake. There are only two times that you should stop before checking other answers. First is when you are positive that the answer choice you have selected is correct. Second is when time is almost out and you have to make a quick guess!

## Check Your Work

Since you will probably not know every term listed and the answer to every question, it is important that you get credit for the ones that you do know. Don't miss any questions through careless mistakes. If at all possible, try to take a second to look back over your answer selection and make sure you've selected the correct answer choice and haven't made a costly careless mistake (such as marking an answer choice that you didn't mean to mark). This quick double check should more than pay for itself in caught mistakes for the time it costs.

## Beware of Directly Quoted Answers

Sometimes an answer choice will repeat word for word a portion of the question or reference section. However, beware of such exact duplication; it may be a trap! More than likely, the correct choice will paraphrase or summarize a point, rather than being exactly the same wording.

## Slang

Scientific sounding answers are better than slang ones. An answer choice that begins "To compare the outcomes…" is much more likely to be correct than one that begins "Because some people insisted…"

## Extreme Statements

Avoid wild answers that throw out highly controversial ideas that are proclaimed as established fact. An answer choice that states the "process should be used in certain situations, if…" is much more likely to be correct than one that states the "process should be discontinued completely." The first is a calm rational statement and doesn't even make a definitive, uncompromising stance, using a hedge word "if" to provide wiggle room, whereas the second choice is a radical idea and far more extreme.

## Answer Choice Families

When you have two or more answer choices that are direct opposites or parallels, one of them is usually the correct answer. For instance, if one answer choice states "x increases" and another answer choice states "x decreases" or "y increases," then those two or three answer choices are very similar in construction and fall into the same family of answer choices. A family of answer choices is when two or three answer choices are very similar in construction, and yet often have a directly opposite meaning. Usually the correct answer choice will be in that family of answer choices. The "odd man out" or answer choice that doesn't seem to fit the parallel construction of the other answer choices is more likely to be incorrect.

# GMAT Analytical Writing Test

Your GMAT exam will begin with the Analytical Writing section. Many students like getting this section out of the way first while others would rather warm up on some easier Quantitative or Verbal Ability questions. In either case, your perceived performance on this section will set the tone for the rest of the exam. This is why it is important to be prepared. This is easier said than done: despite all of the anxiety surrounding the Quantitative Ability section of the GMAT, it may be that the section of the exam for which candidates are least prepared is the Analytical Writing section. One reason for this is that the Analytical Writing section is more a measure of skill than a measure of knowledge and requires a different kind of preparation. Moreover, many students have a general dislike of writing because they associate it with hard labor. Given the choice between composing an essay and answering a series of multiple-choice questions, most students will choose the latter.

Still, the most common reason why students arrive at the testing center unprepared for the Analytical Writing section of the exam is because they simply do not know how to prepare. On the Verbal and Quantitative Ability sections, studying is straightforward: simply learn the types of questions and the content to be covered. This process may not always be easy, but at least it is fairly obvious. For many college students, however, preparing to sit down and write a couple of extended essays can be daunting. Moreover, students whose undergraduate courses did not require a great deal of writing may not have performed such a task since taking a freshman composition course. The basic structure of a persuasive or analytical essay may be long forgotten. Students may get discouraged, feeling that it is impossible to learn to write in a short period of time.

Fortunately, this despair is unnecessary. Even though a crash course in Analytical Writing may not turn you into a best-selling author, it can teach you the fundamentals of composition that can lead you to achieve an excellent score on the GMAT. Preparing for the

Analytical Writing section should not be any more difficult than preparing for the other sections of the GMAT. In fact, it is not much different. To get you ready to excel on the Analytical Writing section, we will take a close look at the two types of essays required and discuss ways to approach each of them. We will then create a basic plan for composing your responses, so that when you enter the testing facility you will have already done most of the hard work.

Before we begin focusing on the essays themselves, we will take a look at the structure of the Analytical Writing section. It is divided into two parts: the Analysis of an Issue essay and the Analysis of an Argument essay. While the Argument essay will require you to critique the reasoning and supporting evidence of a given argument, the Issue essay will require you to present your perspective on an issue effectively. Each of these essays must be completed within 30 minutes. You will not be given a choice of prompt on either of the essays.

Analytical Writing responses are graded according to a simple protocol. Each essay is examined by two readers who give it a holistic score on a scale of zero to six. Some essays will be given one score by a human reader and one score by an automated essay-scoring engine. The automated scoring engine is a computer program that evaluates responses according to more than fifty structural and linguistic features, including syntactic variety, topical analysis, and organization. If the two scores issued for each essay are within one point of each other, they are averaged and finalized. If the difference between the two scores is greater than one point, a third reader is called in to arbitrate. Your final Analytical Writing score will be the average of your scores on the Issue and the Argument essays.

When we say that the scoring of the Analytical Writing responses is "holistic," we mean that it is based on a general view of the responses rather than on any specific or individual criteria. This means that occasional, minor spelling and grammar mistakes will not have an effect on your grade. Instead, your essay is judged on the quality of your thoughts and expression. We can get a specific idea of what the GMAT readers are looking for by examining the description of a superior essay. It is stated that a top-scoring Analysis of an

Issue essay will develop a clear position with persuasive reasons and appropriate examples, convey ideas clearly and articulately, maintain focus on the thesis without introducing irrelevant or extraneous information, and demonstrate command of standard written English, especially in the areas of grammar, sentence structure, and diction. As for the Analysis of an Argument essay, a superior response will do the following: identify the most important features of the given argument, analyze these features thoughtfully, support its critique with insightful reasons and appropriate examples, develop ideas in a lucid and organized manner, connect ideas logically, and demonstrate the same command of standard written English required in the Issue essay. As you can see, the GMAT readers will be looking at a host of factors in judging your essays.

Now for some good news: all of the possible prompts used on the GMAT are listed on the GMAT website. You should spend at least a few hours looking over these prompts, taking a position and imagining a few basic arguments. Look up any words that you do not already know. There are probably too many potential prompts for it to be practical to examine each one in depth, but you can at least familiarize yourself with the question format and the kinds of topics that are likely to appear on the exam. Also, acquainting yourself with the essay prompts will stimulate your brain to start thinking along those lines in the weeks prior to the exam. You may see a newspaper or magazine article that pertains to one of the potential prompts, or you may just find yourself mulling over one of these issues. By giving your brain a chance to process these potential topics, you may improve your chances of producing a thoughtful, well-rounded essay. At the very least, when you finally sit down to take the GMAT, you should have no excuse for being surprised.

## Issue Analysis

According to the GMAT, the Analysis of an Issue task is designed to measure your ability to present a perspective on an issue effectively and persuasively. In other words, this essay is all about expressing your opinion. The prompt will introduce a subjective statement with which you will either agree or disagree. You will then use the time (30 minutes) and space (as much as you can fill) allotted to describe the reasons for your opinion.

At the beginning of the Analysis of an Issue section, the following directions will be posted: This writing task is designed to test your ability to present a position on an issue effectively and persuasively. Your task is to analyze the issue presented, considering various perspectives, and to develop your own position on the issue. In scoring your issue essay, readers will consider how effectively you: recognize and deal with the complexities and implications of the issue; organize, develop, and express your ideas; support your ideas with reasons and examples; control the elements of standard written English.

These directions will be the same for every version of the exam; go ahead and read them a few times, so that you will not need to waste any time during your exam.

Below the directions, there will be a list of basic rules and guidelines for the Issue essay: You are given 30 minutes to write the response. You must not write on any other subject than the one expressed in the prompt. You are allowed to accept, reject, or qualify the statement made by the prompt, though you must be sure to support whatever position you take with reasons and examples from your experience, observation, reading, and/or academic studies. You should take a few minutes to plan your response before typing. You should leave some time at the end of the period to review your response and make any necessary revisions. You can access the directions and guidelines at any time by pressing the HELP button.

Again, these rules and guidelines will be essentially the same for every version of the exam. If you are confident that you understand them as they are written here, there is no need to review them when you sit down to take the GMAT.

Finally, beneath all of this administrative fuss will be the essay prompt. Remember that you will not get a choice of prompt on either of the GMAT exams. The prompt for the Analysis of an Issue essay will consist of a statement of opinion, usually enclosed by quotation marks, and a brief directive. For instance, a hypothetical prompt might begin with the following statement:

"Laws should exist solely to keep people from hurting one another; there should not be laws to prevent people from hurting themselves." Do you agree with this statement? Or do you think that it is appropriate to have laws that prevent individuals from doing themselves harm? Your essay will require you to take a position on the subject and support it with personal or professional experiences, observations, or reading.

The prompts on the GMAT are selected at random, so there is no way of knowing which specific prompt you will receive. As mentioned above, a list of possible prompts can be found at the GMAT website. On the Analysis of an Issue essay, you can be assured that the prompt will be from one of the following topics: advertising and marketing; the influence of technology on business; labor and employment issues; cultural and social values; business organization; productivity, efficiency, and teamwork; government and the legal system; business ethics; and globalization.

## Brainstorm

Spend the first three to five minutes brainstorming out ideas. Write down any ideas you might have on the issue, regardless of which side it supports. Remember that you are under no obligation to argue the point of view with which you personally agree. In fact, if you feel that you can make a better case for a point of view with which you disagree, you should absolutely make that case. The GMAT readers will not be judging you on whether or not your argument is sincere, so you should always pick the position you feel you can best defend. Put the ideas that support one side in one grouping and then further down on your page group the ideas that support the other side. You can use either the scratch paper provided or the word processor to quickly jot down your thoughts and ideas. The word processor is highly recommended though, particularly if you are a fast typist.

## Strength through diversity

First, you should compose a brief summary of the opposing views using as much of the language of the prompt as possible. Summarizing the view expressed by the prompt should be easy enough: There should not be laws to prevent people from harming themselves. To summarize the opposing position, simply reverse this argument: There should be laws to prevent people from harming themselves. Defining both sides of the issue should be your habitual first step. Even if you have already decided which position on the issue you are going to take, it is still helpful to articulate and consider the opposing view.

Indeed, in order to write a conclusive argument for your side, you will have to acknowledge all of the possible arguments against your position and be able to refute these arguments. During this preliminary brainstorming session, make a few brief notes that will remind you of the important arguments and counterarguments on each side. For instance, if you are going to take the position supported by the prompt, you might note that the United States was founded on personal liberty and that the government should not have the right to meddle in the private affairs of individuals. You might also allude to one of the many episodes in history in which a repressive government has restricted the rights of individuals to pursue their own happiness. You might even elaborate on an incident from your own life in which you resented someone for meddling in your private affairs.

For each of these arguments on your side, you will have to acknowledge the corresponding counterargument. For instance, although the United States tries to promote personal liberty, it takes a careful look at how the actions of the individual affect society at large. When someone decides to take illegal drugs, they may believe that their decision does not affect anyone else, but it actually does. They may be contributing to other illegal activities that are funded by drug money, they may be damaging their own ability to be a parent, or they may have to receive medical care that is not only expensive but takes time away from the treatment of other people's medical conditions. For the example of repressive governments, you might note that most governments throughout history have found it necessary to regulate the personal lives of citizens, to some extent, for the well-being of the country as a whole.

The best papers will contain diversity of examples and reasoning. As you brainstorm consider different perspectives. Not only are there two sides to every issue, but there are also countless perspectives that can be considered. On any issue, different groups are impacted, with many reaching the same conclusion or position, but through vastly different paths. Try to "see" the issue through as many different eyes as you can. Look at it from every angle and from every vantage point. The more diverse the reasoning used, the more balanced the paper will become and the better the score.

Example:

> The issue of free trade is not just two sided. It impacts politicians, domestic (US) manufacturers, foreign manufacturers, the US economy, the world economy, strategic alliances, retailers, wholesalers, consumers, unions, workers, and the exchange of more than just goods, but also of ideas, beliefs, and cultures. The more of these angles that you can approach the issue from, the more solid your reasoning and the stronger your position.

Furthermore, don't just use information as to how the issue impacts other people. Draw liberally from your own experience and your own observations. Explain a personal experience that you have had and your own emotions from that moment. Anything that you've seen in your community or observed in society can be expanded upon to further round out your position on the issue.

**Pick a side**

Once you have finished with your creative flow, stop and review it. Which side were you able to come up with more supporting information? It's easy to be biased and to have a side that you believe in and support with your own personal opinion. While enthusiasm for a viewpoint is important, of much more importance is the ability to have a thorough and comprehensive coverage of an issue and the position that you choose. This is not about your personal convictions. Each idea that you can write about and expand upon is a defensive tool. Therefore, pick a side on the issue to defend based upon what you have the most defensive tools to work with. However, you may find that this coincides nicely with what you do believe, since you probably know more information that supports what you believe that detracts from what you believe.

## Weed the garden

Every garden of ideas gets weeds in it. The ideas that you brainstormed over are going to be random pieces of information of mixed value. Go through it methodically and pick out the ones that are the best. The best ideas are strong arguments that it will be easy to write a few sentences or a paragraph about.

## Create a logical flow

Now that you know which side you are going to support and what are the main ideas that you want to focus upon, organize them. You don't want to have a paper that rambles back and forth. Make sure that you align your ideas in a sequence that makes sense and has a sense of flow, so that the reader will go smoothly from one idea to the next in a logical path. The best way to do this is to use your notes and begin to shape them into a rough outline. The outline is your map for writing the essay: it reminds you of where you are trying to go, as well as where you need to make stops along the way. Too often, students will assume that they have a firm grasp over the topic and will just begin writing without creating a basic outline. They may then get distracted by something in the testing center or become overly focused on one aspect of their argument, and they end up forgetting an important part of their response. By composing an outline, you can save yourself the trouble of keeping your entire argument in your head as you write.

The structure of your outline, and hence, of your essay, should be the same no matter what topic or position you are discussing. In the first paragraph, you will lay out the issue to be discussed and indicate your position. In the second, third, and fourth paragraphs, you will give reasons and examples in support of your position. Finally, in the fifth paragraph, you will summarize and generalize your position. There is nothing profound or mysterious about this format: it is the essay structure that has been drilled into your head since middle school. Do not worry about lack of originality; GMAT readers spend five minutes at the most on each essay, and they frankly do not have time to appreciate essays that use unconventional organization. Instead, they look for essays that are easy to read (even if a little dull!) and that are original in their content rather than their structure. Besides, your job becomes much easier when you have a simple template to use no matter what topic you are discussing.

**Start your engines**

Let us take a closer look at the parts of your Issue essay. As mentioned above, in the first paragraph you need to begin by articulating the topic under consideration: in other words, outline the basic issue first without declaring your own position. You do not want to simply duplicate the language used in the prompt. For instance, using the example topic we have been working with, an effective way to introduce the issue might be, "There is a longstanding debate over whether or not laws should extend to the private behavior of citizens." Note how this sentence, bland though it may be, outlines the issue at hand without indicating which side you will be taking. It is important for you to be able to express the topic in an impartial manner so that the reader can become oriented with the discussion. If you simply launch into an impassioned argument, the reader may feel alienated or confused.

After your basic statement of the topic issue, your first paragraph needs to include a summary of your own position. This summary must be clear and concise: there should be no confusion over where you stand after this first paragraph. Continuing with our example, after introducing the topic, the author might write, "It is my belief that since individual behavior, no matter how private, will inevitably affect other people, laws should be extended to prevent self-inflicted damage to individuals and their property." After such a statement, there is no doubt where the author stands: he or she is in favor of legislation forbidding individuals from harming themselves. Also, note the use of the personal pronouns as in, "It is my belief." On the Issue essay, you should feel free to claim your opinions (after all, this essay is all about presenting your perspective). This is preferable to ambiguous expressions like "one believes." The whole point of this first paragraph is to show that you know what you are talking about and to show exactly where you stand on the issue.

Once your position has been clearly articulated, you can move on to supporting it in the subsequent paragraphs. This is when your list of brainstormed ideas will come in handy. Pare the list down to the best three to five ideas or examples, and then rank them from best to worst. You always want to open with your strongest point. In our example, the author's strongest point is probably that self-destructive behavior is actually damaging to other people as well. Therefore, the author will want to make this argument in the second paragraph. When you are establishing the reasons for your position, try to be as specific as possible. This does not mean you need to worry about providing direct quotes or exact numbers, but that you should be able to cite specific instances and trends that support your case.

Also, as you begin to expand your argument in the supporting paragraphs, keep in mind your list of potential counterarguments. The GMAT reader will want you to acknowledge and rebut any obvious arguments that run counter to your own position. If you ignore clear contradictions, the reader will penalize you. For instance, the author of our example essay would need to admit that some people argue that drug abuse, failure to wear a seatbelt, and even suicide are private decisions that only affect the individuals involved. The author might argue that these people ignore the toll that such self-destructive behavior takes on the economy, the community, and the world as a whole. The author might give a couple of quick examples to show how seemingly individual behavior affects other people. By describing the ways in which this counterargument is unreasonable, the author will strengthen his or her own position.

In all of the following support paragraphs, the guidelines are the same. Try to be as specific as possible and be sure to address any legitimate counterarguments to your position. Make sure that all of your examples make sense and have a clear application to the problem being discussed. If you are going to use examples from your personal life, make sure that you can focus on the parts that are relevant to your argument rather than getting bogged down in setting an elaborate scene. As a general rule, if a story or anecdote is going to take more than three sentences to deliver, it is probably not worth the trouble. You want your supporting paragraphs to be brimming with ideas and evidence, not meandering or digressive.

As you are making your argument in the supporting paragraphs, do not be afraid to use clichéd transitional phrases, such as "next," "another," and "finally." Advanced composition classes will try to move students beyond such obvious structural markers, but on the GMAT you can feel free to dust off some of these hackneyed expressions in the interest of clarity. As we have already discussed, the readers of your essay will not be hoping for unorthodox structure: they want a solid essay with good ideas and an easy-to-read format. There is one exception: it is perhaps too formulaic to begin each of your supporting paragraphs with "first," "second," etc. Other than that, go ahead and make your transitions obvious, so that the reader will spend his or her time focusing on the strength of your argument rather than the subtlety of your style.

After you have given three or four specific and detailed arguments or examples in support of your position, it is time to wrap up your essay in a concluding paragraph. Here again, it is acceptable to announce your finale with a phrase like "in conclusion" or "as you can see." (Of course, if you use the latter expression, you had better be confident that your argument was clear!). Then, give a one-sentence recapitulation of your argument. Too often, students take up the entire conclusion giving a complete review of the essay to that point. This is unnecessary: provided you have been clear so far, your reader is only going to be bored by an abridged version of what he or she has already read.

Instead, you should use the concluding paragraph first to summarize and then to generalize your argument. In other words, expand the scope of your argument to take notice of any larger issues or themes. Returning to our hypothetical essay, the author might use the conclusion paragraph to assert that since private self-destructive behavior really does affect other people, individuals should try to be more conscious of the ways in which they mistreat themselves. Note that this kind of generalization can be overdone: it would probably be a bit much, for instance, for the author to declare that his argument proves that all living creatures are one. The GMAT readers do not want you to use your conclusion to advance your vision of the cosmos, but rather to show an awareness of the way that your topic connects with other issues. If you can suggest ways in which your argument resonates beyond the parameters of your essay, then that will be enough.

Pace yourself. Don't spend too much time on any one of the ideas that you are expanding upon. You want to have time for all of them. Make sure you watch your time. If you have twenty minutes to write out your ideas and you have ten ideas, then you can only use two minutes per idea. It can be a daunting task to cram a lot of information down in words in a short amount of time, but if you pace yourself, you can get through it all. If you find that you are falling behind, speed up. Move through each idea more quickly, spending less time to expand upon the idea in order to catch back up.

## Don't panic

Panicking will not put down any more words on paper for you. Therefore, it isn't helpful. When you first see the topic, if your mind goes as blank as the page on which you have to type out your paper, take a deep breath. Force yourself to mechanically go through the steps listed above. Ask yourself who would be impacted by this issue? Would you be impacted? Someone you know? Who stands to benefit or lose from this issue?

Secondly, don't get clock fever. It's easy to be overwhelmed when you're looking at a page that doesn't seem to have much text, there is a lot of blank space further down, your mind is full of random thoughts and feeling confused, and the clock is ticking down faster than you would like. You brainstormed first so that you don't have to keep coming up with ideas. If you're running out of time and you have a lot of ideas that you haven't expanded upon, don't be afraid to make some cuts. Start picking the best ideas that you have left and expand on those few. Don't feel like you have to write down all of your ideas.

## Check your work

It is more important to have a shorter paper that is well written and well organized, than a longer paper that is poorly written and poorly organized. Don't keep writing about a subject just to add words and sentences, and certainly don't start repeating yourself. Expand on the ideas that you identified in the brainstorming session and make sure that you save yourself a few minutes at the end to go back and check your work.

Leave time at the end, at least three minutes, to go back and check over your work. Reread and make sure that everything you've written makes sense and flows. Clean up any spelling or grammar mistakes that you might have made. If you see anything that needs to be moved around, such as a paragraph that would fit in better somewhere else, cut and paste it to that new location. Also, go ahead and delete any brainstorming ideas that you weren't able to expand upon and clean up any other extraneous information that you might have typed that doesn't fit into your paper.

As you proofread, make sure there aren't any fragments or run-ons. Check for sentences that are too short or too long. If the sentence is too short, look to see if you have an identifiable subject and verb. If it is too long, break it up into two separate sentences. Watch out for any "big" words you may have used. It's okay to use difficult vocabulary words, but be positive that you are using them correctly. The position you are defending is important. It needs to be solid and convincing, not fancy. You're not trying to impress anyone with your vocabulary, just your ability to develop and express ideas.

## Shortcut keys

Spend some time on your keyboard getting familiar with the shortcut keys to cut, copy, and paste. It will help you to quickly move text around on your paper. First highlight the text you wish to move or copy and then type:

Ctrl+C = copy

Ctrl+X = cut

Ctrl+V = paste

You must hold down the ctrl key and then tap the "c", "x", or "v" key to perform the desired function.

## Argument Analysis

The Analysis of an Argument essay is a different sort of challenge, but one that many students prefer. You will only have thirty minutes to complete this essay, but it will not require you to do as much brainstorming. Indeed, the secret to success on the Argument essay is to always stay within the boundaries of the prompt. This is because unlike the Issue essay, which asks you to ruminate and take a position on a controversial issue, the Argument essay simply requires you to consider and critique a given position. Simply put, on the Argument essay, your opinion does not matter.

The format of this essay directive will be almost exactly the same as the format for the Analysis of an Issue essay. Once again, you can save yourself some time by previewing the directions that will appear atop your screen:

> This writing task is designed to test your critical reasoning skills as well as your writing skills. Your task is to critique the stated argument in terms of its logical soundness and in terms of the strength of the evidence offered in support of the argument. In scoring your argument essay, the reader will consider how effectively you: identify and analyze the key elements of the argument; organize, develop, and express your critique; support your ideas with reasons and examples; control the elements of standard written English.

Note that there is no requirement here for you to agree or disagree with the opinion expressed in the prompt. Unlike the Analysis of an Issue, in which you were asked to speak for yourself, here you are being asked to write as an impartial observer.

This is stated even more explicitly in the succeeding list of rules and guidelines that will appear roughly as follows: You are not being asked to agree or disagree with any of the statements in the argument. You should only consider the argument's line of reasoning. Specifically, you should consider: questionable assumptions underlying the argument; the extent to which the evidence presented supports the conclusion of the argument; what additional evidence would help to strengthen or refute the argument; and what additional information if any would help you to evaluate the argument's conclusion.

Here again, the GMAT gives us a clear idea of what they are looking for in this essay. In our subsequent consideration of how to write an Analysis of an Argument essay, we will use this description as our guide.

Since your opinion is not required on this essay, from the very beginning your focus should be on the argument advanced in the prompt. Remember that you will not be able to choose from a list of prompts: you will have to work with the one you are given. The prompt will be longer than the ones for the Issue essay, so take your time and read it carefully. It is typical for the prompt to be written from a particular viewpoint. For instance, a prompt might begin by saying that the following statement appeared on the editorial page of a newspaper, in a report published by a certain institution, or in a newsletter distributed by a specific political organization. Pay attention to the source of the argument as this will help you begin your analysis. You want to be sensitive to any prejudices that might be natural to a particular author. As you read the argument that follows, bear the source in mind and see if that generates any insights.

After giving a brief explanation, the prompt will provide a short, paragraph-length argument. Let us look at an example taken from a guide for would-be musicians:

> Fledgling musicians need to establish themselves with small record labels before seeking attention from more well-known entities. However, the rise of the internet and do-it-yourself production have made it easier than ever for novice musicians to create a quality product on a small budget. There is also a much larger market these days for musicians to make and sell their music without any assistance from a label. Some musicians enjoy the process of developing and marketing their songs, while others would rather leave the work to their representatives. The most important thing is to have a good time while you are making music.

## Breakdown

During your first reading, you will probably notice a number of logical errors in this argument. While it is fine to go ahead and jot down any ideas that occur to you immediately, we are going to take a more structured approach to considering the argument.

Spend the first three to five minutes breaking the argument down into little pieces by asking yourself a series of questions.

- What assumptions does the argument make?
- What explanations does it rely upon?
- What authority does it stand upon?
- What supports the reasoning used?
- What evidence is used?
- What examples are provided?

Then ask some follow-up questions.

- What changes to the argument would make it stronger?
- What changes to the argument would make it weaker?
- What would help you to reach a stronger conclusion?
- What would make it more logical?
- What would make it more balanced?

To begin with, let us examine the basic parts of an argument: premise, assumptions, reasoning, and conclusion. Before you create your outline for the Argument essay, you will need to identify these elements within the prompt. The premise of an argument is its starting point, the agreed-upon beginning of its reasoning. In the example, the premise of the argument is that beginning musicians should establish themselves first with a small label. The author has not yet told us why this is necessary or what the benefit of it will be; we are simply supposed to assume the premise to be true as we continue with the argument. Of course, in many cases you will find that the premise of an argument is nonsensical or unsupported. Note that you are not required to agree with the premise of an argument. At this point, it is enough to identify it and move on to an examination of the other components of the argument.

The assumptions of the argument are perhaps the most difficult elements to identify since they are not made explicit. The assumptions are those ideas that the author must take for granted as being true in order to make his or her point. They are all of the unstated bridges between premise and conclusion. As a critical reader, it is your job to articulate the underlying assumptions and decide whether or not they make sense. In the example argument, the author makes a number of assumptions:

- All musicians want to be on a major label.
- All kinds of music can be created on a low budget.
- There is a larger market for all kinds of music.

You could probably find more assumptions implicit in the argument, but three good ones will suffice. It is clear that there are some major problems with these assumptions: specifically, it seems that the author is often guilty of generalizing his beliefs. This is not always a problem: every author must generalize a bit in order to discuss abstract ideas. However, do the assumptions made by this author undermine his or her cause?

Before we go on to consider the reasoning of an argument, we will review some of the most common kinds of faulty assumptions on the GMAT. In the previous paragraph, we saw some good examples of generalization assumptions in which the author makes blanket statements about an entire category. Often, we will find that the exceptions to the author's assumption cast the entire argument into doubt. Another common kind of assumption is the causal assumption in which the author suggests that there is only one cause for a given effect and that the removal of the cause will therefore cause an immediate removal of the effect. For instance, an author might suggest that because smoking causes lung cancer, the prohibition of tobacco would bring an end to the disease. Of course, there are other causes of lung cancer besides tobacco, so this is a faulty causal assumption.

The arguments on the GMAT may also contain faulty sampling assumptions in which the author makes a sweeping statement based on a very small amount of data. One of the most common kinds of sampling assumptions is when the author universalizes his or her own personal experience. For instance, "None of my friends have been harassed on the subway, so to say there is a growing menace there is incorrect." The author erroneously assumes that the experience of his or her friends is a fair representation of the entire subway-riding population. Sampling assumptions may also be faulty when the author uses a particular survey or study to prove something other than what the study set out to prove.

The final kind of assumption that you should be wary of is the analogy assumption. An author will sometimes suggest that two things are comparable when, in fact, they are not. Typically, the author will point out a characteristic of one of the things and then suggest that it must be true of the other as well. Of course, if the things in question are not really analogous, this assumption must be false. For example, consider the following statement: "Cats do not enjoy the heat; after all, dogs try to avoid direct sunlight, and both these animals are common house pets." The author makes a statement about dogs and then asks you to assume it to be true of cats since these are domestic animals as well. Regardless of whether or not you agree that dogs try to avoid direct sunlight, it is clearly absurd to suggest that dogs and cats are exactly the same just because they are both kept as pets. This is an example of a faulty analogy assumption.

After you identify the author's premise and assumptions, you should quickly note his or her conclusion. The conclusion should be the general point supported by all of the author's reasoning. It is usually indicated by words like "therefore," "thus," "as a result," and "hence." The conclusion of the argument is almost always the last sentence; however, the GMAT will occasionally try to confuse you by tacking on an irrelevant final sentence. Indeed, the final sentence in our example prompt somewhat fits this description. Up to that point, the author has been discussing how best to establish oneself in the music industry, and then in the final sentence, he declares that the most important thing in music is to enjoy yourself. This sentence sounds like a conclusion ("The most important thing…"), but it clearly has no relation to the rest of the prompt.

## Findings

Remember that you are not being asked about your personal beliefs or convictions. You are asked whether the argument is well reasoned. Based on the questions that you've asked yourself, you should have a good understanding as to how irrefutable is the argument's logic. The reasoning of an argument is the specific set of ideas and examples that the author uses to move from premise to conclusion. The best kind of reasoning is clear, precise, and relevant to the subject. If the author endeavors to support his or her argument with examples, they must be appropriate. There are a number of ways in which reasoning can be defective. Sometimes, the author will dilute a good argument by including irrelevant information. Other times, an author will have good reasoning but will draw an incorrect conclusion from it. The reasoning, at other times, will contain gaps that require impossible assumptions by the reader.

There are several problems with the reasoning in our example prompt. The author begins by declaring that novice musicians should start with a small record label. He then goes on to undermine this suggestion by asserting that musicians now have the capability to make quality music on their own. Well, one might wonder, which is it? Seek out a small label or do it yourself? The author continues by stating that independent musicians have a much larger market for their products than ever before. This would seem to support the notion of working without a record label. Yet again, the author subsequently weakens this idea by declaring that some musicians would prefer to leave the business and production work to someone else. Finally, as we have already mentioned, the author concludes with a sentence that is basically irrelevant.

## Organize

Make sure that you put these writing points in a logical order. You have your main ideas that you will focus on, and must put them in a sequence that will flow in a smooth, sensible path from point to point, without rambling back and forth. Readers must have a sense of continuity as they read your paper. Since you will have only thirty minutes to complete this essay, it will probably be only four or five paragraphs long. In the first paragraph, you should articulate your general analysis of the argument, making sure to identify the premise and conclusion. You should discuss the specific strengths and weaknesses of the argument's reasoning and assumptions in the succeeding two or three paragraphs. In your final paragraph, you should summarize your analysis and describe ways in which the argument could be improved.

First paragraph: Your first paragraph should have several easily identifiable features. First, it should have a quick description or paraphrasing of the argument. Use your own words to briefly explain what the argument was about.

Second, you should explain your opinion of the argument and give an explanation of why you feel that way. Is the argument well stated? Is the reasoning based upon wild assumptions that have no grounding in reality?

Third, you should list your "writing points". What are the main ideas that you came up with earlier? Which assumptions and explanation do you intend to cover? This is your opportunity to outline the rest of your paper. Have a sentence explaining each assumption on which you intend to go into further depth in additional paragraphs. If someone was to only read this paragraph, they should be able to get an "executive summary" of the entire paper.

Body paragraph: Each of your successive paragraphs should expand upon one of the points listed in the main paragraph. Use your personal experience and knowledge to support the good assumptions that were made and to highlight the weaknesses of any bad assumptions that were made. Give examples to back up each of your points. As with the Issue essay, it is always advisable to lead with your most powerful ideas. (The only exception to this strategy is that you probably do not want to begin by discussing the conclusion of the argument.) For some arguments, the main problem may be faulty assumptions; in others, the most outstanding errors may be in the reasoning. The greatest weakness seems to be that the author argues in favor of two different ideas in the example prompt. In other words, the primary fault of the argument is one of reasoning. The author does make some problematic assumptions, but these are not as worrisome as the ineffective reasoning and nonsensical conclusion. An effective critique of this argument would begin by attacking the poor reasoning that the author uses and the conclusion that the author comes to by using this reasoning. Faulty assumptions should only be discussed if time allows.

Conclusion paragraph: In the concluding paragraph of your Argument essay, summarize your analysis, and more importantly, recommend a few ways to improve the argument. These suggestions should be clear, specific, and restricted to the parameters of the discussion. In other words, do not suggest that the argument be changed in a radical way. Remember that this essay is not meant to be a forum for your opinions. Limit your suggestions to the specific reasoning and assumptions used by the author without distorting the premise or conclusions from the author's basic intent. For instance, a critique of the example prompt might end by suggesting that the author decide which method for success he wants to endorse and then eliminate all of the information that diverges from this thesis. Furthermore, the critique might recommend that the author abandon his conclusion sentence in favor of a recapitulation of the streamlined thesis. In any case, you do not want to spend the conclusion of this essay ruminating on the implications of the argument as you would on the Issue essay. Restrict your remarks to the argument as it is written and you will be rewarded.

**Final review**

Save a few minutes at the end to go back over your paper. It is crucial that you do not leave any obvious spelling or grammar mistakes. Any time spent cleaning up and proofreading is well worth it.

# Final Note

Depending on your test taking preferences and personality, the Analytical Writing test will probably be your hardest or your easiest test. You are required to go through the entire process of writing a paper in 30 minutes or less, which can be quite a challenge.

Focus upon each of the steps listed above. Go through the process of creative flow first, generating ideas and thoughts about the topic. Then organize those ideas into a smooth logical flow. Pick out the ones that are best from the list you have created. Decide upon which side of the issue you will discuss, or your overall impression of the argument. Create a recognizable structure in your paper, with an introductory paragraph explaining what you have decided upon, and what your main points will be. Use the body paragraphs to expand on those main points and have a conclusion that wraps up the issue or argument.

Let's take a moment to consider a few issues of style. Foremost, you should try to make your spelling as perfect as possible without becoming obsessive. The GMAT does not dock your score for misspellings, but readers will admit that serial errors can be distracting and off-putting. The word processing program used on the GMAT does not include a spell-check function, so those students who are used to relying on the computer to correct spelling errors will have to be more diligent. If you suspect that you may be spelling a certain word wrong, see if you can use a synonym instead. If you absolutely have to use the questionable word, do your best and move on. Remember that unless your spelling errors are rampant, you will not be penalized.

Additionally, try to vary the length of your sentences as much as possible. As mentioned in the introduction to this section, one of the criteria judged by the automated essay-scoring engine will be syntactic variety. The degree to which the lengths of your sentences vary says a great deal about you as a writer. Sophisticated writers use sentences of different lengths to create an engaging rhythm. Readers will quickly become bored with writing in which all of the sentences have the same basic structure and length. One common way to avoid monotonous writing is to issue some important statements in short, pithy sentences. For instance, consider the rhythm of the following passage:

When Jack came home from work last Friday, he immediately noticed something different. Usually, his dog Henry would greet him at the door, eyes gleaming and tail wagging. But this night, Henry was gone!

Notice how the author draws attention to the drama in the last sentence by making it short and exclamatory. While you do not need to be quite as melodramatic, you should make use of varying sentence lengths to add drama to your writing.

Another hang-up for many students on the Analytical Writing section is the question of vocabulary. In general, you want to use as many specific and vivid words as possible without overwriting. For example, avoid describing something as "very good" when you could say that it was "fantastic", and do not say "dog" when you really mean "schnauzer." The GMAT readers are trained to pay more attention to your reasoning than to your diction, but they will, nevertheless, reward those students who write energetically and colorfully. There are some limits, however. You should never use a sophisticated word unless you are absolutely sure of the definition and unless it can be used in a natural way. The GMAT readers are extremely sensitive to pretentiousness, and they will be quick to punish you for showing off. If you feel like you are going out of your way to use a particular word, it is probably not worth it. Additionally, slang and inappropriate language should never be used. This may seem obvious, but every year there are students who are penalized for using vulgar or overly-familiar language on the GMAT. The Analytical Writing section is an area in which it can be good to be bland: you do not want to run the risk of offending your reader.

Also, to avoid offending the reader and to prevent digression, make wise choices when using personal anecdotes in the Issue argument. When used properly, illustrative stories are an excellent way to add life to your argument. However, there is a danger of straying too far from the subject matter; be sure to only use anecdotes when you can do so quickly and appropriately. Also, never use personal anecdotes on the Argument essay: this essay is meant to be strictly a critique of the argument presented in prompt.

If you can only remember one piece of advice regarding the Analytical Writing section, it is depth rather than breadth. That is, concentrate on a few great ideas and explicate them fully rather than trying to dazzle the reader with every relevant thought that runs through your mind. In the end, your score will be much higher if you make your points clear, precise, and detailed.

Save a few moments to go back and review what you have written. Clean up any minor mistakes that you might have had and give it those last few critical touches that can make a huge difference. Finally, be proud and confident of what you have written and prepare yourself for the next phase of the test.

# GMAT Quantitative Test

The Quantitative section of the GMAT consists of a 75 minute section with 37 questions. There are two types of questions in the Quantitative section of the GMAT.

1.) Problem Solving (22 or 23 questions)
2.) Data Sufficiency (14 or 15 questions)

The Quantitative Ability (math) section of the GMAT seems to generate the most anxiety among prospective test-takers. Unfortunately, the quantitative ability section of the GMAT is here to stay. The good news is that most experts consider the math included on the GMAT to be significantly less difficult than the math on the SAT. Indeed, this portion of the exam has been developed to be at approximately a ninth-grade level. If you did not take much math as an undergraduate, do not worry. Studying for the Quantitative Ability section of the GMAT is primarily a matter of learning the best strategies for the two types of questions and then brushing up on your skills from junior high and high school math.

Our goal is to show you the simple formulas and methods to solving these problems, so that while you will not gain a mastery of math from this guide, you will learn the methods necessary to succeed on the GMAT. This guide attacks problems that are simple in nature but may have been glossed over during your education.

## Data Sufficiency

The data sufficiency problems on the GMAT are introduced with a rather long and tedious set of directions. Mostly, these directions reiterate the description of data sufficiency questions given above. However, they do impart useful new information, and it is always best to familiarize yourself with the directions beforehand. Here is an example of what you will see on test day:

This Data Sufficiency problem consists of a question and two statements, labeled (1) and (2), in which certain data are given. You have to decide whether the data given in the statements are sufficient for answering the question. Using the data given in the statements plus your knowledge of mathematics and everyday facts (such as the number of days in July or the meaning of counterclockwise), you must indicate whether:

- Statement 1 ALONE is sufficient, but statement 2 alone is not sufficient to answer the questions asked;
- Statement 2 ALONE is sufficient, but statement 1 alone is not sufficient to answer the question asked;
- BOTH statements (1) and (2) TOGETHER are sufficient to answer the question asked; but NEITHER statement ALONE is sufficient;
- EACH statement ALONE is sufficient to answer the question asked;
- Statements (1) and (2) TOGETHER are NOT sufficient to answer the question asked, and additional data specific to the problem are needed.

Also note:

- Numbers: All numbers used are real numbers.
- Figures: A figure accompanying a data sufficiency problem will conform to the information given in the question, but will not necessarily conform to the additional information in statements (1 and 2).
- Lines shown as straight can be assumed to be straight and lines that appear jagged can also be assumed to be straight.
- You may assume that positions of points, angles, regions, etc., exist in the order shown and that angle measures are greater than zero.
- All figures lie in a plane unless otherwise indicated.
- In problems that ask you for the value of a quantity, the data given in the statements are sufficient only when it is possible to determine exactly one numerical value for the quantity.


Obviously, you will want to avoid referring back to these long-winded directions when you are sitting for your timed exam.

At first glance, data sufficiency questions may seem a bit daunting. There is good news, however. For the most part, data sufficiency questions will require less calculation than problem-solving questions; in fact, many data sufficiency questions will not require any calculations at all. The makers of the GMAT acknowledge that the presentation of these questions can be puzzling and purposefully make the problems a bit easier. Once you get the hang of these question types, you will probably be surprised at how well you do.

As indicated above, every data sufficiency problem will be followed by the same five answer choices. They can be simplified as follows:

> A: 1 alone sufficient, 2 alone insufficient
>
> B: 2 alone sufficient, 1 alone insufficient
>
> C: Both together sufficient, neither alone sufficient
>
> D: Each statement alone sufficient
>
> E: Statements together insufficient; more information needed

It is a good idea to memorize these answer choices before the exam so that you can write them down on your scratch paper and cross them out as they are discarded. (As you will discover, process of elimination is a major part of data sufficiency strategy).

**General strategy**

The data sufficiency problems are among the trickiest question on all standardized tests. Not only this, they are mixed in the same section with more straightforward math problems, such that you must ration time between the "normal" problems and these trickier ones.

In general, the data sufficiency problems are a lot easier than they seem at first glance. There is usually some "trick" or thread connecting the statements that reveals the key to a relatively simple problem. If you know to look for a trick, then you have an advantage over 90% of test takers who naively take these problems at face value.

If you have an algebraic mind, you will have the greatest success on these problems, as the quickest way to solve them is to break every statement down into some sort of algebraic statement, then review them analytically and solve the problem. By reducing the problem to variables, you eliminate the need for complex mental acrobatics to keep things arranged properly in your mind while you unlock the enigma. Not only that, you save time as you don't go off on a mental daydream about the problem

Often the best offense is a good defense. If you do well on the normal problems, avoid letting the data sufficiency section steal valuable time from the other quantitative sections, and knock out the easy ones, you can probably get a great GMAT quantitative score even if a moderately difficult data sufficiency problem leaves you clueless.

Now let us consider a simple example. The following is a typical (though easy) data sufficiency problem:

What is the distance from Ted's house to the beach?

> (1)    It takes Ted three hours to drive from his house to the beach.
> (2)    Ted drives at an average of 50 miles per hour.

Although the content of this question is not overly sophisticated, there is a fair amount of information here, so it is important to work through the problem one step at a time. Specifically, we are going to encourage using a basic three-step approach to data sufficiency problems: examine the opening question, examine each statement individually, and then look at the statements together.

Let us use this approach to consider the example problem. The question stem asks us to find the distance from Ted's house to the beach. This is a simple rate question in which distance, speed, and time are considered. We know already that in order to derive the distance driven, we are going to need two pieces of information: the average speed at which Ted drives and the length of time that he drives. Clearly, we are well on our way to answering the problem before we even look at the two statements. For the sake of thoroughness we will examine the two statements in turn. The first statement declares that "It takes three hours for Ted to drive from his house to the beach." This supplies the time component, but since it does not include the average speed, it is not sufficient to answer the question. We can therefore rule out answer choices A and D. Statement 2 asserts that "Ted drives at an average speed of 50 miles per hour." Here is the average speed value we need to answer the question. Note, however, that statement 2 lacks the value for time and is therefore not sufficient by itself to answer the question. We can thus eliminate answer choice B leaving us to choose between answer choices C and E. The essential question we must ask ourselves: is the information contained in the two statements combined sufficient to answer the question? Well, we are looking for a distance, and the two statements provide us with time and speed. They are indeed sufficient, so the answer is C.

In our exposition of this example problem, you may have noticed that we never actually calculated the distance Ted drove. The beauty of data sufficiency questions is that you usually do not have to make a calculation; it is enough to know that you could. This is one of the reasons why, once you get the hang of the format, you should find that you can answer data sufficiency questions more quickly than you can answer problem-solving questions.

Occasionally, you may find that you do not fully understand one of the statements. When this is the case, concentrate on the statement you do understand and narrow your choices from there. For instance, imagine that you do not understand statement 1, but you are able to tell that statement 2, alone, can answer the question; you may assume that the answer will be either B or D. On the other hand, if you cannot understand statement 2, but you can determine that statement 1, alone, is sufficient to answer the question, you then know that the answer must be either A or D. If you only understand statement 2 and determine that it alone is not sufficient to answer the question, the answer must be A, C, or E. If you are only able to ascertain that statement 1 is not sufficient, the answer must be B, C, or E.

Let us assume that in most cases you will be able to work with both of the given statements. There are a few ground rules pertaining to data sufficiency questions that can be helpful.

To begin with, the two statements in a data sufficiency problem will never contradict each other. If you believe that the truth of one statement makes the other statement impossible, you are probably wrong. As an example, consider our example problem. If statement 1 is left as is, statement 2 would never say something such as, "It takes Ted less than an hour to drive to the beach," because this would directly contradict the first statement. In data sufficiency problems, you are to question the relevance rather than the truth of the given statements.

## Variables

Many questions will involve variables (where a letter such as "x" is used to represent any number). Try to solve these problems by plugging in a number for the variable and solving for an answer for both statements 1 and 2. It is best to use different numbers to make sure of your answer. Numbers such as 100, 1, 0, -1, and –100 allow you to check a wide range of possible answers and will keep you from being thrown off by tricky questions. Now you aren't restricted to only using numbers like 100 or 1. Any number is valid. These numbers are only suggested because they are easy to multiply and divide by. Example:

What is the value of a + b?

(1)  $a^2 = 4$
(2)  $b + 6 = 9$

At first glance, it would appear that it is quite possible to solve this question with both statements together. However, remember that the product of two negative numbers is always a positive. In other words, the value for a could be either 2 or -2. For this reason, the two statements together are insufficient, and the answer is E. The GMAT often tries to trip up test-takers with this kind of question, so it is imperative that you consider all possible values for the variables given.

Another similar tactic of the GMAT is to include absolute values in an equation as a means of throwing you off. Consider the following data sufficiency problem:

Which is greater, x or y?

    (1)    $x + 3 = y$

    (2)    $|x| < |y|$

The first statement clearly indicates that y is greater than x. For every possible value of x, y is three greater. Statement 1 alone is sufficient, so you can turn your attention to statement 2. At first glance, this statement would also seem to indicate that y is greater than x. Remember, though, that absolute value is the distance on a number line from zero, not the exact position on the number line. A negative number can have a greater absolute value than a positive number if it is farther away on the number line. Therefore, absolute value cannot give us any definitive information about the relative values of x and y; the answer to this problem, therefore, is A.

Finally, beware of data sufficiency problems in which you are required to substitute values for variables. Consider the following problem:

Is this statement true: $x > y$?

    (1)    $2x = y$

    (2)    $2x + y = 12$

Unfortunately, many students will take a look at this problem and immediately assume that the answer is D. It seems clear that any number multiplied by 2 will produce a greater number, and a little quick substitution in the second statement suggests that the values for x and y are 3 and 6, respectively. However, answer D is wrong because in a data sufficiency question you are asked to consider each statement individually, not to search for conditions in which both statements are true. Statement 1, in fact, does not prove that y is greater than x. Any negative number substituted for x will, in fact, produce a smaller value for y, and additionally, if x = 0, then y = 0. This sort of problem is why you must always substitute a positive number, a negative number, zero, and a fraction any time you attempt to plug in values for a variable. If you do so and derive a consistent result, you can trust the information provided by the statement. Similarly, Statement 2 cannot stand on its own. The values x = 0, y = 12 and the values x = 6, y = 0 both provide solutions to the equation.

Only when both statements are taken together, producing values of x = 3 and y = 6, is there sufficient information, so the answer is C.

## Extra information

Watch out for extra information!  Many questions will have additional information given in notes above the problem.  This additional information is critical to solving the problem.  For example, it may be a comment such as "x > 0".  This means that when you are plugging in a number (such as 100, 1, 0, -1, or –100), only numbers greater than zero (1 or 100) can be used.  Make sure that you read all of the notes and understand what they mean.

Sometimes, the GMAT will include statements that restate or paraphrase some of the information in the question.  Consider the following data sufficiency problem as an example:

If a bag of marbles is three-quarters red marbles, how many red marbles are in the bag?

    (1)  Three out of every four marbles in the bag are red.

    (2)  There are 36 total marbles in the bag.

Statement 1 provides some information that is necessary to answer the question, but it is information that has already been given.  Even though this information is used in answering the question, statement 1 is neither sufficient nor useful in itself.  For this reason, statement 1 (and any other statement that simply reiterates information from the question) is not used to answer the question.  The answer to this example question must therefore be B or E (actually, the answer is B).

Other statements might include information that is irrelevant.  When one of the statements gives information that concerns the terms of the question but does not directly contribute to the answer, it is considered to be unhelpful.  For example, look at the following problem:

    What is the value of x, expressed as a real number?

        (1)    $3x + 5 = 17$

        (2)    $x - 2y = 5$

Statement 2, alone, is not sufficient to answer the question, and it is not helpful when combined with statement 1, which alone is sufficient to answer the question. For this reason, the answer to this problem is A.

Still, other statements will provide information that is redundant. When this is the case, you will choose your answer based on whether the redundant information is sufficient to solve the problem. Consider the following example:

What is the value of b, expressed as a real number?

(1)     $b - 8 = 2$
(2)     $2b = 10$

Both of these statements provide clear ways to calculate the value of b. Indeed, the use of one makes the other unnecessary. That is, both statements alone are sufficient to answer the question: the answer is D.

**Shapes**

Other problems may describe a geometric shape, such as a triangle or circle, but may not include a drawing of the shape. GMAT is testing whether you can read a description and make appropriate inferences by visualizing the object and related information. There is a simple way to overcome this obstacle. DRAW THE SHAPE! A good drawing (or even a bad drawing) is much easier to understand and interpret than a brief description.

Make a quick drawing or sketch of the shape described. Include any angles or lengths provided in the description. Once you can see the shape, you have already partially solved the problem and will be able to determine the right answer. Example:

What is the ratio of the area of a circle A to the area of a square B?

1.) The circle has a radius of 2.

2.) The square has a side of length 2.

Quickly draw a circle and label it with a radius of 2. Then right next to the circle, draw a square that has a side of the same length as the circle's radius. Without knowing either of the formulas for calculating area, you can easily see that the area of both shapes can be determined and therefore the ratio of the two areas can be found.

Be careful though. Shapes can be drawn many different ways. Example:

What is the ratio of the area of a circle A to the area of a rectangle B?

1.) The circle has a radius of 2.

2.) The rectangle has a side of length 2.

This is very similar, but there is a crucial difference. A square has four sides of the same length. A rectangle can have two sides with completely different lengths. If a rectangle has a long side that is length 2, then its area is smaller than a circle. But what if a rectangle has another side that has a length of 100? Suddenly that tiny rectangle becomes a huge rectangle and its area cannot be determined, which means the ratio of the areas can also not be determined. So remember that when shapes are loosely defined, there is flexibility in how they are drawn. In order to be sure of your answer, see if the shape can be drawn differently, just as you should try different numbers to solve for an unknown variable.

In problems involving shapes, it is not always necessary to compute the answer. If your drawings have covered every possibility, the answer will often be clear without calculation. In the example above, once the circle and square are drawn, it is not necessary to calculate that the area of a circle = $\pi r^2$ = 3.14*$(2)^2$ = 12.6 and area of a square = $s^2$ = $2^2$ = 4, in order to determine that it is possible to find the ratio of the areas. From the drawing you can tell that it is solvable.

## Problem Solving

The following directions will precede problem-solving questions:

Solve this problem and indicate the best of the answer choices given. All numbers used are real numbers. A figure accompanying a problem-solving question is intended to provide information useful in solving the problem. Figures are drawn as accurately as possible, except when it is stated in a specific problem that a figure is not drawn to scale. Straight lines may sometimes appear jagged. All figures lie in a plane unless otherwise indicated.

Each problem-solving question will be followed by five answer choices. When these answer choices are real numbers without variables, they will usually be listed in order from least to greatest. One exception to this rule is when a question concerns the relative value of the answer choices. For instance, the answer choices will be listed in a random order for questions asking you to select the greatest of a group of fractions.

As the directions indicate, some of the problem-solving questions will include graphs, charts, or geometric figures. Since there are limitations to the computer program that is used to administer the GMAT, these drawings will not always be perfectly accurate or to scale. You should never make any assumptions about a diagram on the GMAT; only consider information that is either explicitly given by the question or information that can be calculated based on data explicitly given.

The most important thing to remember regarding problem-solving questions is to read the question carefully and make sure you understand what it is asking. For instance, the GMAT is notorious for setting up an equation like $2x = 6$ and then asking you to solve for $x + 2$. Inevitably, many test takers will see the equation and simply solve for $x$; thus, the GMAT punishes those who fail to read the question carefully. Before you even begin to solve the problem or examine the answer choices, make sure you know what the directions are asking you to do.

The GMAT will not require the highest level of specificity on many of the problem-solving questions. For instance, when the answer to a problem is a decimal with nine places, the answer choices will often round to the nearest hundredth or thousandth. Before you go to the trouble of working out the problem to the millionths place, take a look at the answer choices: you may be able to save yourself some labor.

Although calculators are not allowed on the GMAT, scratch paper and pencils will be made available. You should use this scratch paper as much as you can. Do not try to solve complicated problems in your head; put them down on paper so that you can get a visual sense of the problem and leave your mind free to work. The importance of scratch paper is true for the data sufficiency questions as well as the problem-solving questions; on the problem-solving questions, you should use the paper to solve each problem forward and backward. For instance, on a question that asks you to solve for a specific variable, you should solve for the variable, then plug that variable back into the original equation and make sure that it works. After you have reviewed basic arithmetic and algebra, you should have plenty of time to work out problems forwards and backwards on your scratch paper. You can prevent careless mistakes from lowering your score by double checking your work in this way.

## Integers

Quite a few of the questions on the GMAT will require you to understand some of the basic properties of numbers, specifically integers. The set of numbers known as integers is composed of all the so-called counting numbers, both negative and positive, and including zero. Expressed as a mathematical set, integers are {...-3, -2, -1, 0, 1, 2, 3...}. Fractions and decimals are not integers. Any integer that is a multiple of two is called an even integer; all other integers are considered to be odd. Zero is considered to be an even integer. Zero has some special properties: any number multiplied by zero will yield a product of zero, and it is not possible to divide a number by zero. Any groups of integers that are arranged in order from least to greatest, without any gaps, are referred to as consecutive integers.

## Place Value

The value of an integer depends not only on the identity of the digits but also on their placement. For instance, the numbers 0.61 and 0.061 are not the same. The position of a digit in a number is referred to as its place value. In order to answer some of the questions on the GMAT, you may need to be familiar with the more common place values. In a number that does not have a decimal point, the names of the place value increase by powers of ten as you move to the left. For instance, in the number 56,324, four is in the ones place, two is in the tens place, three is in the hundreds place, six is in the thousands place, and five is in the ten thousands place. It is easy to imagine how the progression of increasing places will continue: hundred thousands, millions, ten millions, etc. The place values on the right side of the decimal point also progress by powers of ten, beginning with tenths. As an example, in the number 0.5297, five is in the tenths place, two is in the hundredths place, nine is in the thousandths place, and seven is in the ten thousandths place. Again, it easy to imagine how these decreasing places will continue: hundred thousandths, millionths, ten millionths, etc. Note that all of the place values to the right of the decimal point have a "th" at the end; make sure you do not confuse the thousands and the thousandths place on your exam, for example.

## Prime and Composite Numbers

Any prime number that can only be divided evenly by itself or by one is a prime number. For example, three is a prime number because it can only be divided by three and one; four is not a prime number because it can be divided by two as well as by four and one. All numbers that are not prime numbers are referred to as composite numbers. Prime numbers are always positive whole numbers and are almost always odd (2 is the only even prime number).

## Solving for Variables

Variables are letters that represent an unknown number. You must solve what that number is in single variable problems. The main thing to remember is that you can do anything to one side of an equation as long as you do it to the other.

Example:

Solve for x in the equation 2x + 3 = 5.

Answer: First you want to get the "2x" isolated by itself on one side. To do that, first get rid of the 3. Subtract 3 from both sides of the equation 2x + 3 – 3 = 5 – 3 or 2x = 2. Now since the x is being multiplied by the 2 in "2x", you must divide by 2 to get rid of it. So, divide both sides by 2, which gives 2x / 2 = 2 / 2 or x = 1.

## Basic Algebraic Operations

Remember that algebraic terms can only be combined when the variables are identical. This includes any exponent attached to the variable. For instance, the expression $6x^3 + 4x^2 - 2x^2 + 5x + 4x - 7$ can only be simplified to $6x^3 + 2x^2 + 9x - 7$, and the expression $5x^2 + 4x - 3y^2$ cannot be simplified at all.

Some questions may ask you to factor a given algebraic expression. To factor an algebraic expression means to simplify it by breaking it down into its constituent components. One common form of algebraic expression is $x^2 - y^2$ which can be factored to become $(x + y) (x - y)$. This is true no matter what variable is used or what the value of x or y is, for instance $z^4 - 16 = (z^2 + 4) (z^2 - 4)$.

## Linear equations

When you are given a linear equation, your job is to find the value for each variable that makes the equation true. When the linear equation only has one variable, you should only need one equation to find the value of the variable. An example of a linear equation with one variable is x – 6 = 4. By adding 6 to both sides of the equation, we can see that the only possible value for x that makes this equation true is 10. In a nutshell, this is the method for solving linear equations with one variable: isolate the variable on one side of the equation by removing all of the other values. This is done by adding, subtracting, multiplying, or dividing both sides of the equation by whatever number will remove the extra numbers from the side of the equation with the variable. If you are given the equation $3x + 7 = 19$, you will have to subtract 7 from both sides and then divide both sides by 3, leaving $x = 4$.

The process is slightly more complicated for linear equations including more than one variable. In these cases, you will need more than one equation in order to determine the values of all the variables. The method for solving these equations is to solve for one variable in a given equation, and then substitute for that variable in the second equation and solve for the second variable. As an example, imagine you are given the equations $2x + y = 7$ and $3y + x = 11$. To begin with, solve the first equation for y by subtracting 2x from both sides, leaving an equation of $y = 7 - 2x$. Then substitute this new value for y (i.e., $7 - 2x$), for the y in the second equation [$3(7 - 2x) + x = 11)$]. Distribute the 3 across the parentheses, yielding the equation $21 - 6x + x = 11$. Simplify this to $21 - 5x = 11$, then subtract 21 from both sides, yielding $-5x = -10$. By dividing both sides by -5, we can end with $x = 2$. Now that we have a simple numerical value for x, we can substitute it into the first equation and solve for y. $2x + y = 7$ becomes $2(2) + y = 7$ and can be simplified to $4 + y = 7$; subtracting 4 from both sides yields a final answer of $y = 3$.

**Inequalities**

In most algebraic equations, the two sides will be separated by an equal sign (=). Sometimes, however, the symbol will be one that indicates an inequality. There are five inequality symbols that can appear on the GMAT: <, meaning "is less than"; >, meaning "is greater than"; ≤, meaning "is less than or equal to"; ≥, meaning "is greater than or equal to"; and ≠, meaning "is not equal to." In almost every case, working with an inequality is the same as working with a normal equation (i.e., one with an = sign). The only exception is that when both sides of an inequality are multiplied by a negative number, the direction of the inequality reverses. Therefore, the result of dividing -3 into both sides of the inequality $-6 > -3x$ would be $2 < x$.

# Positive/Negative Numbers

## Multiplication/division

A negative multiplied or divided by a negative = a positive number.  Example:

$$-3 * -4 = 12; -6 / -3 = 2$$

A negative multiplied by a positive = a negative number.  Example:

$$-3 * 4 = -12; -6 / 3 = -2$$

## Addition/subtraction

Treat a negative sign just like a subtraction sign.  Example:

$$3 + -2 = 3 - 2 \text{ or } 1$$

Remember that you can reverse the numbers while adding or subtracting.  Example:

$$-4+2 = 2 + -4 = 2 - 4 = -2$$

A negative number subtracted from another number is the same as adding a positive number.  Example:

$$2 - -1 = 2 + 1 = 3$$

Beware of making a simple mistake!

Example: An outdoor thermometer drops from 42° to –8°.  By how many degrees has the outside air cooled?

Answer:  A common mistake is to say 42° – 8° = 34°, but that is wrong.
It is actually 42° – –8° or 42° + 8° = 50°.

## Absolute value

The absolute value of a number is its distance from zero.  Absolute value is denoted by two vertical lines.  Since absolute value is the measure of distance, it cannot be negative.  Thus, the absolute value of 6 (written |6|), is 6, and the absolute value of -6 is 6 as well.

# Addition and Multiplication Rules

There are a few basic arithmetic properties that, although they are unlikely to be specifically mentioned on the GMAT, may help you to figure out some of the other problems on the test. The associative property of addition asserts that the order of the terms in an addition problem does not matter. Therefore, the various terms can be grouped and organized in any way without affecting the total. As an example, (2 + 5) + 6 = 13; and 2 + (5 + 6) = 13. Also, 2 + 6 + 5 and 5 + 6 + 2 both equal 13. As long as the terms in an addition problem do not change, the sum will not change either.

In a similar vein, the associative property of multiplication asserts that the grouping of the terms in a multiplication problem will not affect the product. For example, 5 (2 x 3) = 30, 3 (2 x 5) = 30, 3 x 2 x 5 = 30, 5 x 2 x 3 = 30, and so on.

The distributive law is only slightly more complicated. It states that any number multiplied by a set of values within parentheses is multiplied by every value within the parentheses. To illustrate, 3 (5 + 4) = 3(5) + 3(4). Occasionally, the GMAT will ask you to transform a problem in the opposite way, as follows: 3(17) + 3 (14) = 3 (17 + 14). The problem may even be written in a slightly more confusing manner, such as 5(12) – 83(5) = 5 (12 – 83).

# Fractions

A fraction, for instance ½, consists of a numerator on top and a denominator on bottom. Fractions are said to be equivalent when they can be reduced to equal the same thing; for example, 5/10 is equivalent to ½ since it can be reduced to ½ by dividing both the numerator and the denominator by 5. Remember that when reducing a fraction, you must divide the numerator and the denominator by the same number. In order to perform addition or subtraction operations with fractions, you must have a common denominator. Once you have a common denominator, you simply perform the operation with the numerators leaving the denominators alone. To multiply two fractions, multiply the numerators together and then multiply the denominators together. To divide one fraction by another, invert the second fraction and then multiply first the numerators and then the denominators. A fraction in which the numerator is greater than the denominator is called an improper fraction. An expression consisting of a whole number and a fraction, for instance 5 ½, is called a mixed number.

## Decimals

Decimals, like fractions, are a way of expressing values other than integers. Every fraction has an equivalent decimal: for instance, the fraction ¼ is equivalent to the decimal 0.25. When working with decimals, it is very important to understand how different operations affect the number of places to the right of the decimal point. When adding or subtracting decimals, the resulting sum or difference should have as many decimal places as the term with the most decimal places in the operation. In the problem 1.5 + 1.05, for example, the answer must have two numbers to the right of the decimal point. One way to simplify such problems is to add zeroes to the ends of those numbers with fewer decimal places; for instance, making our example 1.50 + 1.05. When two decimals are multiplied together, the resulting product will have the sum of the decimal places in the two terms. In other words, the product of 3.55 x 4.785 will have five places to the right of the decimal point since the first term has 2 and the second term has 3. In order to divide decimals, the divisor must be converted into an integer by moving the decimal point to the right. To complete the problem 5.55 ÷ 2.8, we would need to shift the decimal point in both terms one place to the right resulting in the problem 55.5 ÷ 28. The resulting quotient will have one place to the right of the decimal point.

## Exponents

When a number is multiplied by itself several times, we use a form of notation called an exponent. For instance, the number $2^5$ is expressed verbally as "two to the fifth power," and is equivalent to 2 x 2 x 2 x 2 x 2. When a number is raised to the second power (that is, when its exponent is 2), we say that the number is being "squared." When a number is raised to the third power (the exponent being 3), we say that the number is being "cubed." For any number, an exponent of zero makes that number equal to 1. When a number has a negative exponent, it is equal to one over the number raised to the absolute value of the exponent; in other words, $x^{-1} = 1/x$, $x^{-2} = 1/x^2$, $x^{-3} = 1/x^3$...

When exponents are multiplied together, the exponents are added to get the final result. Example:

$$x*x = x^2, \text{ where } x^1 \text{ is implied and } 1 + 1 = 2.$$

When exponents in parentheses have an exponent, the exponents are multiplied to get the final result. Example:

$$(x^3)^2 = x^6, \text{ because } 3*2 = 6.$$

Another way to think of this is that $(x^3)^2$ is the same as $(x^3)*(x^3)$. Now you can use the multiplication rule given above and add the exponents, $3 + 3 = 6$, so $(x^3)^2 = x^6$

## Decimal Exponents (aka Scientific Notation)

This usually involves converting back and forth between scientific notation and decimal numbers (e.g. 0.02 is the same as $2 \times 10^{-2}$). There's an old "cheat" to this problem: if the number is less than 1, the number of digits behind the decimal point is the same as the exponent that 10 is raised to in scientific notation, except that the exponent is a negative number; if the number is greater than 1, the exponent of 10 is equal to the number of digits ahead of the decimal point minus 1.
Example:

Convert 3000 to decimal notation.

Answer: $3 \times 10^3$, since 4 digits are before the decimal, the number is greater than 1, and (4-1) = 3.

Example:

Convert 0.05 to decimal notation.

Answer: $5 \times 10^{-2}$, since the five is two places behind the decimal (remember, the exponent is negative for numbers less than 1).

Any number raised to an exponent of zero is always 1. Also, unless you know what you're doing, always convert scientific notation to "regular" decimal numbers before doing arithmetic, and convert the answer back if necessary to answer the problem.

## Square Roots

The number that when multiplied by the same number as itself would produce a given number is called the "square root" of that given number; for instance, since 2 x 2 = 4, 2 is the square root of 4. Note that -2 could also be considered a square root of 4 since -2 x -2 = 4. Every positive number will have two square roots, one of which will be negative. Also, since any positive or negative number that is multiplied by the same number as itself has a positive product, negative numbers do not have square roots. (This will probably not come up on the GMAT, but the square root of 0 is 0, since $0^2 = 0$). The standard notation for square root is $\sqrt{2}$, which is expressed verbally as "the square root of 2." If a question is specifically asking for the negative square root of 2, this is expressed $-\sqrt{2}$. When two square roots are multiplied together, the numbers are simply multiplied and the resulting product remains as a square root: $\sqrt{2} \times \sqrt{3} = \sqrt{6}$. In like fashion, when one square root is divided by another, the terms inside the root symbol are divided, and the square root sign is left intact: $\sqrt{8}/\sqrt{4} = \sqrt{2}$.

## Order of Operations

There is a specific order in which the various components of an arithmetic problem must be performed. This system is known as the order of operations and is as follows: parentheses, exponents, multiplication/division, and addition/subtraction. The order of operations is easy to follow if you just remember the mnemonic phrase, "Please excuse my dear Aunt Sally." The first letters of the words in this sentence (Please Excuse My Dear Aunt Sally) mirror those of the order of operations: Parentheses, Exponents, Multiplication/Division, and Addition/Subtraction. Multiplication and division have equal priority and should be performed as they appear, working right to left. Similarly, addition and subtraction have equal priority and should be handled in the same way. As an example, take a look at the following arithmetic expression: $3(4 + 3^2) - 2$. In order to derive the correct answer, you would need to begin by determining the value of the parentheses by first calculating the exponent $3^2$ and then by adding 4. Next, you would multiply by 3 (since multiplication preceded subtraction in the order of operations), and then you would subtract 2. The correct value of this expression is 37. Note that if you tried to calculate the value of this expression without observing the proper order of operations (say, by multiplying the 4 inside the parentheses by 3 before finding the total value inside the parentheses), you would not find the same answer.

## Area, Volume, and Surface Area

You will need to know a few basic formulas for calculating the area of various figures. The area of a triangle is calculated by using the formula a = ½(base x height), where the base is one side of the triangle and the height runs perpendicular to the base. The perimeter of the triangle, and indeed the perimeter of any polygon, is the sum of the lengths of the sides. The area of a square, rectangle, or parallelogram can be calculated by multiplying the length by the width. The area of a rhombus can be calculated by multiplying one half by the product of the two diagonals (lines drawn between the vertices of opposing angles). The area of a circle is found by using the formula $a = \pi r^2$, in which r is the radius of the circle. A list of commonly used formulas is provided in the appendix for your convenience.

# Cylinders, Rectangular Solids, and Cubes

Occasionally, the GMAT will require you to work with basic three-dimensional figures like cubes, cylinders, and rectangular solids. A cylinder (shaped like a can) has two parallel circular bases of equal diameter. The height of a cylinder is measured perpendicular to the bases. The surface area of a cylinder is measured with the equation $A = 2(\pi r^2) + 2\pi rh$, in which r is the radius of the bases and h is the height. The volume of a cylinder can be calculated with the equation $V = \pi r^2 h$. A rectangular solid (shaped like a box) has six faces and twelve edges, connected at eight vertices. The volume of a rectangular solid is calculated with the equation $V = lwh$, in which l is length, w is width, and h is height. If these three measurements are equal, the rectangular solid is called a cube. The surface area of a rectangular solid is calculated with the equation $A = 2(wl + lh + wh)$; in other words, surface area is the sum of the areas of the six faces of the rectangular solid.

# Percents

When a number is expressed as a percentage, this means that it is being expressed as a portion of 100. Therefore, 25% is equivalent to 25 hundredths or 0.25. Another way to express this is as a fraction: 25/100. If you prefer, you can always convert the percentages on the GMAT into decimals or fractions. The most common kind of percentage problem you will see on the GMAT is one that asks you to find a certain percentage of a given number. These problems are easily solved by multiplying the decimal equivalent of the percentage by the given number. As an example, imagine you are asked to calculate 25% of 40: you would simply multiply 0.25 by 40, resulting in an answer of 10 (remember the rules for multiplying decimals!). A similar kind of question will ask you to determine what percentage of a given number another number is. For instance, a question might ask what percentage of 40 the number 8 is. The way to solve this kind of problem is to set up a proportional equation, such as 8/40 = x/100. This equation can be expressed as "8 is to 40 as x is to 100." Such an equation can then be solved by cross multiplying and solving for x, yielding an answer of 20%.

A percent can be converted to a decimal simply by dividing it by 100.  Example:

What is 2% of 50?

Answer: 2% = 2/100 or .02, so .02 * 50 = 1

# Word Problems

## Percents

Example: Ticket sales for this year's annual concert at Minutemaid Park were $125,000. The promoter is predicting that next year's sales, in dollars, will be 40% greater than this year's.  How many dollars in ticket sales is the promoter predicting for next year? Answer: Next year's is 40% greater.  40% = 40/100 = .4, so .4 * $125,000 = $50,000. However, the example stated that next year's would be greater by that amount, so next year's sales would be this year's at $125,000 plus the increase at $50,000.  $125,000 + $50,000 = $175,000

## Distances

The most common type of word problem on the GMAT is usually the one that asks you to consider distance, rate, and time.  You will recognize these problems: they begin with something like, "John drives 3 hours at 50 miles per hour.  How many miles does John drive?"  In other words, two values are given and you are asked to find the third.  This is easy to calculate when you remember the simple equation distance = rate x time.  In the example problem, the rate is 50 mph and the time is 3 hours, so the distance is 150 miles. Always make sure that the units in the problem are consistent. You will not get very far trying to convert kilometers per hour into miles.  Also, be aware that the unknown variable will not always be distance, and you will need to rearrange the equation to solve for rate or time.  For instance, if the problem states that "Dale drives 75 miles at 25 miles per hour," and asks you to determine how many hours Dale has been driving, you will need to solve for t, and your equation will be t = d/r.  If the problem asks you to solve for rate, the equation will need to be rearranged to r = d/t.  Example:

In a certain triangle, the longest side is 1 foot longer than the second-longest side, and the second-longest side is 1 foot longer than the shortest side.  If the perimeter is 30 feet, how many feet long is the shortest side.

Answer:  There are three sides, let's call them A, B, and C.  A is the longest, B the medium sized, and C the shortest.  Because A is described in reference to B's length and B is described in reference to C's length, all calculations should be done off of C, the final reference.  Use a variable to represent C's length, "x".  This means that C is "x" long, B is "x + 1" because B was 1 foot longer than C, and A is "x + 1 + 1" because A was 1 foot longer than B.  To calculate a perimeter you simply add all three sides together, so P = length A + length B + length C, or (x) + (x + 1) + (x + 1 + 1) = x + x + x + 1 + 1 + 1 = 3x + 3.  You know that the perimeter equals 30 feet, so 3x + 3 = 30.  Subtracting 3 from both sides gives 3x + 3 – 3 = 30 – 3 or 3x = 27.  Dividing both sides by 3 to get "x" all by itself gives 3x / 3 = 27 / 3 or x = 9.  So C = x = 9, and B = x + 1 = 9 + 1 = 10, and A = x + 1 + 1 = 9 + 1 + 1 = 11.  A quick check of 9 + 10 + 11 = 30 for the perimeter distance proves that the answer of x = 9 is correct

## Ratios

Example:  An architect is drawing a scaled blueprint of an apartment building that is to be 100 feet wide and 250 feet long.  On the drawing, if the building is 25 inches long, how many inches wide should it be.

Answer:  Recognize the word "scaled" to indicate a similar drawing.  Similar drawings or shapes can be solved using ratios.  First, create the ratio fraction for the missing number, in this case the number of inches wide the drawing should be.  The numerator of the first ratio fraction will be the matching known side, in this case "100 feet" wide.  The question "100 feet wide is to how many inches wide?" gives us the first fraction of 100 / x.  The question "250 feet long is to 25 inches long?" gives us the second fraction of 250 / 25.  Again, note that both numerators (100 and 250) are from the same shape.  The denominators ("x" and

25) are both from the same shape or drawing as well. Cross multiplication gives 100 * 25 = 250 * x or 2500 = 250x. Dividing both sides by 250 to get x by itself yields 2500 / 250 = 250x / 250 or 10 = x.

## Interest

Some GMAT word problems will require you to calculate the amount of interest that accrues on a given amount of money over a certain amount of time. In order to solve these problems, you will need to know the equation $I = prt$, in which I is interest, p is principal, r is rate of interest, and t is time. Imagine the following scenario: $20 is placed into an account with an annual interest rate of 5%. How much interest will the money have accrued over 5 years? The principal is $20, the interest rate is 5% (for the purposes of calculation you will want to convert the percentage into a decimal, so 5% becomes 0.05), and the time is 5, so the equation can be set up as $I = 20 \times 0.05 \times 5$, yielding an answer of $5. Remember to make sure that if the interest rate is annual, the time needs to be in units of years as well (for instance, six months would become 0.5). You will not need to worry about compound interest or variable rates: the interest-related questions on the GMAT do not get that complex.

## Special Formulas

### FOIL (first, outer, inner, last)

When you are given a problem such as $(x + 2)(x - 3)$, you should use the FOIL method of multiplication. First, multiply the First parts of each equation $(x*x)$. Then multiply the Outer parts of each equation $(x*-3)$. Note that you should treat the minus 3 in the second equation as a negative 3. Then multiply the Inner parts of each equation $(2*x)$. Finally, multiply the Last parts of each equation $(2*-3)$. Once you are finished, add each part together $(x*x)+(x*-3)+(2*x)+(2*-3) = x^2 + -3x + 2x + -6 = x^2 - 3x + 2x - 6 = x^2 - 1x - 6 = x^2 - x - 6$.

Also, the GMAT may give you the following variation involving FOIL: you may be given a quadratic equation and asked to convert it back into an equation with two parenthetical expressions. If you are given the equation x2 + 6x + 9 = 0, for example, you must find values that have a sum of 6 and a product of 9. The only values that can fit this description are 3 and 3, so the equivalent equation is (x + 3) (x + 3) = 0. If you try factoring this new equation with FOIL, you will arrive at the original version. Some versions of this problem will include negatives and will therefore be slightly more difficult. For example, x2 + 4x – 5 = 0 can be converted to (x + 5) (x – 1) = 0. Remember that this is true because 5 and -1 have a sum of 4 and a product of -5.

## Slope-Intercept formula

$y = mx + b$, where m is the slope of the line and b is the y-intercept.
Example:

  In the (x,y) coordinate plane, what is the slope of the line 2y = x – 4?
Answer: First this needs to be converted into slope intercept form. Divide both sides by 2, which gives 2y/2 = (x-4)/2 or y= x/2 – 2. x/2 is the same as ½ *x, so since m in the formula y = mx+b is the slope, then in the equation y = ½ * x – 2, ½ is the slope.

Example:

  In the (x,y) coordinate plane, where does the line y = 2x – 3 cross the y-axis?
Answer: In the formula y = mx + b, b is the y – intercept, or where the line crosses the y-axis. In this case, b is represented by –3, so –3 is where the line crosses the y-axis.

Example:

  In the (x , y) coordinate plane, what is the slope of the line y = x + 2?
Answer: This is already in the slope intercept form of y = mx + b. Whenever x does not have a number in front of it, you can always assume that there is a 1 there. Therefore, this equation could also be written as y = 1x + 2, which means m = 1, and the slope is 1.

**Slope formula**

$m = (y_1 - y_2)/(x_1 - x_2)$, where m is the slope of the line and two points on the line are given by $(x_1,y_1)$ and $(x_2,y_2)$. This can sometimes be remembered by the statement "rise over run", which means that the "y" values represent the "rise" as they are the up and down dimension and the "x" values represent the "run" as they are the side to side dimension. Example: What is the slope of a line that passes through points (5,1) and (-2, 3).
Answer:  $m = (y_1 - y_2)/(x_1 - x_2)$ or $(1 - 3)/(5 - -2)$ or $-2 / (5 + 2)$ or $-2 / 7$

# Line Plotting

Coordinate geometry is the placement of points, lines, and figures on a coordinate axis. On the GMAT, you are only going to work with coordinate geometry on a plane (i.e., in two dimensions). The two dimensions of a plane are defined with an x-axis which runs horizontally, and a y-axis which runs vertically. These two lines intersect at the origin and divide the plane into four quadrants. The quadrants are numbered in a counterclockwise fashion beginning with quadrant I in the upper right. Any point on the coordinate plane can be described with a pair of numbers: one indicates the point's placement on the x-axis, and the other indicates the point's placement on the y-axis. All the values on the x-axis that are to the left of the origin are negative. All of the values on the y-axis that are below the origin are negative. The point at which a line intersects the x-axis is known as the x-intercept, and the point at which the line intersects the y-axis is known as the y-intercept.

If you are trying to plot a line, there is an easy way to do it. First convert the line into slope intercept form ($y = mx + b$). Then, put a dot on the y-axis at the value of b. For example, if you have a line given by $y= 2/3x + 1$, then the first point on the line would be at (0,1), because 1 is the y-intercept, or where the line crosses the y-axis. To find the next point on the line, use the slope, which is 2/3. First go 2 increments up, and then 3 increments to the right. To find the next point on the line, go 2 more increments up, and then 3 more increments to the right. You should always go either up or down depending on the numerator in the slope fraction. So if the slope is 3/5, then the numerator is 3, and you should go 3 increments up and 5 increments to the right. You should always go to the right the amount of the denominator. So if the slope is –2, then first you should remember that –2 is the same as –2/1. Since –2 is the numerator, you should go down 2 increments and then 1 increment to the right.

Remember that positive slopes slope upward from left to right and that negative slopes slope downward from left to right.

## Mean, Median, Mode

Some questions on the GMAT may present you with a set of data and ask you to name the mean, median, or mode of the set. The mean of a set is the same thing as the average and is calculated in the same way, namely by adding together all the values in the set and dividing that sum by the number of values in the set. For instance, in the set of data {5, 6, 4, 9}, the mean would be calculated as follows: (5 + 6 + 4 + 9)/ 4 = 6. The median of a set is the middle value when the set is arranged from least to greatest. In the set {1, 3, 5}, the median is 3. If the set contains an even number of values, the median is calculated by adding together the 2 middle values and dividing by 2. For the set {2, 4, 6, 8}, the median would be calculated as follows: (4 + 6)/2 = 5. Finally, the mode of a set of data is the value within the set that occurs most frequently. Sometimes, a set will have more than one mode. If every value within the set appears only once, it will not have a mode at all.

## Average

The word average is synonymous with the word median. The basic rule for finding the average of a set of data is to add up all the members of the set and then divide by the number of members. The average of a set containing 1, 3, 6, and 6 would be calculated as follows: (1 + 3 + 6 + 6)/4 = 4.

Some problems will give you the average of an incomplete set of data and ask you to identify the missing term. You can solve this kind of problem by rearranging the equation for finding an average. Instead of average = sum/# of members, use sum = average x # of members. For instance, if you are told that the average of a set containing 7, 5, x, and 20 is 10, you can determine that the sum of the members of the set must be 10 x 4 = 40. Since the known members of the set add up to 32, the missing member of the set must be 8.

On rare occasions, you may have to deal with weighted averages in which some of the values in the set are given more importance than others. For example, imagine that during the last ten games a certain baseball team scored 8 runs one time, 4 runs three times, 2 runs five times, and 0 runs one time. You cannot simply add up 8, 4, 2, and 0 and divide by 4 to find the average number of runs scored over the last ten games. Instead, you need to establish a set of ten members and then multiply each value by its number of occurrences before adding. Therefore, the average would be calculated as follows: [1(8) + 3(4) + 5(2) + 1(0)]/10 = 3.

## Simple Probability

The probability problems on the GMAT are fairly straightforward. The basic idea is this: the probability that something will happen is the number of possible ways that something can happen divided by the total number of possible ways for all things that can happen. Example: I have 20 balloons, 12 are red, 8 are yellow. I give away one yellow balloon; if the next balloon is randomly picked, what is the probability that it will be yellow?
Answer: The probability is 7/19, because after giving one away, there are 7 different ways that the "something" can happen, divided by 19 remaining possibilities.

## Ratios

A ratio is simply a comparison between numbers. Indeed, ratios are noted in the same way as verbal analogies since both involve a consideration of the relationship between two things.  The ratio 4 to 5 would be expressed as 4:5.  Ratios can also be expressed as fractions, for example 4/5.  Some ratios can be simplified.  For instance, in the ratio 8:12, both terms are divisible by 4, so we can simplify the ratio to 2:3.

When a question asks about two similar shapes, expect a ratio problem.
Example: The figure below shows 2 triangles, where triangle ABC ~ A'B'C'.  In these similar triangles, a = 3, b = 4, c = 5, and a' = 6.  What is the value of b'?
Answer:  You are given the dimensions of 1 side that is similar on both triangles (a and a').
You are looking for b' and are given the dimensions of b.  Therefore you can set up a ratio of a/a' = b/b' or 3/6 = 4/b'.  To solve, cross multiply the two sides, multiplying 6*4 = 3*b' or 24 = 3b'.  Dividing both sides by 3 (24/3 = 3b'/3) makes 8 = b', so 8 is the answer.

Note many other problems may have opportunities to use a ratio.  Look for problems where you are trying to find dimensions for a shape and you have dimensions for a similar shape.  These can nearly always be solved by setting up a ratio.  Just be careful and set up corresponding measurements in the ratios.  First decide what you are being asked for on shape B, represented by a variable, such as x.  Then ask yourself, which side on similar shape A is the same size side as x.  That is your first ratio fraction, set up a fraction like 2/x if 2 is the similar size side on shape A.  Then find a side on each shape that is similar.  If 4 is the size of another side on shape A and it corresponds to a side with size 3 on shape B, then your second ratio fraction is 4/3.  Note that 2 and 4 are the two numerators in the ratio fractions and are both from shape A.  Also note that "x" the unknown side and 3 are both the denominators in the ratio fractions and are both from shape B.

## Graphs

The graphs used on the GMAT will be the kinds most familiar to students: circle/pie graphs, double axis line graphs, triple axis line graphs, and bar graphs.  Remember that on a circle or pie graph, the circle itself represents 1 or 100%.  A double axis graph, otherwise known as a line graph, has a horizontal and a vertical axis, each of which represents an individual variable. A triple axis graph has an additional vertical axis on the right side which is used to mark a third variable. A bar graph is composed of vertical or horizontal bars representing certain values. In rare cases, a question may include two kinds of graphs. When confronting this sort of problem, be sure that the units and scale used by the two graphs are consistent. If they are not, you will need to make adjustments in order to make accurate comparisons of data from each of the graphs.

## Lines

The basic unit of geometry is the line. Unless it is specified otherwise, lines are assumed to travel in opposite directions infinitely. Lines that are finite are called line segments. Where two lines intersect, angles are formed.

## Midpoints

To find a midpoint, find the difference in the x-direction between the two endpoints given, and divide by two. Then add that number to the leftmost endpoint's x coordinate. That will be the x coordinate of the midpoint. Next find the difference in the y-direction between the two endpoints given, and divide by two. Then add that number to the lower endpoint's y coordinate. That will be the y coordinate of the midpoint.

Example: What is the midpoint of the line segment with endpoints of (-2 , 5) and (4 , 1)?

Answer: First, subtract the leftmost endpoint's x coordinate from the rightmost endpoint's x coordinate 4 - -2 = 4 + 2 = 6. Then divide by two, 6 / 2 = 3. Then add that number to the leftmost x coordinate -2 + 3 = 1, which is the midpoint's x coordinate. Second, subtract the lower endpoint's y coordinate from the higher endpoint's y coordinate 5 – 1 = 4. Then divide by two, 4 / 2 = 2. Then add that number to the lower y coordinate 1 + 2 = 3, which is the midpoint's y coordinate. So the midpoint is given by (1 , 3).

# Geometry

## Angles

A right angle is one in which the two sides of the angle are perpendicular to one another; a right angle measures 90°. An acute angle has a measurement between 0° and 90°. An obtuse angle has a measure between 90° and 180°. An angle with a measure of 180° is called a straight angle, although for all intents and purposes, this is just a straight line. Two or more angles that add up to 90° are referred to as complementary angles. Two or more angles that add up to 180° are referred to as supplementary angles. There is no such thing as a negative angle or an angle measuring 0°. When two lines intersect and form 4 angles, the angles opposite one another are referred to as vertical angles; vertical angles are always equal. When two parallel lines (i.e., lines extending infinitely in either direction but never touching) are intersected by a third line, known as a transversal, the corresponding angles formed are called transverse angles.

If you have a two intersecting lines, remember that the sum of all of the angles can only be 360°. In fact, the two angles on either side of each line will add up to 180°. In the example below, on either side of each line, there is a 137° angle and a 43° angle (137° + 43°) = 180°. Also note that opposite angles are equal. For example, the 43° angle is matched by a similar 43° angle on the opposite side of the intersection.

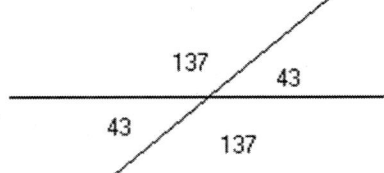

Additionally, parallel lines intersected by a third line will share angles. In the example below, note how each 128° angle is matched by a 128° angle on the opposite side. Also, all of the other angles in this example are 52° angles, because all of the angles on one side of a line have to equal 180° and since there are only two angles, if you have the degree of one, then you can find the degree of the other. In this case, the missing angle is given by 180° – 128° = 52°.

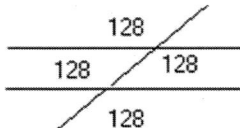

In every triangle, the largest angle is opposite the longest side. The sum of the lengths of the two smallest sides of a triangle will be greater than the length of the longest side. When the measurements of the angles inside a triangle are added up, the sum is always 180°. A triangle with three equal sides and three equal angles is known as an equilateral triangle. A triangle with two equal angles and two equal sides is referred to as an isosceles triangle. A triangle that has no equal sides and no equal angles is referred to as a scalene triangle.

Example:

If you have a triangle with two given angles of 20° and 130°, what degree is the third angle?

Answer: All angles must add up to 180°, so 180° – 20° – 130° = 30°.

## Right triangles

Whenever you see the words "right triangle" or "90° angle," alarm bells should go off. These problems will almost always involve the law of right triangles, AKA The Pythagorean Theorem:

$A^2 + B^2 = C^2$

Where A = the length of one of the shorter sides

B = the length of the other shorter side

C = the length of the hypotenuse or longest side opposite the 90° angle

**Make sure you know this formula.** At least 3-5 questions will reference variations on this formula by giving you two of the three variables and asking you to solve for the third.

Example: A right triangle has sides of 3 and 4; what is the length of the hypotenuse?

Answer: Solving the equation, $A^2=9$, $B^2=16$, so $C^2=25$; the square root of 25 is 5, the length of the hypotenuse C.

Example: In the rectangle below, what is the length of the diagonal line?

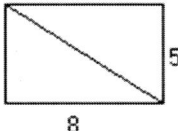

Answer: This rectangle is actually made of two right triangles. Whenever you have a right triangle, the Pythagorean Theorem can be used. Since the right side of the triangle is equal to 5, then the left side must also be equal to 5. This creates a triangle with one side equal to 5 and another side equal to 8. To use the Pythagorean Theorem, we state that $5^2 + 8^2 = C^2$ or $25 + 64 = C^2$ or $89 = C^2$ or C = Square Root of 89

**Quadrilaterals and Other Polygons**

A quadrilateral is any figure with four sides in which the four interior angles add up to 360°. There are a few special quadrilaterals. A quadrilateral with four equal sides and four right angles is called a square. A quadrilateral with four equal sides and four interior angles that are not equal is called a rhombus. A quadrilateral with four equal angles and two opposite and equal pairs of sides is called a rectangle. All the angles in a rectangle are right angles. A quadrilateral with two opposite and equal pairs of sides and two opposite and equal pairs of non-right angles is called a parallelogram. A quadrilateral with four unequal angles and one pair of parallel sides is called a trapezoid.

Triangles and quadrilaterals are the types of polygons (closed figures) you are most likely to encounter on the GMAT. You should know the names of some other regular polygons, however. A regular polygon is one in which all the sides and all the angles are equal. A regular polygon with five sides is called a pentagon. A regular polygon with six sides is called a hexagon. A regular pentagon with seven sides is called a heptagon. A regular polygon with eight sides is called an octagon. A regular polygon with nine sides is called a nonagon. A regular polygon with ten sides is called a decagon. There is a simple formula

- 79 -

for determining the sum of the interior angles in a regular polygon: simply subtract two from the number of sides and multiply by 180°. The sum of the interior angles of a pentagon, for instance, would be (5 – 2) 180° = 540°. You can find the measurement of each interior angle by dividing the sum of the interior angles by the number of sides in the figure: 540°/5 = 108°.

## Circles

In geometry, a circle is defined as all of the points in a plane that are the same distance from a given point (the center of the circle). The distance from the center of a circle to any point on its border is known as the radius. Any line that passes from one edge of the circle to another is called a chord. The length of a line extending from one edge of the circle to another and passing through the center is known as the diameter. The diameter is the longest chord in any given circle. The diameter of a circle is twice the radius. The distance around the edge of the circle is known as the circumference of the circle. The circumference of a circle can be determined with the following equation: c = 2πr, in which r is the radius of the circle. The set of points including and connecting any two points on the edge of the circle is called an arc of the circle. Like angles, arcs are measured in degrees; the largest possible arc is 360°. Any line that meets with a circle in exactly one point is called a tangent of that circle. The radius running from the center of the circle to the point at which a tangent touches the edge of the circle will be perpendicular to the tangent. Two or more circles that share a center but have different diameters are referred to as concentric circles.

Many students have never seen the formula for a circle:
$$(x-A)^2 + (y-B)^2 = r^2$$

This looks intimidating, but it's really not:

A = the coordinate of the center on the x-axis

B = the coordinate of the center on the y-axis

r = the radius of the circle

Example:

What is the radius of the circle described by: $(x+2)^2 + (x-3)^2 = 16$

Answer: Since $r^2 = 16$, r, the radius, equals 4.

Also, this circle is centered at (-2,3) since those must be the values of A and B in the generic equation to make it the same as this equation.

## Final note

Always draw out shape problems. Approach problems systematically. Take time to understand what is being asked for. In many cases there is a drawing or graph that you can write on. Draw lines, jot notes, do whatever is necessary to create a visual picture and to allow you to understand what is being asked. Even if you have always done well in math, you may not succeed on the GMAT. While math tests in high school and college test specific competencies in specific subjects, the GMAT frequently tests your ability to apply math concepts from vastly different math subjects in one problem. However, in few cases is any GMAT Quantitative problem more than two "layers" deep. What does this mean for you? You can easily learn the GMAT Quantitative through taking multiple practice tests. If you have some gaps in your math knowledge, we suggest you buy a more basic study guide to help you build a foundation before applying our secrets. Check out our special report to find out which books are worth your time.

# GMAT Verbal Test

The Verbal section of the GMAT consists of a 75 minute section with 41 questions.

There are three types of questions in the Verbal section of the GMAT.

    1.) Reading Comprehension

    2.) Critical Reasoning

    3.) Sentence Correction

## Reading Comprehension

The reading comprehension questions are the component of the Verbal Ability section that requires the most work. On your GMAT, you will be asked 12 or 13 questions based on four different passages, each of which will be approximately 350 words in length. These passages will pertain to topics in the physical sciences, social sciences, and in business. The reading comprehension exercises on the GMAT are designed to assess your ability to read carefully, analyze the relationships between different parts of a passage, and draw inferences from the material in the passage. The reading comprehension questions on the GMAT are of four basic types: main idea, detail, tone, and extending the author's reasoning. Each type of question calls for a slightly different approach.

The format of reading comprehension questions should not pose any problems. The passages of text will appear on the left side of the screen, and the questions will appear on the right. The directions preceding the questions will state the following, "The questions in this group are based on the content of a passage. After reading the passage, choose the best answer to each question. Answer all questions on the basis of what is stated or implied in the passage." You will be able to scroll back through the passage as much as you like. For the most part, questions pertaining to the beginning of the passage will come before questions pertaining to the end of the passage. The reading comprehension questions on the GMAT are meant to be comprehensible to a general audience and will not contain any specialized jargon. Also, you will not need any outside information or experience: all of the information required to answer the questions will be found in the passages. Now we will take a quick look at the content of the passages that will appear on the GMAT.

The biological and physical science passages are probably the most daunting for the majority of test-takers. Those students whose undergraduate careers did not include a great deal of hard science may be taken aback by the rigid structure and torrent of facts in a science passage. Remember, though, that the questions on the GMAT will not require any outside knowledge. It is also wise to keep in mind that you do not need to memorize the information in the passage since you will be able to refer to the text as much as you like. The science passages on the GMAT will be either specific or general. A specific science passage usually describes a particular study or set of research data without mentioning any ideas or ramifications outside the boundaries of the study. A specific passage will be akin to an article in a scientific journal. A general science passage, on the other hand, will be similar to an article in a scientific magazine. That is, it will describe a science-related topic in a manner that is more accessible to a general audience. It is typical for a general science article to focus the discussion on the possible consequences of research or on general theories that have arisen out of recent studies. Regardless of whether the science passage on the GMAT is specific or general, try to pay attention to the main theme of the passage without getting mired in excessive details. The questions following a science passage will most likely pertain to the elements of the passage that are most obvious to a reader with a non-science background.

The second content area from which reading comprehension passages may be drawn is the social sciences. The social sciences include sociology, psychology, history, business, and anthropology, among others. By and large, the social science passages will be similar to other science passages in the way the topics are addressed: that is, they will be either specific or general. One difference is that the authors of the GMAT will expect you to be a little bit better at extrapolating and making inferences based on the information in a social science passage. The authors assume that your common sense will enable you to evaluate a social science passage with more insight. For this reason, you are more likely on a social science passage to be asked to extend the reasoning of the passage or to describe the attitude of the author.

The third and final content area from which reading comprehension passages are drawn is business. These passages can be about anything remotely connected to business, including but not limited to government regulation, business ethics, and the use of technology in the workplace. Business passages will not be similar to the white papers or quarterly reports you may be familiar with from your own business experience. The passages on the GMAT will be much less technical. Indeed, these passages will most closely resemble magazine articles about business. Like a magazine article, most of these passages will be primarily descriptive and impartial. Some passages, however, will argue a particular position. In any case, you will not need to have any specialized knowledge of business or industry in order to understand the content of business passages.

## Directions

The questions in this group are based on the content of a passage. After reading the passage, choose the best answer to each question. Answer all questions following the passage on the basis of what is stated or implied in the passage.

## Types of Questions

Now that we have covered the content areas from which the reading comprehension passages will be drawn, let us consider the types of questions that you will encounter. The first and most basic kind of reading comprehension question will ask you to define the main idea of the passage. This question may arrive in any of a few different forms. The question may ask you for the "best summary," the "salient point," or the "overarching theme" of the passage. Do not be baffled by this language: this is a main idea question. As you no doubt have learned by now, the main idea of a passage is most likely to appear in either the first or the last sentence. As you are reading a passage for the first time, pay special attention to the beginning and the end. Whether the main idea is offered first or last will depend on the type of passage: expository passages tend to give a main idea first and spend the rest of the sentences defending it, and critical or argumentative essays will often begin with a set of loose facts and end with a summarizing conclusion. In any case, be prepared to refer back to the text in search of the main idea.

On occasion, the authors of the GMAT will try to fool you by asking you to provide the main idea of a specific part of the passage rather than of the passage as a whole. Similarly, they may try to confuse you with answer choices that, while true, do not express the main idea of the passage. For this reason, it is imperative that you read the question carefully and do not assume that the first or last sentence of the paragraph is the main idea. The main idea is not just any true statement contained within the passage: it is the idea that most effectively summarizes the entire passage.

It is certain that at least a couple of the reading comprehension questions will ask you to determine the main idea. In addition, it is quite likely that a few of the questions will ask you to recall specific details from the passage. This would appear to be the easiest kind of question to answer, but many students go astray by relying on memory instead of scrolling back up to find the pertinent details in the passage. As mentioned above, both the computer and paper versions of the GMAT allow you to refer to the text at will. Take advantage of this freedom. Remember also that specific questions are likely to have specific answers just as general questions are likely to have general answers. In other words, if the question asks for the identity of a concept, the answer will probably not be a piece of specific data.

A more subtle form of questioning will require speculation on the author's attitude. As with the main idea question, this kind of question can take a number of different forms. It may ask you to describe the "tone," "opinion," "feeling," or "mood" of the author or passage. All of these questions are essentially asking you to assess how the author feels about his or her topic. In order to answer such a question, you will have to pay attention to the specific language used by the author and the point of view that the language conveys. For instance, if the author is describing a small person, he or she would create a sharply different tone by using the word puny than would be created by using the word petite. Puny suggests a shriveled, scrawny individual while petite conjures daintiness and delicacy. It may take a little bit of practice before you habitually notice these shades of meaning, but you should try to be conscious of the ways in which language can be used to subtly indicate attitude.

When dealing with questions of tone, you should also consider the genre of the passage. For instance, specific science passages, whether in biology, physical sciences, or the social sciences, are almost always written in an objective, nonjudgmental tone. These passages will rarely demonstrate a strong opinion, so you should avoid any answer choices that suggest a positive or negative view on the part of the author. Business essays, on the other hand, can often be quite opinionated. Even general passages on the sciences may evince a clear positive or negative disposition. However, the GMAT typically avoids passages that are highly opinionated or controversial. Answer choices suggesting that the author holds an opinion that could be considered radical or offensive are most likely incorrect.

The final category of question types that you may encounter on the GMAT is one that asks you to extend the author's reasoning. Put another way, these questions require you to consider the information provided in the passage and then use this information to consider a problem that is not mentioned in the passage. For instance, a specific science passage about the migratory patterns of a certain predatory bird might ask you to consider the effects of these migrations on the populations of rodents in various regions. Even if the passage has not mentioned rodents up to this point, you should be able to guess that more rodents will be killed when the predatory birds are in the area. The most common problem students have with questions asking them to extend the reasoning of the passage is that they attempt to find the answer explicitly in the passage. Remember that even though all of the information needed to answer every question can be found in the text, some questions will require you to do some independent thinking.

## Skimming

Your first task when you begin reading is to answer the question "What is the topic of the selection?" This can best be answered by quickly skimming the passage for the general idea, stopping to read only the first sentence of each paragraph. A paragraph's first sentence is usually the main topic sentence, and it gives you a summary of the content of the paragraph. Once you've skimmed the passage, stopping to read only the first sentences, you will have a general idea about what it is about, as well as what is the expected topic in each paragraph.

Each question will contain clues as to where to find the answer in the passage. Do not just randomly search through the passage for the correct answer to each question. Search scientifically. Find **key word**(s) or ideas in the question that are going to either contain or be near the correct answer. These are typically nouns, verbs, numbers, or phrases in the question that will probably be duplicated in the passage. Once you have identified those key word(s) or idea, skim the passage quickly to find where those key word(s) or idea appears. The correct answer choice will be nearby.

Example:

What caused Martin to suddenly return to Paris?

The key word is Paris. Skim the passage quickly to find where this word appears. The answer will be close by that word.

### General Idea

However, sometimes key words in the question are not repeated in the passage. In those cases, search for the general idea of the question. Example:

Which of the following was the psychological impact of the author's childhood upon the remainder of his life?

Key words are "childhood" or "psychology". While searching for those words, be alert for other words or phrases that have *similar meaning*, such as "emotional effect" or "mentally" which could be used in the passage, rather than the exact word "psychology".

Numbers

Numbers or years can be particularly good key words to skim for, as they stand out from the rest of the text. Example:

Which of the following best describes the influence of Monet's work in the 20th century?

20th contains numbers and will easily stand out from the rest of the text. Use 20th as the key word to skim for in the passage.

Punctuation

Other good key word(s) may be in quotation marks. These identify a word or phrase that is copied directly from the passage. In those cases, the word(s) in quotation marks are exactly duplicated in the passage. Example:

In her college years, what was meant by Margaret's "drive for excellence"?

"Drive for excellence" is a direct quote from the passage and should be easy to find.

**Beware of Directly Quoted Answers**

Once you've quickly found the correct section of the passage to find the answer, focus upon the answer choices. Sometimes a choice will repeat word for word a portion of the passage near the answer. However, beware of such duplication – it may be a trap! More than likely, the correct choice will paraphrase or summarize the related portion of the passage, rather than being exactly the same wording.

## True does not equal correct

For the answers that you think are correct, read them carefully and make sure that they answer the question. An answer can be factually correct, but it MUST answer the question asked. Additionally, two answers can both be seemingly correct, so be sure to read all of the answer choices, and make sure that you get the one that BEST answers the question.

## When there's no key word

Some questions will not have a key word. Example:

> Which of the following would the author of this passage likely agree with?

In these cases, look for key words in the answer choices. Then skim the passage to find where the answer choice occurs. By skimming to find where to look, you can minimize the time required.

Sometimes it may be difficult to identify a good key word in the question to skim for in the passage. In those cases, look for a key word in one of the answer choices to skim for. Often the answer choices can all be found in the same paragraph, which can quickly narrow your search.

## Paragraph focus

Focus upon the first sentence of each paragraph, which is the most important. The main topic of the paragraph is usually there.

Once you've read the first sentence in the paragraph, you have a general idea about what each paragraph will be about. As you read the questions, try to determine which paragraph will have the answer. Paragraphs have a concise topic. The answer should either obviously be there or obviously not. It will save time if you can jump straight to the paragraph, so try to remember what you learned from the first sentences.

Example:

The first paragraph is about poets; the second is about poetry. If a question asks about poetry, where will the answer be? It will be in the second paragraph.

The main idea of a passage is typically spread across all or most of its paragraphs. Whereas the main idea of a paragraph may be completely different than the main idea of the very next paragraph, a main idea for a passage affects all of the paragraphs in one form or another.

Example:

What is the main idea of the passage?

For each answer choice, try to see how many paragraphs are related. It can help to count how many sentences are affected by each choice, but it is best to see how many paragraphs are affected by the choice. Typically the answer choices will include incorrect choices that are main ideas of individual paragraphs, but not the entire passage. That is why it is crucial to choose ideas that are supported by the most paragraphs possible.

**Eliminate choices**

Some choices can quickly be eliminated. "Andy Warhol lived there." Is Andy Warhol even mentioned in the article? If not, quickly eliminate it.

When trying to answer a question such as "the passage indicates all of the following EXCEPT" quickly skim the paragraph searching for references to each choice. If the reference exists, scratch it off as a choice. Similar choices may be crossed off simultaneously if they are close enough.

Watch for answers that are similarly worded. Since only one answer can be correct, if there are two answers that appear to mean the same thing, they must BOTH be incorrect, and can be eliminated.

Example Answer Choices:

A. changing values and attitudes

B. a large population of mobile or uprooted people

These answer choices are similar; they both describe a fluid culture. Because of their similarity, they can be linked together. Since the answer can have only one choice, they can also be eliminated together.

## Contextual clues

Look for contextual clues. An answer can be right but not correct. The contextual clues will help you find the answer that is most right and is correct. Understand the context in which a phrase is stated.

When asked for the implied meaning of a statement made in the passage, immediately go find the statement and read the context. Also, look for an answer choice that has a similar phrase to the statement in question. Example:

In the passage, what is implied by the phrase "Churches have become more or less part of the furniture"?

Find an answer choice that is similar or describes the phrase "part of the furniture" as that is the key phrase in the question. "Part of the furniture" is a saying that means something is fixed, immovable, or set in their ways. Those are all similar ways of saying "part of the furniture." As such, the correct answer choice will probably include a similar rewording of the expression. Example:

Why was John described as "morally desperate"?

The answer will probably have some sort of definition of morals in it. "Morals" refers to a code of right and wrong behavior, so the correct answer choice will likely have words that mean something like that.

**Fact/opinion**

Remember that answer choices that are facts will typically have no ambiguous words. For example, how long is a long time? What defines an ordinary person? These ambiguous words of "long" and "ordinary" should not be in a factual statement. However, if all of the choices have ambiguous words, go to the context of the passage. Often a factual statement may be set out as a research finding. Example:

"The scientist found that the eye reacts quickly to change in light."

Opinions may be set out in the context of words like thought, believed, understood, or wished. Example:

"He thought the Yankees should win the World Series."

## Sentence Correction

Each question includes a sentence with part or all of it underlined. Your five answer choices will offer different ways to reword or rephrase the underlined portion of the sentence. The first answer choice merely repeats the original underlined text, while the other four offer different wording.

Sentence correction questions specifically target your command of the English language and the norms of standard written English. Some sentence correction questions will test your knowledge of specific rules of grammar while others will gauge your ability to notice errors of style or tone in a sentence. Do not be alarmed if you do not remember your grammar instruction from high school: sentence correction questions on the GMAT are limited to a few clear and basic rules of style and grammar. After taking a quick look at the format of the sentence correction questions, we will cover all of the content you will need for this portion of the exam.

The structure of sentence correction questions is laid out in detail in the directions preceding these questions:

This question presents a sentence, all or part of which is underlined.

Beneath the sentence you will find five ways of phrasing the underlined part. The first of these repeats the original; the other four are different. If you think the original is best, choose the first answer; otherwise, choose one of the other answers. This question tests correctness and effectiveness of expression. In choosing your answer, follow the requirements of standard written English; that is, pay attention to grammar, choice of words, and sentence construction. Choose the answer that produces the most effective sentence; this answer should be clear and exact, without awkwardness, ambiguity, redundancy, or grammatical error.

You should not have any trouble deciphering the structure of a sentence correction question. The only important point to remember is that the first answer choice is always exactly the same as the given sentence. You should only choose this answer choice when you believe the sentence is correct as written.

Your approach to sentence correction exercises should be simple: read the original sentence carefully, mentally substitute each of the answer choices, eliminate wrong answers, and confirm your judgment by reading to yourself the corrected sentence. You should be able to articulate a reason for eliminating or selecting a given answer choice.

Remember that sentence correction questions will not concern issues of vocabulary, slang, or punctuation. In some cases, the correct answer choice will produce a sentence that remains awkward or inelegant; do not get hung up on aesthetics. Other times, more than one answer choice will produce a sentence that is grammatically correct. If this is the case, try to determine which of the new sentences is more fluent. The good news about sentence correction questions is that they only cover a limited number of linguistic topics. Indeed, when making the sentence correction questions, the writers of the GMAT refer to a short list of structural and grammatical issues that we will now cover in some detail.

## Use your ear

Read each sentence carefully, inserting the answer choices in the blanks. Don't stop at the first answer choice if you think it is right, but read them all. What may seem like the best choice, at first, may not be after you have had time to read all of the choices. Allow your ear to determine what sounds right. Often one or two answer choices can be immediately ruled out because it doesn't sound logical or make sense.

## Contextual clues

It bears repeating that contextual clues offer a lot of help in determining the best answer. Key words in the sentence will allow you to determine exactly which answer choice is the best replacement text. Example:

> Archeology has shown that some of the ruins of the ancient city of Babylon are
> approximately 500 years <u>as old as any supposed</u> Mesopotamian predecessors.
> A. as old as their supposed
> B. older than their supposed

In this example, the key word "supposed" is used. Archaeology would either confirm that the predecessors to Babylon were more ancient or disprove that supposition. Since supposed was used, it would imply that archaeology had disproved the accepted belief, making Babylon actually older, not as old as, and answer choice "B" correct.

Furthermore, because "500 years" is used, answer choice A can be ruled out. Years are used to show either absolute or relative age. If two objects are as old as each other, no years are necessary to describe that relationship, and it would be sufficient to say, "The ancient city of Babylon is approximately as old as their supposed Mesopotamian predecessors," without using the term "500 years".

## Simplicity is Bliss

Simplicity cannot be overstated. You should never choose a longer, more complicated, or wordier replacement if a simple one will do. When a point can be made with fewer words, choose that answer. However, never sacrifice the flow of text for simplicity. If an answer is simple, but does not make sense, then it is not correct.

Beware of added phrases that don't add anything of meaning, such as "to be" or "as to them". Often these added phrases will occur just before a colon, which may come before a list of items. However, the colon does not need a lengthy introduction. The italics phrases in the below examples are wordy and unnecessary. They should be removed and the colon placed directly after the words "sport" and "following".

Example 1:

> There are many advantages to running as a sport, *of which the top advantages are*:

Example 2:

> The school supplies necessary were the following, *of which a few are*:

## Sentence fragments

A sentence fragment is one of the easiest errors to spot. Sentences are considered fragments when they are missing either a subject or a predicate. For instance, look at the following fragment: General Davis, having learned about the possible ambush. There is a subject (General Davis) and a supporting clause, but there is no predicate telling us what he did with the information he learned. Remember that having a verb does not guarantee that a sentence will also have a predicate. The verb must be in agreement with the subject. Since sentence fragments are fairly easy to spot, the GMAT will often try to camouflage them by making them extremely long. Remember that no matter how many words it contains, a sentence is a fragment if it does not contain both a subject and a predicate.

## Parallel construction error

When two or more words or phrases are being placed in the same grammatical position in a sentence, they are said to be parallel. Words or phrases that are parallel need to receive the same grammatical treatment. Several of the sentence correction exercises on the GMAT will concern the two main forms of parallel construction: lists and correlatives. When a sentence contains a list, all of the items in the list need to receive the same grammatical treatment. As an example, read the following sentence: Andrew had all the symptoms of influenza: headache, fever, and he was nauseous. Notice how the first two items in the list are simply named while the last item includes the words he was. A grammatically-correct version of this list would read: headache, fever, and nausea. Of course, it would also be possible to correct the list as follows: he had a headache, he had a fever, and he was nauseous. This is a more awkward wording, but it is a consistent parallel construction. The essential point about parallel constructions is that they must be consistent for all of the items in a list.

The second way in which parallel constructions will be covered on the GMAT is linked with correlatives. Ideas that are parallel in a sentence must be given the same grammatical treatment. For instance, read the following sentence: Most people think it is easier to read a book than writing one. Since the infinitive form to read is used in the first part of the sentence, the words to write should be substituted for writing. Here is another example: Dr. Baker asked us either to study for the test or wait a week. The incorrect parallel construction is a little more subtle here, but if the infinitive form to study is used then the word to should also be inserted before wait. Whenever you believe a sentence correction exercise may hinge on an incorrect parallel construction, scan the parallel components of the sentence and determine whether or not they are receiving the same grammatical treatment.

## Faulty comparison

The GMAT will often contain sentences in which a faulty comparison is made. A faulty comparison exists when the author unintentionally creates a comparison between two unlike ideas or things. Consider the comparison made by the following sentence: Some people think that the citizens of America are healthier than other countries. Notice that the author is technically comparing the citizens of America with other countries. The author's intent is made clear in the corrected sentence. Some people think that the citizens of America are healthier than the citizens of other countries. Always make sure that the comparison being made in a sentence is between the right ideas or things.

## Punctuation

If a section of text has an opening dash, parentheses, or comma at the beginning of a phrase, then you can be sure there should be a matching closing dash, parentheses, or comma at the end of the phrase. If items in a series all have commas between them, then any additional items in that series will also gain commas. Do not alternate punctuation. If a dash is at the beginning of a statement, then do not put a parenthesis at the ending of the statement.

## Word confusion

"Which" should be used to refer to things only.

> "John's dog, which was called Max, is large and fierce."

"That" may be used to refer to either persons or things.

> "Is this the only book that Louis L'Amour wrote?"

> "Is Louis L'Amour the author that [or who] wrote Western novels?"

"Who" should be used to refer to persons only.

> "Mozart was the composer who [or that] wrote those operas."

## Adjective/adverb error

Once you know what to look for, spotting errors in the use of adjectives and adverbs should be easy. An adjective describes a noun while an adverb may describe a verb, adjective, or another adverb. In general (but not always), an adverb will end with –ly. The sentence correction exercises on the GMAT will probably include a couple of sentences in which the wrong part of speech is used. For instance, look at the following sentence: The end of the song was beautifully. This sentence sounds wrong to the ear because the adverbial form is inappropriate for modifying the noun phrase end of the song. The correct word would be the adjective beautiful.

One common exception to the –ly rule regarding adverbs involves two adverbs in a row. In such a case, it is typical for the –ly to be eliminated from the second adverb. Consider the following sentence: I didn't feel particularly sadly about the cancelled party. Even though particularly and sadly are both adverbs, the sentence is incorrect until the –ly is removed from sadly: I didn't feel particularly sad about the cancelled party.

## Correct pronoun usage

Personal pronouns are words like we, him, it, and our that substitute for individuals or groups of people. Occasionally, in a complicated sentence, it can be difficult to determine the appropriate personal pronoun. In order to confidently assert the correct personal pronoun, you need to know the different cases in which a pronoun can be used. The first of these is the subjective case that includes I, we, you, he/she/it, and they. These words are used when the pronoun is functioning as the subject of the sentence, as in the following: Jim and he were the winners. The subjective case is also used when the pronoun is used as a complement to the subject, as in Steve told us that the winners were Jim and he, in which he is a substitute for Steve.

The pronouns me, us, you, him/her/it, and them are used in the objective case. Pronouns are placed into the objective case when they are used as the direct object, indirect object, or object of a preposition. The following is an example of a pronoun being used as a direct object: Sarah called Bob and invited him to the party. Here is an example of a pronoun being used as an indirect object: Yancey gave me a wonderful present. This is an example of a pronoun being used as the object of a preposition: Sally decided that the gift must be for her.

Finally, pronouns may also be used in the possessive case, as in the forms my, our, your, his/her/its, and their. These are used when the pronoun is establishing ownership of something, as in the sentence Dave looked high and low for his lunch.

The personal pronoun errors on the GMAT will usually be fairly obvious. One helpful way to identify a personal pronoun error is to consciously consider the case in which the pronoun is being used. For instance, look at the following sentence: I can't see anything wrong with you being here. The pronoun I is correct because it is being used as a subject, but since it describes your being here, you actually needs to be in the possessive case your. If you think the sentence may have a personal pronoun error, see if you can pinpoint the exact error of case.

Another way in which pronouns can be used incorrectly is in relation to their antecedents. A pronoun's antecedent is the word to which it refers. A pronoun must always have a clear antecedent, and it must always agree with this antecedent in number. Consider the following sentence: Darryl and Dirk went to the beach, but he didn't go swimming. To which person does the pronoun he refer? This sentence needs to be corrected to make the tie between pronoun and antecedent clear. A possible correction could be Darryl and Dirk went to the beach, but they didn't go swimming.

Pronouns must also agree with their antecedents in number. Consider the following sentence: A student must realize that not every teacher will be right for them. This is actually one of the more common errors in written English: the pronoun them is plural, but it refers to a singular student. A corrected version of the sentence would read as follows: A student must realize that not every teacher will be right for him or her. Whenever you are unsure about pronoun-antecedent agreement, isolate the components and make sure that they have the same number.

## Disagreement between subject and verb

The subject and verb in a sentence or clause should always agree in number. This is a fairly basic point of grammar, so the GMAT will try to disguise disagreement by inserting prepositional phrases between the subject and the verb. For instance, read the following sentence: The child with young parents have more life skills than other children. Because have is placed after parents, it almost sounds correct. Remember, though, that the subject and simple predicate (verb) of this sentence is "child have", which is clearly incorrect. The best way to diagnose disagreement between subject and verb is to eliminate any extra diction and to consider the relation of the subject to the simple predicate.

## Verb tense error

The GMAT frequently contains errors of verb tense in the sentence correction exercises. Although these mistakes will often be obvious, in some cases they will be hidden by extraneous clauses and prepositional phrases. A good rule of thumb regarding verb tense is that a sentence should maintain the same verb tense throughout. Consider the following sentence: Dale spent a year in college and had read several books on the subject. The first verb (spent) is in the past tense while the second (had read) is in the past perfect. In order to correct this sentence, the verb tenses need to be made consistent, as in the following: Dale spent a year in college and read several books on the subject.

There are some exceptions to the rule of consistency in verb tenses. Occasionally, a sentence will indicate that two or more things are happening at different times, as in the following: Please tell me when you will mow the grass. Obviously, the present tense (tell) and future tense (will mow) are appropriate when the speaker is requesting information about something in the future. Therefore, look for consistency in verb tenses, unless the sentence is clearly establishing two different time periods.

## Misplaced modifier

A modifier is any word, phrase, or clause that alters the meaning of another word in the sentence. A modifier can be an adjective, an adverb, or a participial expression. The GMAT frequently includes sentences with misplaced modifiers. There are a few different ways that modifiers can be misplaced. One common modifier error is when a participial phrase modifies the wrong word, as in: While looking for the restaurant, John's car got pulled over. The participial phrase that begins this sentence should modify the first word after the comma; in this construction, the sentence implies that John's car was looking for the restaurant!

Other forms of misplaced modifier errors will feature participial phrases, adjectives, and adjectival phrases that modify the wrong noun or pronoun. For instance, read this sentence: Tender-hearted, the movie brought Fred to tears several times. Obviously, the sentence means to imply that Fred, not the movie, is tender-hearted. The corrected version would read: Tender-hearted, Fred was brought to tears several times by the movie.

## Incorrect idiomatic expression

One of the trickier areas that the GMAT occasionally covers is idiomatic expression. This topic is difficult to study because it relies more on an acquired sense of written English than on any consistent rules of grammar. For instance, there is no clear reason why we say that something is defined as or results in. Surely, it would make no less sense to say defined of or results by, but these constructions are plainly incorrect. Because idiomatic expression is such a vague subject, you should only consider it as a possibility when you have exhausted all of the other possible errors in the sentence. To get the best sense of whether an underlined expression "sounds" right, try isolating it from the rest of the sentence and saying it aloud (quietly, of course!).

# Commas

**Flow**

Commas break the flow of text. To test whether they are necessary, while reading the text to yourself, pause for a moment at each comma. If the pauses seem natural, then the commas are correct. If they are not, then the commas are not correct.

**Nonessential clauses and phrases**

A comma should be used to set off nonessential clauses and nonessential participial phrases from the rest of the sentence. To determine if a clause is essential, remove it from the sentence. If the removal of the clause would alter the meaning of the sentence, then it is essential. Otherwise, it is nonessential. Example:

John Smith, who was a disciple of Andrew Collins, was a noted archeologist.

In the example above, the sentence describes John Smith's fame in archeology. The fact that he was a disciple of Andrew Collins is not necessary to that meaning. Therefore, separating it from the rest of the sentence with commas, is correct.

Do not use a comma if the clause or phrase is essential to the meaning of the sentence. Example:

Anyone who appreciates obscure French poetry will enjoy reading the book.

If the phrase "who appreciates obscure French poetry" is removed, the sentence would indicate that anyone would enjoy reading the book, not just those with an appreciation for obscure French poetry. However, the sentence implies that the book's enjoyment may not be for everyone, so the phrase is essential.

Another perhaps easier way to determine if the clause is essential is to see if it has a comma at its beginning or end. Consistent, parallel punctuation must be used, and so if you can determine a comma exists at one side of the clause, then you can be certain that a comma should exist on the opposite side.

**Independent clauses**

Use a comma before the words and, but, or, nor, for, yet when they join independent clauses. To determine if two clauses are independent, remove the word that joins them. If the two clauses are capable of being their own sentence by themselves, then they are independent and need a comma between them. Example:

He ran down the street, and then he ran over the bridge.

He ran down the street. Then he ran over the bridge. These are both clauses capable of being their own sentence. Therefore a comma must be used along with the word "and" to join the two clauses together.

If one or more of the clauses would be a fragment if left alone, then it must be joined to another clause and does not need a comma between them. Example:

He ran down the street and over the bridge.

He ran down the street. Over the bridge. "Over the bridge" is a sentence fragment and is not capable of existing on its own. No comma is necessary to join it with "He ran down the street".

Note that this does not cover the use of "and" when separating items in a series, such as "red, white, and blue". In these cases a comma is not always necessary between the last two items in the series, but in general it is best to use one.

## Parenthetical expressions

Commas should separate parenthetical expressions such as the following: after all, by the way, for example, in fact, on the other hand. Example:

By the way, she is in my biology class.

If the parenthetical expression is in the middle of the sentence, a comma would be both before and after it. Example:

She is, after all, in my biology class.

However, these expressions are not always used parenthetically. In these cases, commas are not used. To determine if an expression is parenthetical, see if it would need a pause if you were reading the text. If it does, then it is parenthetical and needs commas. Example:

You can tell by the way she plays the violin that she enjoys its music.

No pause is necessary in reading that example sentence. Therefore the phrase "by the way" does not need commas around it.

## Hyphens

Hyphenate a compound adjective that is directly before the noun it describes.

Example 1: He was the best-known kid in the school.

Example 2: The shot came from that grass-covered hill.

Example 3: The well-drained fields were dry soon after the rain.

# Semicolons

## Period replacement

A semicolon is often described as either a weak period or strong comma. Semicolons should separate independent clauses that could stand alone as separate sentences. To test where a semicolon should go, replace it with a period in your mind. If the two independent clauses would seem normal with the period, then the semicolon is in the right place. Example:

> The rain had finally stopped; a few rays of sunshine were pushing their way through the clouds.

The rain had finally stopped. A few rays of sunshine were pushing their way through the clouds. These two sentences can exist independently with a period between them. Because they are also closely related in thought, a semicolon is a good choice to combine them.

## Transitions

When a semicolon is next to a transition word, such as "however", it comes before the word. Example:

> The man in the red shirt stood next to her; however, he did not know her name.

If these two clauses were separated with a period, the period would go before the word "however" creating the following two sentences: The man in the red shirt stood next to her. However, he did not know her name. The semicolon can function as a weak period and join the two clauses by replacing the period.

# Critical Reasoning

The skills you will need to succeed on critical reasoning questions will be basically the same as those required for the Analysis of an Argument essay. The questions will ask you to critique a given argument, suggest ways to make it stronger or weaker, and draw basic inferences from it. The format of critical reasoning questions is simple. In fact, the directions consist of the single sentence, "For this question, select the best of the answer choices given."

These directions will be followed by a short passage of text, either three or four sentences in length. You will then be asked one or two questions about the passage. The topics of the textual passages are of little importance, and they may concern any number of subjects. You will not be required to possess any specialized knowledge to answer critical reasoning questions. Your focus should be placed squarely on the structure and quality of the argument rather than on the particular topic under consideration.

## Types of Questions

The first and most common type of critical reasoning question concerns the assumptions made by the argument. Assumptions, of course, are anything that is not explicitly stated but must be believed to be true in order for the reasoning of the argument to make sense. In order to judge the validity of an argument, you will need to understand and affirm the assumptions made by the argument. Many arguments that seem conclusive will fall apart when it is discovered that they rest on faulty assumptions. For this reason, the makers of the GMAT want to ensure that you are skilled at identifying and evaluating assumptions. To get an idea of the kinds of assumptions that are integral to the GMAT, we will take a look at an example prompt:

> Providing children with an hour of free time during the school day is beneficial to learning. Recent studies indicate that if children get an hour of cardiovascular

exercise before learning, they are more likely to retain the material learned. For this reason, teachers should make sure their pupils get free time during the school day.

This argument makes a number of assumptions. To begin with, it assumes that students will use an hour of free time to exercise. It also assumes that teachers will be able to give their students free time early in the day or at least before intense learning situations. Finally, it assumes that the decision as to whether or not to give students free time is left up to teachers.

These assumptions affect the strength of the argument to varying degrees. The most dubious assumption is that students will use free time to get vigorous exercise. It seems quite likely that many students will not exercise unless they are directly encouraged to do so. The assumption that teachers will be able to give students free time at the most beneficial point in the day is also questionable. The argument does not go into enough detail to indicate whether an hour of free time/exercise could be fit into a normal school day. The assumption that teachers have the power to grant free time does not exactly weaken the argument, but it might raise doubts in the mind of the reader. In order to be air-tight, the author would need to show that this decision is made by teachers.

Therefore, the strength of an argument depends not only on the validity of its premises and conclusions, but on how reasonable its assumptions are. A typical assumption question on the GMAT will ask you to identify which assumptions make either the whole argument or a particular part of the argument possible. It is common for the assumption in question to be faulty or doubtful. Remember the four common types of faulty assumptions we outlined in the Analytical Writing section: generalization, causal, sampling, and analogy. A generalization assumption is faulty when it makes a blanket statement about an entire category based on observations about one member of that category. For instance, if in the above example the author wrote, "All children enjoy vigorous exercise," he would be guilty of a faulty generalization assumption. A poor causal assumption suggests that one event happens as a result of another, even though this connection is not obvious. The above example contains the weak causal assumption that if children are given an hour of free time, they will use it to exercise. A third kind of assumption that is often dubious is the sampling assumption in which the author assumes that what is true for a small number of a population is also true for the population as a whole. The author of our example would be guilty of a poor sampling assumption if it was determined that the study to which he referred had actually focused on only a small group of children of a specific age. The last kind of assumption that you should be wary of is the analogy assumption, in which the argument assumes similarities between two things. The example argument would be guilty of an erroneous analogy assumption if it suggested that since hamsters are calmer after vigorous exercise, young children would be as well. There are too many differences between hamsters and young children for this to be a strong assumption.

The second common type of critical reasoning question asks you to identify additional information that would weaken the argument. You will be presented with five pieces of additional evidence or reasoning and asked to name the one that would most seriously undermine the argument. Specifically, you are looking for the statement that does the most damage to the conclusion of the argument.

There are a number of ways that additional information can weaken an argument. In order to examine these ways more closely, we will look at another example of a critical reasoning prompt:

> The Hendersonville Hornets have been a much better team ever since they signed the starting pitcher known as "Hurricane" Robinson. When he joined the team, they were in last place in the division, but they are now in second place and gaining fast on the first-place Tigers. Robinson has single-handedly brought the Hornets back to life.

Clearly, this argument is resting on a number of assumptions, and one of the main ways in which additional information can weaken an argument is by disproving or contradicting these assumptions. For instance, the argument states that Robinson has single-handedly made the team better, but it does not specifically demonstrate that he has been a great player or that the other players on the team have not improved their play. A potentially damaging piece of information could possibly be a statistic indicating that Robinson has only been decent while his teammates have vastly improved since his arrival.

Another assumption made by this argument is that the other teams in the division have remained the same while the Hornets have improved. The author indicates that the Hornets have improved their position in the division standings, but he asserts rather than proves that this is because of Robinson. It would be quite possible to weaken the argument by indicating that while the Hornets have improved a little bit, the other teams in the division have gotten much worse.

It is also possible for a statement to weaken an argument by challenging the premises. For instance, the information that a starting pitcher only plays once every five games would seem to suggest that Robinson cannot be the only reason for the Hornets' success. Also, the author states that the Hornets started out in last place, but does not indicate how many teams are in the division. If there are only three teams in the division, a move up to second place does not indicate as much improvement as it would if there were seven teams.

In order to find the statement that most effectively weakens an argument, you should be looking for the statement that contradicts or undermines the assumptions or premises. The GMAT will try to confuse you by including answer choices that seem to be correct at first glance. It is common for the answer choices to include statements that could either strengthen or weaken the argument, depending on unknown facts. For instance, one of the answer choices for our example prompt might be, "First baseman Ted Flanders has not missed a game since Robinson joined the team." This is a good thing only if Flanders has been playing well during this period; if not, the fact that he has not missed a game might be hurting the team.

It is also common for answer choices on a weakening-argument question to consist of irrelevant information. The answer choice you select must directly affect the conclusion of the argument given. For instance, one of the answer choices for our example prompt might be, "In his career, Robinson has won 68 games and lost 58." This information may suggest that Robinson is not a dominant pitcher, but it neither undermines nor supports the reasoning in the passage. It is irrelevant. Remember that the information that most firmly weakens the argument is the information that directly contradicts either the premises or the assumptions.

Another similar sort of question will ask you to identify the statement that most effectively strengthens the argument. We will not need to spend a great deal of time considering this type of question since it simply involves identifying the opposite of evidence that weakens the argument. In many cases, the correct answer will supply an assumption or a piece of evidence that makes the conclusion stronger. In some instances, though, the correct answer will simply support a pre-existing assumption or reason.

Let us examine a case in which additional information could strengthen an argument:

> A series of earthquakes in South America have decimated the avocado harvest, resulting in skyrocketing prices. This means that guacamole manufacturers will have to pay much more for their main ingredient, and store-bought guacamole will become much more expensive for the average consumer.

Before we determine the information that would most effectively strengthen this argument, we will consider the reasoning and assumptions in it. To start with, this argument assumes that all avocadoes come from South America. If guacamole manufacturers really have no other choice than to buy from South America, they will be forced to pay the elevated prices. Besides this assumption, the argument also depends on the reasoning that the price of store bought guacamole will inevitably rise due to increases in the price of avocadoes.

When we are looking for an answer choice that strengthens this argument, we will be looking for the statement that supports its reasoning and assumptions. Perhaps the most supportive information would be that all avocadoes come from South America. This would affirm that guacamole manufacturers must buy their ingredients from South America and cannot avoid being affected by the earthquakes. Another strengthening statement would state that the price of store-bought guacamole is inextricably linked to the price of South American avocadoes. If we knew this to be the case, we could not imagine other ways for the manufacturers to maintain their current prices.

So far we have covered questions that identify assumptions and questions that ask you to weaken or strengthen an argument. The fourth and final of the common question types asks you to make an inference based on the reasoning of the argument. In other words, you will be asked to determine which of the answer choices is most likely to be true if you assume that the argument is valid. A good inference is something that is probable in light of the evidence and reasoning of the argument, but it does not have to be something that is necessary. It should be possible to support your answer choice with evidence taken directly from the passage.

To begin with, inference questions assume that everything in the critical reasoning passage is correct. Unlike the strengthening or weakening evidence questions in which you are asked to consider the merit of an argument, in inference questions you are supposed to accept the argument at face value. Let us look at an example passage:

> In the last four presidential elections, the number of voters between the ages of 18 and 25 has gone up, as has the number of total voters. At the same time, the number of people under 25 who are registered to vote has stayed the same.

An inference question will often be phrased as follows: "If the statements above are all true, they provide the most support for which of the following conclusions about the last four presidential elections?"

As we begin to consider inferences that can be made from the above argument, keep in mind that inferences are things that we can expect to be true, not things that we know to be true. Often, the correct answer will simply be the inference that is most probable. Also, you will find that on inference questions it is less efficient to come up with your own hypothetical answer before looking at the answer choices given. There are just too many possible inferences for you to expect your hypothetical inference to appear among the possible answers.

A good rule of thumb to use when considering the relative merits of inferences is that a narrow inference is more likely than a general inference to be correct. This is true as long as the facts of the argument support the narrow inference. For instance, the example argument asserts that both the number of voters between the ages of 18 and 25 and the number of total voters have risen while the number of registered voters between 18 and 25 has stayed the same. Perhaps the most obvious inference that can be drawn is that the percentage of registered voters between 18 and 25 who actually vote in presidential elections has increased. This would make it possible for the number of voters to increase even as the number of registered voters remains the same.

The important thing about this inference is that it is fully supported by the facts of the argument. Incorrect inferences are usually those that could be true but are not fully substantiated by the given argument. If an inference requires additional information, it is incorrect. There are a number of erroneous inferences that can be made based on the given passage. For instance, one might try to infer that the number of voters above the age of 25 has stayed the same, meaning that the increase in total voters is entirely due to the increase in voters between the ages of 18 and 25. Of course this could be true, but it is also possible that the number of voters above the age of 25 has risen. Another false inference would be that presidential candidates have made an increasing effort to appeal to young voters. Again, this could be true, but it is not directly substantiated by the facts of the argument. This is the kind of sweeping inference that is usually incorrect. When a passage contains specific facts, make sure that your answer choice is an inference that springs directly out of these facts.

While these four question types will be predominant in the critical reasoning section, there are a few other types you should recognize. The GMAT will occasionally include a strategy question in which you are asked to decide which of five given strategies or plans would be most effective at resolving the situation described in the prompt. Obviously, strategy questions will only be asked when the prompt describes a negative state of affairs. For example, the prompt might outline an environmental problem, a downward trend in business productivity, or an obstacle to better human relations. Your job will be to select the strategy that would be most appropriate and effective at solving the problem discussed; in other words, you should look for the answer choice that would resolve the problem as it is described in the passage. Do not allow your thinking to stray outside the facts given by the prompt. The correct answer to a strategy question is usually a general plan that could solve the entire problem rather than a specific plan that will resolve only part of the problem. The incorrect answers on a strategy question are usually plans that have no clear relation to the problem described, plans that could either solve or worsen the problem depending on other factors, or plans that only treat a component of the problem.

Another question type that you may see occasionally in the critical reasoning section of the GMAT is the hypothesis question that asks you to choose the statement that most effectively explains a problematic set of information in the prompt. Typically, hypothesis questions will follow prompts composed of two conflicting sets of observations or reasoning. For instance, the prompt might contain the results of two different experiments on the same subject. The hypothesis question will ask you to identify the statement that most effectively reconciles these opposing viewpoints. In order to find the right answer, you must restrict your thinking to the facts presented in the prompt. As usual, the GMAT will try to fool you with answer choices that require information not given in the passage. Other incorrect answers will either be inappropriate or irrelevant to the conclusions of the prompt.

On rare occasions, the GMAT will ask you to select the answer choice that most closely mimics the reasoning of the given argument. In order to solve this kind of problem, you will need to discover the underlying structure of the given argument. For instance, consider the following argument:

Reading books will make you a better student. A recent study indicated that high-achieving students are more likely to be recreational readers. Therefore, you should read books in your spare time.

The structure of this argument can be summarized in the following way: If A, then B. If B, then most likely A. To produce B, do A. You can then examine the answer choices to find the one that most closely shares this reasoning structure. An example of a similar argument might be the following:

> Reducing waste makes a factory more efficient. Research suggests that efficient factories are more likely to have minimum waste. For this reason, factories should strive to reduce waste.

Note how this argument has the same basic structure. Although mimic the reasoning questions are rare on the GMAT, you can be prepared for them if you can practice outlining the essential pattern of an argument.

## Opposites

Answer choices that are direct opposites are usually correct. The paragraph will often contain established relationships (when this goes up, that goes down). The question may ask you to draw conclusions for this and will give two similar answer choices that are opposites. Example:

> A. if other factors are held constant, then increasing the interest rate will lead to a decrease in housing starts
>
> B. if other factors are held constant, then increasing the interest rate will lead to an increase in housing starts

Often these opposites will not be so clearly recognized. Don't be thrown off by different wording, look for the meaning beneath. Notice how these two answer choices are really opposites, with just a slight change in the wording shown above. Once you realize these are opposites, you should examine them closely. One of these two is likely to be the correct answer. Example:

> A. if other factors are held constant, then increasing the interest rate will lead to a decrease in housing starts

B. when there is an increase in housing starts, and other things remain equal, it is often the result of an increase in interest rates

## Make predictions

One convenience of having only a short paragraph to contain information is that you can easily remember the few facts presented, compared to a much longer reading passage full of much more information. As you read and understand the passage and then the question, try to guess what the answer will be. Remember that four of the five answer choices are wrong, and once you begin reading them, your mind will immediately become cluttered with answer choices designed to throw you off. Your mind is typically the most focused immediately after you have read the passage and question and digested its contents. If you can, try to predict what the correct answer will be. You may be surprised at what you can predict.

Quickly scan the choices and see if your prediction is in the listed answer choices. If it is, then you can be quite confident that you have the right answer. It still won't hurt to check the other answer choices, but most of the time, you've got it!

## Answer the Question

It may seem obvious to only pick answer choices that answer the question, but GMAT can create some excellent answer choices that are wrong. Don't pick an answer just because it sounds right, or you believe it to be true. It MUST answer the question. Once you've made your selection, always go back and check it against the question and make sure that you didn't misread the question, and the answer choice does answer the question posed.

## Benchmark

One disadvantage of taking a computer based test, as opposed to a traditional paper and pencil test, is that you can't make notes directly on the page. More specifically, you can't cross out answers you believe to be wrong as you read through the list of possible answer choices. The computer offers another solution though. After you read the first answer choice, decide if you think it sounds correct or not. If it doesn't, move on to the next answer choice. If it does, click beside the choice to select it. This doesn't mean that you've definitely selected it as your answer choice, it just means that it's the best you've seen thus far. Go ahead and read the next choice. If the next choice is worse than the one you've already selected, keep going to the next answer choice. If the next choice is better than the choice you've already selected, change your selection.

As you read through the list, highlight the choice you think is right. That is your new standard. Every other answer choice must be benchmarked against that standard. That choice is correct until proven otherwise by another answer choice beating it out. Once you've decided that no other answer choice seems as good, do one final check to ensure that it answers the question posed.

**New information**

Correct answers will usually contain the information listed in the paragraph and question. Rarely will completely new information be inserted into a correct answer choice. Occasionally the new information may be related in a manner than GMAT is asking for you to interpret, but seldom. Example:

> The argument above is dependent upon which of the following assumptions?
> A.) Scientists have used Charles's Law to interpret the relationship.

If Charles's Law is not mentioned at all in the referenced paragraph and argument, then it is unlikely that this choice is correct. All of the information needed to answer the question is provided for you, and so you should not have to make guesses that are unsupported or choose answer choices that have unknown information that cannot be reasoned.

## Key words

Look for answer choices that have the same key words in them as the question. Example:

Which of the following, if true, would best explain the reluctance of politicians since 1980 to support this funding?

Look for the key words "since 1980" to be referenced in the correct answer choice. Most valid answer choices would probably include a phrase such as "since 1980, politicians have..."

## Valid information

Don't discount any of the information provided in the paragraph. They are short to begin with and every piece of information may be necessary to determine the correct answer. None of the information in the paragraph is there to throw you off (while the answer choices will certainly have information to throw you off). If two seemingly unrelated topics are discussed, don't ignore either. You can be confident there is a relationship, or it wouldn't be included in the paragraph, and you are probably going to have to determine what is that relationship for the answer.

# Time Management

In technical passages, do not get lost on the technical terms. Skip them and move on. You want a general understanding of what is going on, not a mastery of the passage. When you encounter material in the selection that seems difficult to understand, it often may not be necessary and can be skipped. Only spend time trying to understand it if it is going to be relevant for a question. Understand difficult phrases only as a last resort.

Identify each question by type. Usually the wording of a question will tell you whether you can find the answer by referring directly to the passage or by using your reasoning powers.

# Final Warnings

## Hedge phrases revisited

Once again, watch out for critical "hedge" phrases, such as likely, may, can, will often, sometimes, etc, often, almost, mostly, usually, generally, rarely, sometimes. Question writers insert these hedge phrases, to cover every possibility. Often an answer will be wrong simply because it leaves no room for exception. Example:

Animals live longer in cold places than animals in warm places.

This answer choice is wrong, because there are exceptions in which certain warm climate animals live longer. This answer choice leaves no possibility of exception. It states that every animal species in cold places live longer than animal species in warm places. Correct answer choices will typically have a key hedge word to leave room for exceptions. Example:

In severe cold, a polar bear cub is likely to survive longer than an adult polar bear.

This answer choice is correct, because not only does the passage imply that younger animals survive better in the cold, it also allows for exceptions to exist. The use of the word "likely" leaves room for cases in which a polar bear cub might not survive longer than the adult polar bear.

## Word usage questions

When asked how a word is used in the passage, don't use your existing knowledge of the word. The question is being asked precisely because there is some strange or unusual usage of the word in the passage. Go to the passage and use contextual clues to determine the answer. Don't simply use the popular definition you already know.

## Switchback words

Stay alert for "switchbacks". These are the words and phrases frequently used to alert you to shifts in thought. The most common switchback word is "but". Others include although, however, nevertheless, on the other hand, even though, while, in spite of, despite, regardless of.

## Avoid "fact traps"

Once you know which paragraph the answer will be in, focus on that paragraph. However, don't get distracted by a choice that is factually true about the paragraph. Your search is for the answer that answers the question, which may be about a tiny aspect in the paragraph. Stay focused and don't fall for an answer that describes the larger picture of the paragraph. Always go back to the question and make sure you're choosing an answer that actually answers the question and is not just a true statement.

# Special Report: What Your GMAT Score Means for Admissions and Scholarships

Based on the distribution of GMAT scores, an admissions officer will classify a student into one of five score regions:

| GMAT Score Range | Description | Likely Result |
|---|---|---|
| 260-360 | College competent | Admission to mildly selective graduate school |
| 370-470 | Prepared for graduate school | Admission to somewhat selective graduate school |
| 480-580 | Excellent preparedness | Admission to somewhat selective graduate school, possible partial scholarship |
| 590-690 | Superior preparedness | Admission to selective graduate school, "full ride" possible at less selective graduate schools |
| 700-800 | Exceptional top student | Admission to very selective graduate school, "full ride" possible from selective graduate schools |

If you are on the upper edge of one of these categories, it is definitely profitable to work your way into the next one by studying and practicing. If you are only concerned about admission, check the latest US News statistics for the 75th percentile GMAT score. A score above this virtually guarantees admission.

# Special Report: Area, Volume, Surface Area Formulas

These are VERY valuable to memorize for the GMAT Quantitative Test.

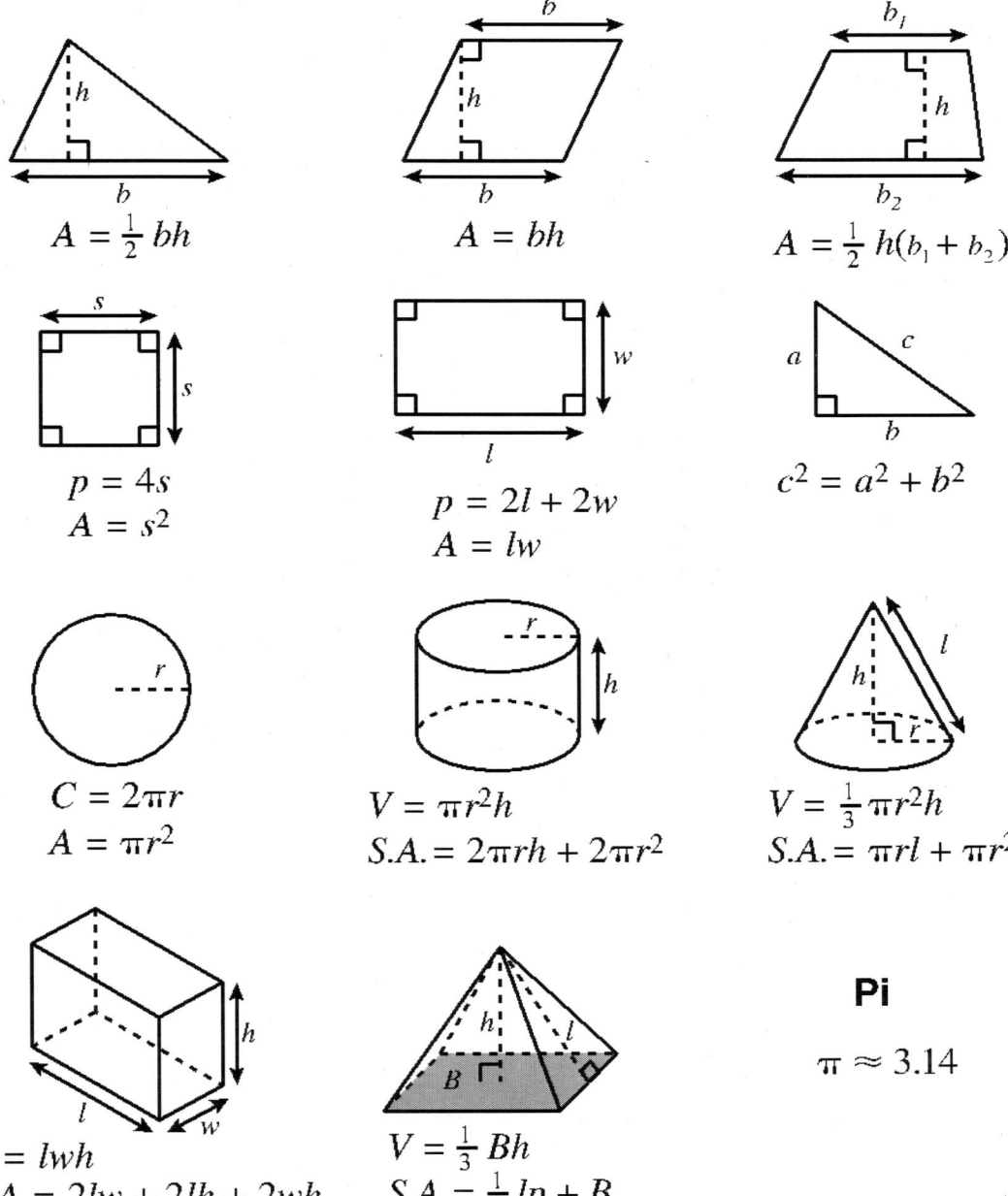

$$A = \frac{1}{2}bh$$

$$A = bh$$

$$A = \frac{1}{2}h(b_1 + b_2)$$

$$p = 4s$$
$$A = s^2$$

$$p = 2l + 2w$$
$$A = lw$$

$$c^2 = a^2 + b^2$$

$$C = 2\pi r$$
$$A = \pi r^2$$

$$V = \pi r^2 h$$
$$S.A. = 2\pi rh + 2\pi r^2$$

$$V = \frac{1}{3}\pi r^2 h$$
$$S.A. = \pi rl + \pi r^2$$

$$V = lwh$$
$$S.A. = 2lw + 2lh + 2wh$$

$$V = \frac{1}{3}Bh$$
$$S.A. = \frac{1}{2}lp + B$$

**Pi**

$$\pi \approx 3.14$$

# Special Report: GMAT Secrets in Action

This section will walk you through techniques that can help you to answer specific types of questions. The following section will provide you with the opportunity to practice these skills in a practice test modeled after the GMAT.

## Verbal Subtest

## *Sample Sentence Correction Question*

Choose which of five ways of writing the underlined part of the sentence is correct.

> <u>While a leader, one can decide</u> to allow the group to determine its course by a simple vote of majority, or we can choose to guide the group without allowing the opportunity for discussion.

- A. While a leader, one can decide
- B. While leaders, we can decide
- C. While a leader, we can decide
- D. While leaders, one can decide
- E. While leading, one can decide

Let's look at a couple of different methods and steps to solving this problem.

### Agreement in Pronoun Number

All pronouns have to agree in number to their antecedent or noun that they are representing. In the underlined portion, the pronoun "one" has as its antecedent the noun "leader".

Go through and match up each of the pronouns in the answer choices with their antecedents:

    A.  leader,  one – correctly matches singular antecedent to singular pronoun

    B.  leaders, we – correctly matches plural antecedent to plural pronoun

    C.  leader, we – incorrectly matches singular antecedent to plural pronoun

    D.  leaders, one – incorrectly matches plural antecedent to singular pronoun

    E.  one – no antecedent

Based on pronoun number agreement, you can eliminate choices C and D from consideration, because they fail the test.

## Parallelism

Not only do the pronouns and antecedents in the underlined portion of the sentence have to be correct, but the rest of the sentence has to match as well.  The remainder of the sentence has to be parallel to the underlined portion.  Part of the sentence that is not underlined has the phrase "we can choose."  Notice how this phrase uses the plural pronoun "we".  This means that the underlined portion of the sentence has to be plural to agree with the rest of the sentence and have matching plural pronouns and nouns as well.

Quickly review the answer choices and look for whether the nouns and pronouns in the answer choices are singular or plural:

    A.  leader, one – singular noun, singular pronoun

    B.  leaders, we – plural noun, plural pronoun

    C.  leader, we – singular noun, plural pronoun

    D.  leaders, one – plural noun, singular pronoun

    E.  one – singular pronoun

Only choice B has both a plural noun and a plural pronoun, making choice B correct.

## Sample Reading Comprehension Question

Mark Twain was well aware of his celebrity. He was among the first authors to employ a clipping service to track press coverage of himself, and it was not unusual for him to issue his own press statements if he wanted to influence or "spin" coverage of a particular story. The celebrity Twain achieved during his last ten years still reverberates today. Nearly all of his most popular novels were published before 1890, long before his hair grayed or he began to wear his famous white suit in public. We appreciate the author but seem to remember the celebrity.

Based on the passage above, Mark Twain seemed interested in:
- A. maintaining his celebrity
- B. selling more of his books
- C. hiding his private life
- D. gaining popularity
- E. writing the perfect novel

Let's look at a couple of different methods of solving this problem.

## Key Words

Identify the key words in each answer choice. These are the nouns and verbs that are the most important words in the answer choice:
- A. maintaining, celebrity
- B. selling, books
- C. hiding, life
- D. gaining, popularity
- E. writing, novel

Now try to match up each of the key words with the passage and see where they fit. You're trying to find synonyms and/or exact replication between the key words in the answer choices and key words in the passage:

A. maintaining – no matches; celebrity – matches in sentences 1, 3, and 5

B. selling – no matches; books – matches with "novels" in sentence 4.

C. hiding – no matches; life – no matches

D. gaining – no matches; popularity –matches with "celebrity" in sentences 1, 3, and 5, because they can be synonyms

E. writing – no matches; novel – matches in sentence 4

At this point there are only two choices that have more than one match, choices A and D, and they both have the same number of matches, and with the same word in the passage, which is the word "celebrity" in the passage. This is a good sign, because Praxis will often write two answer choices that are close. Having two answer choices pointing towards the same key word is a strong indicator that those key words hold the "key" to finding the right answer.

Now let's compare choice A and D and the unmatched key words. Choice A still has "maintaining" which doesn't have a clear match, while choice D has "gaining" which doesn't have a clear match. While neither of those have clear matches in the passage, ask yourself what are the best arguments that would support any kind of connection with either of those two words.

- "Maintaining" makes sense when you consider that Twain was interested in tracking his press coverage and that he was actively managing the "spin" of certain stories.

- "Gaining" makes sense when you consider that Twain was actively issuing his own press releases, however one key point to remember is that he was only issuing these press releases after another story was already in existence.

Since Twain's press releases were not being released in a news vacuum, but rather as a response mechanism to ensure control over the angle of a story, his releases were more to maintain control over his image, rather than gain an image in the first place.

Furthermore, when comparing the terms "popularity" and "celebrity", there are similarities between the words, but in referring back to the passage, it is clear that "celebrity" has a stronger connection to the passage, being the exact word used three times in the passage.

Since "celebrity" has a stronger match than "popularity" and "maintaining" makes more sense than "gaining," it is clear that choice A is correct.

## Process of elimination

The process of elimination for this passage could follow these lines:

A. maintaining his celebrity – The passage discusses how Mark Twain was both aware of his celebrity status and would take steps to ensure that he got the proper coverage in any news story and maintained the image he desired.  This is the correct answer.

B. selling more of his books – Mark Twain's novels are mentioned for their popularity and while common sense would dictate that he would be interested in selling more of his books, the passage makes no mention of him doing anything to promote sales.

C. hiding his private life – While the passage demonstrates that Mark Twain was keenly interested in how the public viewed his life, it does not indicate that he cared about hiding his private life, not even mentioning his life outside of the public eye.  The passage deals with how he was seen by the public.

D. gaining popularity – At first, this sounds like a good answer choice, because Mark Twain's popularity is mentioned several times.  The main difference though is that he wasn't trying to gain popularity, but simply ensuring that the popularity he had was not distorted by bad press.

E. writing the perfect novel – Though every author of fiction may strive to write the perfect novel, and Mark Twain was a famous author, the passage makes no mention of any quest of his to write a perfect novel.

## Sample Critical Reasoning Question

The cost of producing radios in Country Q is ten percent less than the cost of producing radios in Country Y. Even after transportation fees and tariff charges are added, it is still cheaper for a company to import radios from Country Q to Country Y than to produce radios in Country Y.

The statements above, if true, best support which of the following assertions?
   A. Labor costs in Country Q are ten percent below those in Country Y.
   B. Importing radios from Country Q to Country Y will eliminate ten percent of the manufacturing jobs in Country Y.
   C. The tariff on a radio imported from Country Q to Country Y is less than ten percent of the cost of manufacturing the radio in Country Y.
   D. The fee for transporting a radio from Country Q to Country Y is more than ten percent of the cost of manufacturing the radio in Country Q.
   E. It takes ten percent less time to manufacture a radio in Country Q than it does in Country Y.

Let's look at a couple of different methods of solving this problem.

**Eliminate Choices**

When in doubt, eliminate what you can first. Go through each answer choice and see if you can eliminate it from consideration:

- Answer choice A mentions labor costs, although labor costs are not even mentioned in the question. Rarely will GMAT try to trick you by bringing up an unmentioned variable, therefore answer choice A can be eliminated.
- Answer choice B mentions manufacturing jobs, and answer choice E mentioned manufacturing time, neither of which were mentioned in the question, and both answer choices can be eliminated.

Now you're down to just answer choice C and D, making your task much easier.

- Answer choice D states that the transportation fee is more than ten percent of the cost of manufacturing the radio. However, if that were true, then the total cost of importing a radio from Country Q would exceed the manufacturing cost in Country Y, making choice D incorrect, because the question clearly states that the importing cost is still less, even after the transportation and tariff costs are added in.

This makes answer choice C the default correct answer.

## Plug and Chug

Take some sample numbers and plug them into the problem. Rather than having to remember the relationships, writing them down with real numbers helps a lot of students understand the problem better. Use round number like 100 that are easy to use in calculations, especially with percents.

In this case, you could write:

> Country Y - $100 is the cost to produce 1 radio
> Country Q - $90 is the cost to produce 1 radio (10% less)

The question states that even if transportation fees and tariff charges are added to the cost of producing radios in Country Q, radios are still cheaper to import. Since that would mean that the total cost from Country Q could not exceed $100 (the cost in Country Y), then the transportation and tariff costs could not exceed $10, because the manufacturing cost is already $90, and $90 + any number greater than $10 would exceed $100.

Since the upper limit of the transportation and tariff costs of $10 is 10% of $100, that means that the tariff costs alone would definitely have to be less than 10%, which makes answer choice C correct.

# Quantitative Subtest

## *Sample Problem Solving Question*

Three coins are tossed up in the air.  What is the probability that two of them will land heads and one will land tails?

  A.  0
  B.  1/8
  C.  1/4
  D.  3/8
  E.  1/2

Let's look at a few different methods and steps to solving this problem.

### Reduction and Division

Quickly eliminate the probabilities that you immediately know.  You know to roll all heads is a 1/8 probability, and to roll all tails is a 1/8 probability.  Since there are in total 8/8 probabilities, you can subtract those two out, leaving you with 8/8 – 1/8 – 1/8 = 6/8.  So after eliminating the possibilities of getting all heads or all tails, you're left with 6/8 probability.  Because there are only three coins, all other combinations are going to involve one of either head or tail, and two of the other.  All other combinations will either be 2 heads and 1 tail, or 2 tails and 1 head.  Those remaining combinations both have the same chance of occurring, meaning that you can just cut the remaining 6/8 probability in half, leaving you with a 3/8 chance that there will be 2 heads and 1 tail, and another 3/8 chance that there will be 2 tails and 1 head, making choice D correct.

## Run Through the Possibilities for that Outcome

You know that you have to have two heads and one tail for the three coins. There are only so many combinations, so quickly run through them all.

You could have:

H, H, H

H, H, T

H, T, H

T, H, H

T, T, H

T, H, T

H, T, T

T, T, T

Reviewing these choices, you can see that three of the eight have two heads and one tail, making choice D correct.

## Fill in the Blanks with Symbology and Odds

Many probability problems can be solved by drawing blanks on a piece of scratch paper (or making mental notes) for each object used in the problem, then filling in probabilities and multiplying them out. In this case, since there are three coins being flipped, draw three blanks. In the first blank, put an "H" and over it write "1/2". This represents the case where the first coin is flipped as heads. In that case (where the first coin comes up heads), one of the other two coins must come up tails and one must come up heads to fulfill the criteria posed in the problem (2 heads and 1 tail). In the second blank, put a "1" or "1/1". This is because it doesn't matter what is flipped for the second coin, so long as the first coin is heads. In the third blank, put a "1/2". This is because the third coin must be the exact opposite of whatever is in the second blank. Half the time the third coin will be the same as the second coin, and half the time the third coin will be the opposite, hence the "1/2". Now multiply out the odds. There is a half chance that the first coin will come up "heads", then it doesn't matter for the second coin, then there is a half chance that the third coin will be the opposite of the second coin, which will give the desired result of 2 heads and 1 tail. So, that gives 1/2*1/1*1/2 = 1/4.

But, now you must calculate the probabilities that result if the first coin is flipped tails. So draw another group of three blanks. In the first blank, put a "T" and over it write "1/2". This represents the case where the first coin is flipped as tails. In that case (where the first coin comes up tails), both of the other two coins must come up heads to fulfill the criteria posed in the problem. In the second blank, put an "H" and over it write "1/2". In the third blank, put an "H" and over it write "1/2". Now multiply out the odds. There is a half chance that the first coin will come up "tails", then there is a half chance that the second coin will be heads, and a half chance that the third coin will be heads. So, that gives 1/2*1/2*1/2 = 1/8.

Now, add those two probabilities together. If you flip heads with the first coin, there is a 1/4 chance of ultimately meeting the problem's criteria. If you flip tails with the first coin, there is a 1/8 chance of ultimately meeting the problem's criteria. So, that gives 1/4 + 1/8 = 2/8 + 1/8 = 3/8, which makes choice D correct.

## Sample Data Sufficiency Question

If a real estate agent received a commission of 6 percent of the selling price of a certain house, what was the selling price of the house?

    (1) The selling price minus the real estate agent's commission was $84,600.

    (2) The selling price was 250 percent of the original purchase price of $36,000.

  A. Statement (1) ALONE is sufficient, but statement (2) alone is not sufficient.

  B. Statement (2) ALONE is sufficient, but statement (1) alone is not sufficient.

C. BOTH statements TOGETHER are sufficient, but NEITHER statement ALONE is sufficient.

D. EACH statement ALONE is sufficient.

E. Statements (1) and (2) TOGETHER are NOT sufficient.

Let's look at a few different methods and steps to solving this problem.

## Use Algebra

If the answer isn't immediately apparent, creating an algebra problem allows you to logically dissect the problem and statements into pieces that can be put together to solve whether or not the statement is sufficient to find the answer to the question.

Create an algebra problem out of both statements.

*First Statement:* The first statement is that "The selling price minus the real estate agent's commission was $84,600." You can convert this into:

x (the selling price) – y (the commission) = $84,600.

This alone doesn't tell you enough, yet you do have another piece of information that you can plug in. The question told you that the real estate agent's commission was 6% of the selling price. Since we set the variable "x" as the selling price, that makes the agent's commission ".06*x". This allows us to replace "y" in the equation above, with ".06*x".

Our equation is now:

x – .06*x = $84,600.

"x" can be factored out, leaving x(1–.06) = $84,600 or .94*x = $84,600.

Solving for x gives us:

.94*x/.94 = $84,600/.94 or x = $90,000

- 132 -

This is the selling price, meaning that statement 1 is sufficient to answer the question, but what about statement 2?

*Second Statement:* The second statement is that "The selling price was 250 percent of the original purchase price of $36,000." You can convert this into:

$$x \text{ (the selling price)} = 250\% * \$36,000.$$

This becomes:

$$x = 2.5*\$36,000 \text{ or } x = \$90,000$$

This is the selling price, meaning that statement 2 is also sufficient to answer the question, making answer choice D correct.

## Single Variable Logic

A method that works even faster than setting up equations is using simple logic. Whenever you are able to create an equation, if you know that you will only have a single variable to work with, then you can solve for that variable. In the first statement, you have, "The selling price minus the real estate agent's commission was $84,600." Quickly looking at this statement it appears that you will have two variables. However, once you realize that you can substitute the variable for the agent's commission with a 6% multiplier based on the selling price (using the information in the question) then you know that you are actually down to just a single variable, meaning this statement alone is sufficient to solve for the answer.

In the second statement, you have, "The selling price was 250 percent of the original purchase price of $36,000." A quick view of this statement reveals that you are going to have a simple equation with only a single variable and will be able to solve for the answer, meaning that this statement is also sufficient.

**Warning:** Make sure that the single variable you've identified is the variable asked about in the question. In this question, you are asked for the selling price. Therefore, the single variable in each statement must be the selling price. Don't make this simple mistake!

## Analytical Writing subtest

### *Sample Analysis of an Issue Topic*

Possessions can be extremely difficult to give up or lose. Some people believe that is an evolutionary adaptation to cling to assets which are necessary for survival. Others feel that it is due to a personal attachment that develops over the years as emotional memories become linked to inanimate objects.

Which do you find more compelling, the belief that attachment to possessions is an evolutionary adaptation for survival or that the attachment stems from a more human element of emotions? Explain your position, using relevant reasons and/or examples from your own experience, observations, or reading.

Let's look at a few different methods and steps to writing your analysis.

**What's the Goal?**

Remember that on the essay portion of the GMAT, there isn't a "correct" answer. The response you choose to give to the topic provided does not have to be the first thing that comes to your mind. In fact, the side or response you pick doesn't even have to support the side of the topic that you actually believe in. It is better to have a good explanation for the position, rather than to actually believe in the position on the topic. However, typically you will find that the side you believe in is also the side that you have the most information that you can write about.

To go through some of the steps that you could walk through as you develop your response, let's choose to support the belief that the attachment develops from emotional memories slowly becoming linked to inanimate objects.

As you consider some good examples of possessions, your first thought might be the importance of your home or car, which are necessary for the basic functions of life, such as providing a roof over your head and a method of transportation. Yet, what would be your supporting answer about why your car is important and would be difficult to give up? Some possibilities might be: "it gets me where I need to go, it is brand new, it is expensive, I like it a lot, it would be difficult to replace, it's shiny."

These answer choices may fill up some space, but don't have much meaning. There are other possessions in your life that have much more meaning and priority in other ways that would be better to write about.

Think of possessions that have meaning beyond the mere basics of shelter or transportation. You want examples that you could potentially write pages and pages about, filling each of them with depths of passionate detail. While you probably won't have time to write pages and pages, it's good to have a examples that have plenty of room to be expanded upon.

**Make a Short List**

The best way to think of examples you would want to include might be to create a short list of possibilities. What are some that you would truly hate to give up? What are things that you would regret and miss for years to come? What are items that would fit the description of having an emotional attachment develop over the years? Perhaps a precious heirloom, a family antique, or a faded photograph would be suitable examples. After you've made your list, look back over it and see which possessions you could write the most information about. Those are the ones you would want to include as examples.

## Answer "Why"

Notice that choosing possessions and writing about them is not the only thing that you have to do. You have to explain your position. You have to answer the "Why." That is an all-important question. If you wrote a sentence as part of your response and one of the essay scorers looked over your shoulder and said, "but why?" would your next sentence answer their question. For example, suppose you wrote, "The old chair that used to belong to my grandfather has a lot of meaning." If someone asked why, would your next sentence answer it? Your next sentence should say, "It has meaning because it was the one chair that my grandfather would sit in every day and tell stories from." Answering the "Why" question is crucial to your success at writing a great essay. It doesn't do any good to write a good essay if it doesn't answer that question.

# Practice Test #1

## Practice Questions
## Analytical Writing Assessment

**Analysis of an Issue**

This writing task is designed to test your ability to present a position on an issue effectively and persuasively. Your task is to analyze the issue presented, considering various perspectives, and to develop your own position on the issue. In scoring your issue essay, readers will consider how effectively you: recognize and deal with the complexities and implications of the issue; organize, develop, and express your ideas; support your ideas with reasons and examples; control the elements of standard written English. You are given 30 minutes to write the response. You must not write on any other subject than the one expressed in the prompt. You are allowed to accept, reject, or qualify the statement made by the prompt, though you must be sure to support whatever position you take with reasons and examples from your experience, observation, reading, and/or academic studies. You should take a few minutes to plan your response before typing.

*Issue*: Although elementary education proposals have typically emphasized math and science, there is a growing movement to restore fine arts education in the early grades. Many education experts assert that neglecting music, dance, and painting produces students who have a great deal of knowledge but little capability of expression. Furthermore, they argue, the creativity and free-thinking required for the practice of the fine arts leads to innovation and progress in other areas. Critics of these proposals argue that the United States still lags behind other countries in science and mathematics test scores, and should focus on improving performance in these areas before allocating extra funds to arts programs.

## Analysis of an Argument

This writing task is designed to test your critical reasoning skills as well as your writing skills. Your task is to critique the stated argument in terms of its logical soundness and in terms of the strength of the evidence offered in support of the argument. In scoring your argument essay, the reader will consider how effectively you: identify and analyze the key elements of the argument; organize, develop, and express your critique; support your ideas with reasons and examples; control the elements of standard written English.

You are not being asked to agree or disagree with any of the statements in the argument. You should only consider the argument's line of reasoning. Specifically, you should consider: questionable assumptions underlying the argument; the extent to which the evidence presented supports the conclusion of the argument; what additional evidence would help to strengthen or refute the argument; and what additional information if any would help you to evaluate the argument's conclusion.

*Argument*: According to the author of a recent editorial, most of the problems in the United States are a consequence of the national dependence on oil. Oil consumption is expensive, damaging to the environment, and requires the United States to do business with some unsavory regimes. The United States should therefore impose strict gas-mileage requirements on automobiles, effective immediately. Although this would pose some temporary problems for the economy, in the long run it would be the best solution to American oil addiction.

# Quantitative
# Problem Solving

1. The number 2 + 0.4 is how many times the number 1 − 0.2?

    a. $1\frac{1}{3}$

    b. 2

    c. $2\frac{2}{5}$

    d. $2\frac{1}{2}$

    e. 3

2. If a movie reached the 90-minute mark 12 minutes ago, what minute mark had it reached *m* minutes ago?

    a. $m - 102$

    b. $m - 78$

    c. $102 - m$

    d. $78 - m$

    e. $90 - m$

3. A bull's-eye with a 4-inch diameter covers 20 percent of a circular target. What is the area, in square inches, of the target?

    a. $0.8\pi$

    b. $32\pi$

    c. $10\pi$

    d. $20\pi$

    e. $80\pi$

4. Which of the following is less than $\frac{5}{8}$ ?

    a. $\frac{7}{10}$

    b. $\frac{4}{5}$

    c. $\frac{6}{11}$

    d. 0.625

    e. 0.65


5. A wholesale bakery marks up the price of a loaf of bread by 20 percent. The grocery store that resells that bread then marks up the increased price by 20 percent. This series of successive markups is equivalent to what single markup?

    a. 20 percent

    b. 22 percent

    c. 30 percent

    d. 40 percent

    e. 44 percent


6. If line AB perpendicularly bisects line CD at point O, which of the following is true of $\Delta$ AOD?

    a. $40° < \Delta\ AOD \le 50°$

    b. $80° < \Delta\ AOD \le 90°$

    c. $170° < \Delta\ AOD \le 180°$

    d. $215° < \Delta\ AOD \le 225°$

    e. $260° < \Delta\ AOD \le 270°$

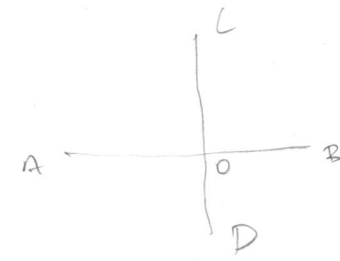

7. The volume in a water drum is halved every 2 days of a drought. If the volume of water in the drum was initially $10^6$ gallons, what was the volume after 10 days?

   a. $(\frac{1}{2})^{10}(10^6)$

   b. $(\frac{1}{2})^5(10^6)$

   c. $2^5(10^6)$

   d. $2^{10}(10^6)$

   e. $(10^6)^5$

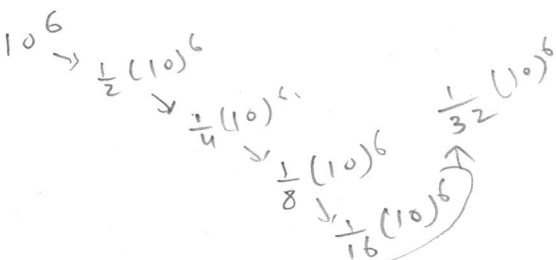

8. At a wedding reception, only 60 percent of the 750 invited guests show up. Of those in attendance, 46 percent are males. How many of the guests in attendance are female?

   a. 207
   b. 243
   c. 345
   d. 405
   e. 450

9.

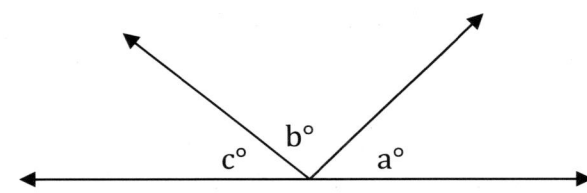

In the figure above, if $\frac{b}{a+b+c} = \frac{3}{5}$, then $b$ = ?

   a. 60
   b. 72
   c. 108
   d. 120
   e. 180

10. Abby is selling magazine subscriptions. She has turned in 3 order forms totaling $75, $40, and $107. She has 1 additional order pending. If Abby's average (arithmetic mean) order is to be exactly $80 on 4 forms, the fourth order must total how much?

    a. $18
    b. $74
    c. $80
    d. $98
    e. $101

$$320$$
$$147$$
$$\overline{173}$$
$$75$$
$$\overline{98}$$

11. $3y - 2x = 9$

    $2x + y = -5$

$$3y = 9 + 2x$$
$$y = \frac{9}{3} + \frac{2}{3}x = 3 + \frac{2}{3}x$$

In the system of equations above, what is the value of $y$?

    a. $-3$
    b. $-\frac{1}{7}$
    c. $-1$
    d. $1$
    e. $3$

$$2x + 3 + \frac{2}{3}x = -5$$

$$2y + \frac{2}{3}x = -8$$

$$\frac{6x + 2x}{3} = -8$$

$$\frac{8x}{3} = -8$$

$$8x = -24$$

$$x = -3$$

12.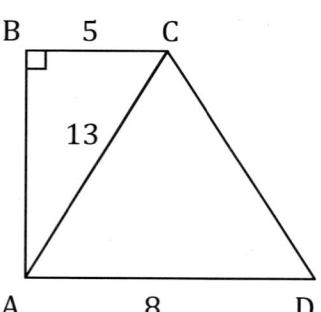

In the figure above, what is the area of triangular region ACD?

    a. 13
    b. 30
    c. 48
    d. 60
    e. 96

- 142 -

13. What is the maximum number of $6\frac{3}{4}$ inch strips that can be cut from a spool of ribbon that is 10 yards long?

    a. 1
    b. 17
    c. 18
    (d.) 53
    e. 54

14. A pilot traveled the first 1,500 miles of a 3,000-mile journey with an average speed of 400 miles per hour. At what speed must the pilot travel the remaining 1,500 miles to record an average speed of 500 miles per hour for the entire flight?

    a. $261\frac{2}{3}$ MPH
    b. 600 MPH
    (c.) $666\frac{2}{3}$ MPH
    d. 800 MPH
    e. 5,625 MPH

15. If the radius of circle O is one-quarter the diameter of circle P, what is the ratio of the circumference of circle O to the circumference of circle P?

    a. $\frac{1}{4}$

    (b.) $\frac{1}{2}$

    c. 1
    d. 2
    e. 4

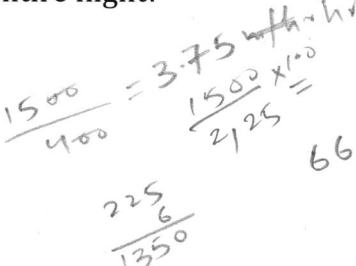

16. If $\frac{3}{8}$ of the money in a certain college fund was spent on tuition, $\frac{1}{4}$ was spent on room and board, $\frac{1}{5}$ was spent on books, and the remaining $7,000 remained in the fund, what was the total amount of the college fund?

    a. $7,000
    b. $8,485
    c. $33,000
    (d.) $40,000
    e. $47,000

- 143 -

17. If $x^2 + 3x - 18 = 0$ and $x < 0$, which of the following must equal 0?

 I. $x^2 - 36$

 II. $x^2 - 2x - 3$

 III. $x^2 + 5x - 6$

 a. I only
 b. II only
 c. III only
 d. I and III only
 e. I, II, and III

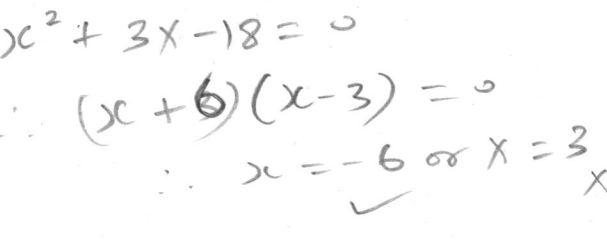

18. The length of the edge of cube A is three-quarters the length of the edge of cube B. What is the ratio of the volume of cube B to the volume of cube A?

 a. $\dfrac{1}{64}$

 b. $\dfrac{1}{4}$

 c. $\dfrac{27}{64}$

 d. $\dfrac{3}{4}$

 e. $\dfrac{64}{27}$

19. If the fractions $\dfrac{5}{9}$, $\dfrac{6}{11}$, $\dfrac{1}{2}$, $\dfrac{9}{16}$, and $\dfrac{3}{5}$ are numbered from least to greatest, the second fraction of the resulting sequence would be?

 a. $\dfrac{5}{9}$

 b. $\dfrac{6}{11}$

 c. $\dfrac{1}{2}$

 d. $\dfrac{9}{16}$

 e. $\dfrac{3}{5}$

20. If x > 2500, then the value of $\frac{x}{1-2x}$ is closest to

    a. –1

    b. $-\frac{50}{99}$

    c. $-\frac{1}{2}$

    d. $\frac{50}{99}$

    e. $\frac{1}{2}$

21. If the area of a rectangular game board is 336 square inches and its perimeter is 76 inches, what is the length of each of the shorter sides?

    a. 10 inches
    b. 14 inches
    c. 19 inches
    d. 24 inches
    e. 65 inches

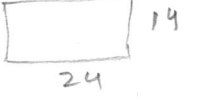
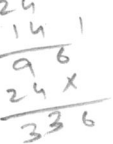

22. In a spelling bee, Anish's placement is both the 11th highest and the 25th lowest among all the spellers who participated. How many spellers participated in the spelling bee?

    a. 33
    b. 34
    c. 35
    d. 36
    e. 37

23. If c is to be chosen at random from the set {1, 2, 3, 4} and d is to be chosen at random from the set {1, 2, 3, 4}, what is the probability cd will be odd?

    a. $\frac{1}{4}$

    b. $\frac{1}{3}$

    c. $\frac{3}{4}$

    d. 4

    e. 12

**24.** The length ($l$) of a rectangle is three times its width. What is the length of the diagonal in terms of the length ($l$)?

a. $\frac{\sqrt{10}}{3}l$

b. $\frac{10}{3}l$

c. $\frac{10}{9}l$

d. $\sqrt{10}\,l$

e. $10l$

$l = 3w$

$\therefore w = \frac{1}{3}l$

$l^2 + w^2 = d^2$

# Data Sufficiency

This Data Sufficiency problem consists of a question and two statements, labeled (1) and (2), in which certain data are given. You have to decide whether the data given in the statements are sufficient for answering the question, using only the data given in the statements and your knowledge of mathematics and everyday facts (such as the number of days in July or the meaning of counterclockwise).

A. Statement (1) ALONE is sufficient, but statement (2) is not sufficient.
B. Statement (2) ALONE is sufficient, but statement (1) is not sufficient.
C. BOTH statements TOGETHER are sufficient, but NEITHER statement ALONE is sufficient.
D. EACH statement ALONE is sufficient.
E. Statements (1) and (2) TOGETHER are NOT sufficient.

25. What is the value of $\frac{q}{5} - \frac{r}{5}$?

(1) $\frac{q-r}{5} = 3$

(2) $q - r = 15$

a.        b.        c.        (d.)        e.

26. If Barry is $y$ years old and Charisse is $z$ years old, what is their combined age?

(1) Barry is 16 years older than Charisse.

(2) Ten years from now, Barry will be twice Charisse's age.

a.        b.        (c.)        d.        e.

27. If $l$, $w$, and $h$ represent the length, width, and height respectively of a rectangular solid, what is the volume of the solid?

(1) $lw = 40$

(2) $\frac{1}{2} lwh = 30$

a.        (b.)        c.        d.        e.

$z = x + 50000$

$z = \frac{3}{4} y$

28. What were the net proceeds from a fundraiser on the third day it was held?

(1) Net proceeds on the third day were $50,000 more than the first day.

(2) Net proceeds on the third day were three-quarters the second day's net proceeds.

a.         b.         c.         d.         (e.)

29. What is the value of $x$?

(1) $1 - 3x = 7x + 5$

(2) $\frac{4}{x} = -10$

a.         b.         (c.)         (d.)         e.

30.

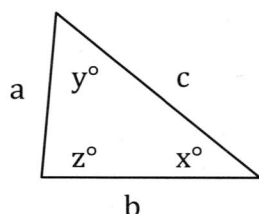

Is the triangle above a right triangle?

(1) $a = 5$, $b = 12$, $c = 13$

(2) $x = 45$

(a.)         b.         c.         d.         e.

31. If a total of 1,500 Democrats, Republicans, and Independents participated in a voters' survey, how many Independents were surveyed?

(1) 40 percent of the voters were Republicans.

(2) The number of Independents surveyed was 25 percent of the combined total of Democrats and Republicans surveyed.

a.         (b.)         c.         d.         e.

32. Is the value of *p* closer to 10 than to 25?

(1) $25 - p < p - 10$

(2) $p < 20$

a. (circled)　　　b.　　　c.　　　d.　　　e. (circled)

33. What is the radius of circle O?

(1) The ratio of circle O's area to its circumference is 2.

(2) The area of circle O is $16\pi$.

a.　　　b.　　　c.　　　d. (circled)　　　e.

34. If the average (arithmetic mean) of *m* consecutive integers is 7, what is the greatest of the integers?

(1) The range of the *m* integers is 8.

(2) The least of the *m* integers is 3.

a.　　　b. (circled)　　　c.　　　d. (circled)　　　e.

35. Janika buys fabric in each of her three school colors: black, white, and red. If the total yardage of the fabric is 19, how much white fabric did she buy?

(1) The amount of white fabric is 1.5 times the amount of black fabric and two-thirds the amount of red fabric.

(2) The sum of the amounts of white and black fabric is 1 yard more than the amount of red fabric.

a. (circled)　　　b.　　　c. (circled)　　　d.　　　e.

$W + B + R = 19$

$W = 1.5\,B = \frac{2}{3}R$

$W + B = R + 1$

$R + 1 + R = 19$

$2R = 18$

$R = 9$

$W + B = 9 + 1 = 10$

$1.5B + B = 10$

$2.5B = 10$

$B = 4$

36.

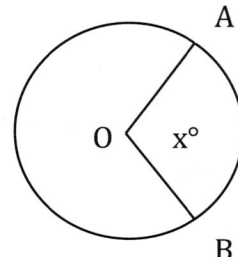

What is the measure of x in the circle with center O above?

(1) The circumference of the circle is $6\pi$.

(2) The length of arc AB is $2\pi$.

a.          b.          c.          d.          e.

37. If $q$ is an integer between 2 and 9 inclusive and $q$ is also the square root of an integer, what is the value of $q$?

(1) $q$ is even.

(2) The cube root of $q$ is an integer.

a.          b.          c.          d.          e.

# Verbal
# Reading Comprehension

*Questions 1 – 4 pertain to the following passage:*

One of the key features of the music scene in the past decade has been the increasing popularity of outsiders, especially those with a career. In previous decades, amateur status was seen as a lower calling or, at best, a step on the way to professional status, but many musical insiders now believe that amateurs actually constitute an elite group within the music scene, with greater chances of eventual success. Professionals, once able to fully devote themselves to the advancement of their musical careers, now find themselves hamstrung by a variety of factors that were not issues even a decade ago, giving the edge to people who do not depend on music for a livelihood. A number of technological, demographic, and economic factors are to blame for this change.

Full-time musicians always had difficulties making ends meet, but these difficulties have been vastly increased by a changing music scene. The increased popularity of electronic music, mega-bands, and other acts that rely heavily on marketing, theatrics, and expensive effects has made it harder than ever for local acts to draw crowds. The decreasing crowds at coffee houses, bars, and other small venues leave the owners without the ability to pay for live music. Amateurs can still play the same coffee houses as ever, and the lack of a hundred-dollar paycheck at the end of the night is hardly noticed. Professionals, however, have to fight more desperately than ever for those few lucrative gigs.

An even bigger factor has been the rise of digital media in general and digital file sharing in particular. People have been trading copies of music for decades, but in the days of analog tapes there was always a loss. The tape one fan burned for another would be of lesser quality than the original, prompting the recipient to go out and buy the album. Now that music fans can make full-quality copies for little or nothing and distribute them all over the world, it can be very hard for bands to make any money on music sales. Again, this does not make much difference to amateurs, but it robs the professionals of what has traditionally been one of their biggest sources of revenue.

All of this results in a situation so dire for professional musicians that their extra experience often doesn't balance out their lack of economic resources. The amateurs are the only ones who can afford to buy new gear and fix broken equipment, keep their cars in working order to get to shows, and pay to promote their shows. The professionals tend to have to fall back on "day jobs," typically at lower rates and with less opportunity for advancement. Even those professional musicians who are able to supplement their incomes with music lessons, wedding shows, and other traditional jobs are often living at such a low level that they cannot afford to buy the professional equipment they need to keep the higher-paying gigs. A fairly skilled amateur, by contrast, may not have the same level of virtuosity but will be able to fake his way through most of what a professional does at a more competitive rate, which will allow him to play professional shows.

1. The author of this essay is mainly
   a. arguing for a return to a climate more favorable to professional musicians
   b. examining the causes of the increasing success of amateur musicians over professionals
   c. revealing the psychological toll the current economy takes on professional musicians
   d. disputing the claim that unsuccessful professional musicians simply don't work hard enough
   e. comparing the relative contributions of professional and amateur musicians

2. Which of the following statements about musicians does the essay most directly support?

 a. Bars and coffee houses should be willing to pay a fair wage to professional musicians

 b. The most popular professional bands have not been affected by the changes that plague most professional musicians

 c. It is much easier for amateur musicians to book shows than it was a decade ago

 d. Professional musicians have recently lost some of their most important sources of income

 e. With the shrinking music scenes, it is nearly impossible for a modern musician to support himself on music alone

3. In his discussion of professional musicians in the last paragraph, the author

 a. indicates that amateurs deserve their new, higher status

 b. shows that in the current climate, professionals may not have the ability to purchase and maintain the tools that they need

 c. points out the decrease in the market for wedding gigs and lessons

 d. questions an assumption about the status of professional musicians

 e. predicts a decline in the number of professional musicians

4. According to the essay, amateur musicians are becoming more successful at both amateur and professional gigs because professionals

 a. exclusively performs high-paying gigs and are unwilling to play in clubs

 b. are not able to relate to ordinary people as well as amateurs can

 c. have financial needs that they are not able to meet in the current musical climate

 d. are in an industry that is particularly susceptible to economic changes

 e. don't receive the same respect as people with more lucrative careers

*Questions 5 – 7 pertain to the following passage*:

 A meeting of the High Tribal Council of Urk in the year 5543 addressed parliamentary critiques of the 5542 Freedom of Thought Law. The law's complete exemption of any thoughts believed to be libelous or licentious from protection—e.g., negative opinions about major political and religious figures or daydreams about taboo or illegal subjects—caused the Council to redraft portions of the law and overturn convictions of many currently incarcerated under it. Supreme councilor Snort McGuinn stated that the law provided "no way to selectively pardon thoughts thought in the pursuit of artistic creativity or legitimate political activity." Members of Parliament also testified that the overly broad provisions of the law were sometimes used by corrupt bureaucrats as a way to stifle political dissent and to dispossess wealthy artists for personal gain.

As a reply, the Terrestrial House of Parliament drafted PT 5x23, which included numerous proposed changes to the text of the law. A section was written to ensure the liberty to ponder even controversial ideas if the thinker was able to furnish a general explanation as to how his thought process could lead to the betterment of society without compromising social order. In this version, citizens would no longer be required to specifically catalog, register, and answer for each thought they had, but they would instead be able to defend ideas and avenues of inquiry as a whole. Both the Low and High Tribal Councils would be empowered to review these defenses, speeding up the review process considerably. The Orbiting House of Parliament bill, PO 2D54 included all of the changes in the Terrestrial bill but went even further. It provided a legal process to punish bureaucrats using thought restrictions for personal gain, designated free thought zones within personal residences, and a special Civilian Thought Review Council with the ability to permanently legalize new ideas on a case-by-case basis.

The Urk Homeland Security Department strongly objected to the proposed changes, calling them "dangerous, unenforceable, and ill-defined." They argued that the new laws might actually limit protections for freedom of thought by moving many previously illegal thoughts into a gray area where they could be found either legal or illegal, hampering the efforts of citizens to restrict their thought-processes to wholly legal topics. The elite Department of Friendly and Secret Enforcement further stated that the review of thoughts set up in the new laws could pose a threat to Urk national safety and security.

Both parliamentary laws were passed later that year after a considerable amount of further negotiation and discussion. One key amendment added to the bill was the Sol amendment, which required that bureaucrats detail any possible personal benefit before dispossessing a thought criminal unless detailing those benefits could cause a breach in state security. The president himself objected strongly to this, saying that the amendment would potentially expose huge numbers of government contacts and connections to public view unless the bureaucrats were able to show that each individual secret was exempt from the law.

Before the law was submitted to the president and the High Tribal Council for ratification, the two versions of the bill were combined into one compromise bill. It addressed the president's concern by making it somewhat easier for bureaucrats to gain exemptions to the disclosure law. It also worked with the Urk Homeland Security Department to tighten the definitions of what constituted thought crime. The bill passed by an overwhelming majority, and the council and president had no choice but to ratify it.

5. The Urk Homeland Security Department opposed the bill because its members felt that the bill would
    a. curtail the public's right to security
    b. undermine existing national security laws
    c. pose legal problems for ordinary citizens
    d. weaken their own power in enforcing security measures
    e. undermine the authority of the High Tribal Council

6. Of the statements below, which best supports that "the review of thoughts set up in the new laws could pose a threat to Urk national safety and security"?

    a. Civilians do not have the knowledge required to judge whether a thought is dangerous or not

    b. Some of the thoughts that are currently labeled dangerous are actually no longer threatening to the political establishment

    c. A civilian board would need a huge amount of resources to review all of the thoughts currently labeled illegal

    d. Civilians can be influenced by government pressure not to legalize a thought

    e. The High Tribal Council has the power to veto all Civilian Thought Review Council decisions

7. Judging by the president's statement on the Sol amendment, with which statement would he most likely agree?

    a. Bureaucratic conflicts of interest should be exempt from any public scrutiny

    b. Bureaucratic conflicts of interest should be released into the public eye unless doing so would threaten national security

    c. It would be impractical for bureaucrats to have to justify withholding each individual secret from public disclosure

    d. Protection of public safety comes before protection of bureaucratic secrets

    e. Bureaucratic secrets should not be examined individually before being released

*Questions 8 – 11 pertain to the following passage:*

Current theories of linguistic evolution state that language change, rather than being the result of incorrect language use or sloppy speech, is part of the continual evolution and progression of the structure of language. As languages are influenced by other cultures they come into contact with, dialectical variations occur. It can take anywhere from a century in intensely multicultural areas to millennia in isolated communities for the standard spoken language to change so much that it would be unrecognizable to speakers of the original tongue. In either case, the accumulation of new

- 156 -

words is accompanied by the proliferation of subtle grammatical variations that indicate a deeper language change.

Language changes in multicultural regions—like the Balkans of Europe—are quite drastic and rapid; linguists studying language change in these areas can observe the process as it occurs much more readily. When the language seems to be evolving much more gradually, however, as in Iceland and the other Scandinavian countries, locating current linguistic trends is just the surface. Verb morphology irregularities, vowel shifts, and recently introduced words all help to show how the language may change next, as do areas where the language has remained surprisingly consistent over the past several centuries. When the historical record is available, linguists rely on it. Early writings can vary from fragments of stories on scraps of parchment to well-preserved, detailed accounts of the proper use and pronunciation of the ancient tongue, as is the case with the ancient Romans.

Once the boundaries and characteristics of a language community are established, linguistic scholars can gather data from subcultures within that community. The linguists must attempt to study every group within a community, while staying within a linguistically well-defined area. Changes in the speech of young or marginalized subcultures or groups that have an unusual amount of contact with outsiders are great early indicators of looming language shifts. Phonological drift—a gradual change in the way certain sounds or combinations of sound are pronounced by speakers within the community—can be accurately measured and recorded through computer voice analysis measuring the pronunciations of hundreds of volunteers saying the same sentences. In theory, if the linguists posit a definition of a critical language shift—the amount of change in a given language before it would become unrecognizable to current speakers—they can predict when this will occur by extrapolating current rates of change. All things being equal, this can predict the time it will take for a completely new language to evolve.

Massive migrations, occupations, and social collapse are some phenomena that can trigger a more rapid language change. Many are only just being investigated as modern linguists observe cultures in crisis. Watching for these sorts of drastic upheavals helps linguists select potential regions for current studies. The effects of these events are still being discovered. For example, linguists are currently studying the declines of Meso-American languages under the influence of Spanish-speaking Mexican linguistic and cultural hegemony.

8. The text says that a main difference between multicultural regions like the Balkans and isolated regions like Iceland is that in multicultural regions
   a. there are no precursors to change
   b. there are fewer language changes
   c. languages change more rapidly
   d. there are no subtle changes before big language shifts
   e. the cultural forces that underlie language change are less powerful

9. The essay is written to
   a. show how languages change in isolated areas
   b. argue that language change is a normal thing
   c. examine the phenomena that cause language change in multicultural areas
   d. assert that it is impossible to predict when a language will change
   e. describe how linguists study language change

10. The third paragraph serves primarily to

   a. describe the relationship between phonological drift and language change

   b. explain the difficulty of studying language change in a given community

   c. contrast language communities in isolated and multicultural areas

   (d.) examine some of the ways linguists study language change in different parts of a
   community to get a picture of the community as a whole

   e. suggest that language change is a much more pervasive phenomenon than most
   scholars think

11. According to the essay, information about phonological drift within a community can
help linguists

   (a.) predict when a new language will evolve

   b. assess how important a new word is in the evolution of the language

   c. measure social and cultural upheaval

   d. come up with more accurate ways to measure language change

   e. estimate the rate of language change in similar cultures

*Questions 12 – 14 pertain to the following passage:*

   Although technological tools like polygraph tests, psychological theories, and
   interrogation techniques have resulted in slightly greater accuracy for law
   enforcement agents catching liars, it is still important to understand the
   nature of lies and check unfounded assumptions that can lead to
   unquestioning acceptance of false statements. Because intentional deception
   is one of the biggest obstacles to a successful criminal investigation,
   developing the ability to separate dubious or outright false statements from
   true ones has to be one of the main goals of every police officer and law
   enforcement investigator. In addition, an officer must be able to quickly sort
   out the possible repercussions of a false statement and the ways it can affect
   the rest of an investigation, should one slip by police screening. This is the
   only way to punish the guilty, exonerate the innocent, and do the most
   possible good in preventing future crimes.

The most difficult lie to catch is the half-truth. Half-truths are distortions constructed by using a seed of truth as a way to sprout a more convincing lie. A half-truth may incorporate intentional exaggeration or understatement, lies of omission, false implications, or outright lies mixed in with actual facts. Half-truths that slip past the detectives investigating a case are classified as either "smoke" lies or "mirror" lies. Smoke refers to half-truths that slow down an investigation by casting doubt on otherwise promising leads or angles of investigation. Mirrors are lies that manage to send the detective off in the wrong direction altogether, usually by linking a fact to a false supposition.

Most other lies are overt and intentional. Usually, they are told as a way for a suspect or witness to protect himself or his friends or, more rarely, to cast suspicion on a rival. In some cases, these sorts of lies can be compounded by overzealous or corrupt police who want to earn a conviction of a supposed perpetrator at any cost. Particularly in high-profile cases with gruesome details, this sort of lie results in more false convictions than any other type of distortion.

12. Which statement most accurately conveys the essay's main idea?
    a. New police techniques have been ineffective at helping investigators catch liars
    b. The worst lies aren't outright lies, but sneaky half-truths
    c. People in law enforcement need to be able to recognize lies to be effective and just
    d. There are only two primary types of lies
    e. Most overt lies are told to protect a suspect or a witness

13. The essay's writer would be most likely to say that a police officer's ability to recognize both lies and half-truths is

    a. indispensable in a criminal investigation

    b. difficult because of the sophistication of some liars

    c. the most important tool that law enforcement has

    d. important only when investigating a crime

    e. crucial, but beyond the abilities of most officers

14. According to the essay, "smoke"

    a. is the most frequently told type of half-truth

    b. never contains outright lies mixed in with truth

    c. can slow down an investigation

    d. is used to protect the guilty

    e. sends detectives off in the wrong direction altogether

# Sentence Correction

These questions present a sentence, all or part of which is underlined. Beneath each sentence you will find five ways of phrasing the underlined part. The first of these repeats the original; the other four are different. If you think the original is best, choose the first answer; otherwise, choose one of the other answers.

These questions test correctness and effectiveness of expression. In choosing your answer, follow the requirements of standard written English; that is, pay attention to grammar, choice of words, and sentence construction. Choose the answer that produces the most effective sentence; this answer should be clear and exact, without awkwardness, ambiguity, redundancy, or grammatical error.

15. Skeptical visitors often dismiss the Castle Blood hauntings on the basis of the lack of <u>a tangible experience, such as spirit knockings, that are called conclusive evidence of the occult, and ignore less obvious phenomena, such as</u> faint whisperings and cold mists.

    a. a tangible experience, such as spirit knockings, that are called conclusive evidence of the occult, and ignore less obvious phenomena, such as

    b. a tangible experience, such as spirit knockings, that are called conclusive evidence of the occult, and ignore less obvious phenomena, such as what is experienced as

    c. a tangible experience, such as spirit knockings, that is called conclusive evidence of the occult, and ignore less obvious phenomena, such as

    d. what they think of as tangible experience, such as spirit knockings, that are called conclusive evidence of the occult, and ignore less obvious phenomena, such as what is experienced as

    e. what they think of as tangible experience, such as spirit knockings, that are called conclusive evidence of the occult, and ignore less obvious phenomena, such as

16. A frequent source of stress for entering freshmen happens <u>when students enroll in out-of-state schools, and it makes them grow apart</u> from their high school friends.

    a. when students enroll in out-of-state schools, and it makes them grow apart

    b. by a student enrolling in an out-of-state school, which makes him grow apart

    c. when students enroll in out-of-state schools, thereby growing apart

    d. when a student who enrolls in out-of-state schools, and so grows apart

    e. if a student enrolls in an out-of-state school, he would grow apart


17. Egyptologists believe that the desiccated bodies recently found in an Egyptian tomb, <u>evidently those of servants who are believed to have been buried</u> nearly 4,000 years ago, remained intact and undisturbed by rot or scavengers because of their dry, stable, and isolated environment

    a. evidently those of servants who are believed to have been buried

    b. those of servants, evidently, who were believed to have been buried

    c. those of evident servants who were believed to have been buried

    d. those of servants who are believed to have been evidently buried

    e. those of servants who were evidently believed to have been buried


18. Unlike Hakim Bey, <u>Robert Anton Wilson felt how late 20<sup>th</sup>-century technology not as an inherently alienating force, and</u> something that could potentially liberate people from their hang-ups, isolation, and prejudices.

    a. Robert Anton Wilson felt how late 20<sup>th</sup>-century technology not as an inherently alienating force, and

    b. Robert Anton Wilson saw late 20<sup>th</sup>-century technology not as an inherently alienating force, but as

    c. Robert Anton Wilson felt that late 20<sup>th</sup>-century technology was not as an inherently alienating force, and

    d. it was felt by Robert Anton Wilson that late 20<sup>th</sup>-century technology was not an inherently alienating force, but

    e. late 20<sup>th</sup>-century technology was felt by Robert Anton Wilson to be not an inherently alienating force, and be

19. Federal investigators surveying the crash scene noted that only one-third of the passengers on board the plane had been issued life jackets. <u>At the least as many as 80 or more other ones had not been given any</u> flotation device whatsoever.

    a. At the least as many as 80 or more other ones had not been given any

    b. At the least as many as more than 80 other ones had not been given any

    c. More than 80 other ones had not been given any

    d. At least 80 had not been given any

    e. There were at the least 80 or even more who had not been given any


20. Historians have discovered that fighting was a popular sport for ancient cultures, <u>as that of modern civilizations</u>.

    a. as that of modern civilizations

    b. like that for modern civilizations

    c. exactly like modern civilizations do

    d. as modern people do

    e. as it still is for modern civilizations


21. Born John Joseph Lydon in North London in 1956, <u>Johnny Rotten's first number 1 song, *God Save the Queen* was released during the week of Queen Elizabeth II's Silver Jubilee when the musician was 21</u>.

    a. Johnny Rotten's first number 1 song, *God Save the Queen* was released during the week of Queen Elizabeth II's Silver Jubilee when the musician was 21

    b. Johnny Rotten's first number 1 song, *God Save the Queen*, released during the week of Queen Elizabeth II's Silver Jubilee when the musician was 21

    c. Johnny Rotten's *God Save the Queen*, his first number 1 song was released during the week of Queen Elizabeth II's Silver Jubilee when the musician was 21

    d. Johnny Rotten released his first number 1 song, *God Save the Queen*, during the week of Queen Elizabeth II's Silver Jubilee when the musician was 21

    e. during the week of Queen Elizabeth II's Silver Jubilee, Johnny Rotten released his first number 1 song, *God Save the Queen* when the musician was 21

22. In musical recording, one advantage of simultaneous multi-track recording over recording one musician at a time is that the harmonies are blended as the music is played <u>rather than</u> a digital simulation requiring extra processing and remixing.

    a. rather than

    b. rather than in

    c. as opposed to

    d. and not

    e. instead of having been with


23. The Discordian Society believes that, since the untimely demise of their leader Kerry Thornley, <u>they did and will keep continuing the chaotic goals of Thornley and his cabal, the Legion of Dynamic Discord</u>, who have begun to sow the seeds of worldwide anarchy.

    a. they did and will keep continuing the chaotic goals of Thornley and his cabal, the Legion of Dynamic Discord

    b. they did and will keep continuing Thornley's, and his cabal the Legion of Discord's, chaotic goals

    c. it did and will keep continuing the chaotic goals of Thornley and his cabal, the Legion of Dynamic Discord

    d. it has maintained and will continue to maintain the chaotic goals of Thornley and his cabal, the Legion of Dynamic Discord

    e. it has continued the chaotic goals of Thornley and his cabal, the Legion of Dynamic Discord

24. Environmentalists studying global climate change have scientifically determined that global warming is accelerating, and <u>the Kyoto protocols and other environmental treaties of the latter half of the 20<sup>th</sup> century is only slowing, rather than stopping, the acceleration of climate change.</u>

    a. the Kyoto protocols and other environmental treaties of the latter half of the 20<sup>th</sup> century is only slowing, rather than stopping, the acceleration of climate change

    b. in the latter half of the 20<sup>th</sup> century, the Kyoto protocols and other environmental treaties is only slowing, rather than stopping, the acceleration of climate change

    c. the Kyoto protocols and other environmental treaties of the latter half of the 20<sup>th</sup> century have only slowed, rather than stopped, the acceleration of climate change

    d. in the latter half of the 20<sup>th</sup> century, the Kyoto protocols and other environmental treaties have only been slowing, rather than stopped, the acceleration

    e. the latter half of the 20<sup>th</sup> century's Kyoto protocols and other environmental treaties only were slowing, rather than stopping, climate change's acceleration


25. <u>All of Lloyd Kaufman's most successful movies—*Class of Nuke 'em High, Toxic Avenger,* and *Tromeo and Julliet*—takes place in a high school setting</u>, a fact that suggests that his high school experiences may have played a formative role in his film-making career.

    a. All of Lloyd Kaufman's most successful movies—*Class of Nuke 'em High, Toxic Avenger,* and *Tromeo and Julliet*—takes place in a high school setting

    b. *Class of Nuke 'em High, Toxic Avenger,* and *Tromeo and Julliet*—each of them among Lloyd Kaufman's most successful movies—takes place in a high school setting

    c. Lloyd Kaufman's most successful movies—*Class of Nuke 'em High, Toxic Avenger,* and *Tromeo and Julliet*—all take place in a high school setting

    d. The movies by Lloyd Kaufman—*Class of Nuke 'em High, Toxic Avenger,* and *Tromeo and Julliet*—each one of these successful movies takes place in a high school setting

    e. Movies Lloyd Kaufman made—*Class of Nuke 'em High, Toxic Avenger,* and *Tromeo and Julliet*—all of them successful, take place in a high school setting

26. Still using classic forms dating from before the age of Shakespeare, <u>new metric forms and approaches to rhythm allow 21<sup>st</sup>-century poets not only to write artful verse, but also to express</u> the rhythms of modern life.

    a. new metric forms and approaches to rhythm allow 21<sup>st</sup>-century poets not only to write artful verse, but also to express

    b. 21<sup>st</sup>-century poets using new metric forms and approaches to rhythm write not only artful verse, but also can express

    c. employing new metric forms and approaches to rhythm allows 21<sup>st</sup>-century poets not only to  write artful verse, but also to express

    d. employing new metric forms and approaches not just for artful verse, 21<sup>st</sup>-century poets are able to express

    e. the poets of the 21<sup>st</sup> century are empowered by new metric forms and approaches not just for writing artful verse, but also for expressing

27. Unlike their Scandinavian counterparts, British teens <u>have force to compete</u> from an early age, with no regard given to the value of cooperation.

    a. have force to compete

    b. are forced to compete

    c. are forced of competing

    d. are under force to compete

    e. have force that they must compete

**28.** In the early 1960s, <u>when the Scratching Post was a small, recently opened, hole-in-the-wall pub, the club booked as many local bands in a typical month as they do now, despite</u> the fact that they are a much more popular club in a better location.

   a. when the Scratching Post was a small, recently opened, hole-in-the-wall pub, the club booked as many local bands in a typical month as they do now, despite

   b. when the Scratching Post was a small, recently opened, hole-in-the-wall pub, the club booked as many local bands in a typical month as they do in a typical month now, despite

   c. when the Scratching Post was a small, recently opened, hole-in-the-wall pub, the club booked a quantity of local bands in a typical month as so they do now, despite

   d. whereas the Scratching Post was a small, recently opened, hole-in-the-wall pub, the club booked such a number of local bands in a typical month as do they now, in spite of

   e. when the Scratching Post was a small, recently opened, hole-in-the-wall pub, the club booked a quantity of local bands just as great in a typical month as the number that they do now, despite

**29.** The writing of novelist Philip K. Dick works as an interrogation of consensus reality and the category of the real <u>more than it does as a response to the particular wars and struggles of late 20<sup>th</sup>-century society.</u>

   a. more than it does as a response to the particular wars and struggles of late 20<sup>th</sup>-century society.

   b. more than it did as a response to the particular wars and struggles of late 20<sup>th</sup>-century society.

   c. more than it did respond, during the late 20<sup>th</sup> century, to the particular wars and struggles of society.

   d. more than it was responsive to the particular wars and struggles of late 20<sup>th</sup>-century society.

   e. more than, in late 20<sup>th</sup>-century society, responding to the particular wars and struggles.

**30.** Just as the rarity of musical all-ages venues contributes to the dullness of life for teens in the Detroit suburbs, <u>so the absence of public transportation further restricts the ability of young people to enjoy an active and varied social life.</u>

- a. so the absence of public transportation further restricts the ability of young people to enjoy an active and varied social life.
- b. just the same, public transportation being absent further restricts the ability of young people to enjoy an active and varied social life.
- c. so the absence of public transportation further restricting the ability of young people to enjoy an active and varied social life.
- d. in identical manner, potentials for an active and varied social life are restricted by the absence of public transportation.
- e. so it is in other aspects of life, where the absent public transportation aids the further restricting of the ability of young people to enjoy an active and varied social life.

# Critical Reasoning

31. A recent exposé reported that a new series of television commercials makes deceptive claims about the health benefits of a new cereal. The reporter drew the conclusion that the commercials could cause consumers to actually choose a less healthful cereal for its supposed health benefits.

*Which of the following choices would best reinforce the reporter's conclusion?*

   a. Television stations rely heavily on food commercials as a source of revenue

   b. Television executives have little idea whether a particular commercial is true or false

   c. Viewers depend on commercials as a way to understand the health benefits of new foods

   d. Television commercials tend to distort information more than print ads do

   e. All food ads are carefully screened by a panel of experts for accuracy before they are put on the air

32. A state senator asserts that her state's ban on smoking marijuana is unprincipled and backwards, since more dangerous drugs like nicotine and alcohol are legal. She argues that instead of futilely struggling to enforce the ban, the government should lift all drug prohibition. She asserts that legalization would provide a further benefit by reducing crime.

*Assuming the following statements are true, which does the most to weaken the senator's argument?*

   a. Many people use drugs because of the thrill of getting away with it. Therefore, legalizing drug use would drive these people away, lowering the rate of drug use.

   b. The senator's state already makes drug enforcement a low priority. Therefore, legalization wouldn't have much effect on the law enforcement budget.

   c. Since marijuana was first outlawed, the number of users has increased substantially every year.

   d. If drugs were legalized, users from neighboring states would be drawn in. Many of them are involved in racketeering and other serious illegal activities.

   e. Many illegal drug users argue that they can get high on cough syrup and other legal pharmaceuticals.

**33.** Scientists studying the CPUs (equivalent to the brains) of killer robots discovered that the robots receive just as many commands to crush humans when recharging as when actively crushing. In order to discover why the robot's massive steel claws don't respond to the crush command when the bot recharges, a scientist removed a chip in the primary sympathetic processor (PSC), a module that connects the robot's body to the CPU. Without leaving recharge mode, the robot grabbed the scientist, threw him to the ground, stomped him repeatedly, and then proceeded to crush several imaginary people while stomping around the room. *In combination with the account above, which statement lends most support to the conclusion that the recharging robot was acting out some sort of evil robot dream?*

    a. The chip that was removed from the primary sympathetic processor normally triggers the robotic recharge state and the diminished activity that accompanies it

    b. The PSC can pass on data even if the robot is recharging

    c. The chip that was extracted normally transmits commands from the CPU to the robot body

    d. The chip that was extracted normally stops commands from moving from the CPU to the robot body

    e. The CPU seems to select different targets for crushing when asleep than when awake

34. A widely believed anthropological theory states that the Hill People, an early culture on Mucky Muck Island, fought with and were eventually wiped out by the Lothars whose culture dominates the island today. More recently, however, anthropologists have proposed that modern Mucky Muck culture is more complex than they previously thought. The theory states that the Lothars, the Hill People, and several other tribes lived side-by-side for a long time and that the modern culture shows influences from several societies. *Which piece of evidence would most strongly support the more modern theory about the culture of the Mucky Muck Islanders?*

    a. Archaeological evidence shows that both the Hill People and the Lothars originated in Central Europe at least 10,000 years before they arrived on Mucky Muck Island

    b. The Hill People and the Lothars had similar height, build, and facial features

    c. A modern Mucky Muck myth incorporates a Hill People hero, one of the gods of the Lothars, as well as fertility rituals used by other cultures in the area

    d. The Hill People culture remained a primitive hunter-gatherer culture, while the Lothars learned agriculture and advanced tool-making skills

    e. The Lothars were willing to trade with strangers, while the Hill People were culturally insular and suspicious


35. Radiation is not the cause of the increase in mutations in the area around the abandoned weapons testing facility. Instead, the increase is caused by the fact that more thrill-seekers have recently moved to the area. Statistics show that thrill-seekers are more likely to undergo genetic mutations, and these thrill-seekers comprise a greater proportion of the population around the facility than ever. *A flaw in this argument is that it fails to account for the possibility that*

    a. thrill-seekers were born as normal, non-thrill-seeking children

    b. there are plenty of citizens around the plant who are not thrill-seekers

    c. the increase in radiation may just be a fluke

    d. thrill-seekers are not statistically more likely to have drastic mutations than other people

    e. thrill-seekers are more likely to expose themselves to radioactive environments such as the abandoned facility than other people are

36. Until Congress began offering bailouts to insolvent lenders, risky loans were limited by the fear that corporate directors had of becoming insolvent. Since the bailouts began, however, high risk strategies have boomed and corporate bankruptcies have crippled the economy. *Assuming that all of the following solutions are possible to carry out, which would have the best chance of stopping the problem of corporate bankruptcy?*

    a. stopping companies from expanding current high-risk loan programs

    b. using economic modeling software to predict how likely risky loans are to lead to lender bankruptcy

    c. requiring the establishment of a low-risk loan program for every new high-risk loan program

    d. offering to buy high-risk loans from lenders and passing a law to ban further bailouts

    e. requiring lenders to adopt a more diverse economic program in exchange for eligibility for future bailouts


37. Victims of Marah's disease, a virtually unknown neurological condition, appear pain-free and content. Often, they also have a desire to engage in vigorous physical activities such as contact sports. Beneath it all, they are in great physical pain but have an inability to express it or act to reduce it, making diagnosis difficult. As a result, they are inaccurately diagnosed as very low on the pain scale, their discomfort level much lower than victims of severe sprains, despite the fact that sprains, although more painful, are temporary and comparatively easy to manage nature. *This passage makes the argument that*

    a. the pain scale is not an accurate or adequate way to measure the physical discomfort of certain people, such as those suffering from Marah's disease

    b. sprain victims have more intense pain than Marah's sufferers, but they can manage their pain more easily

    c. the pain scale seems to put more emphasis on intensity of pain than duration

    d. victims of Marah's syndrome are often unable to deal effectively with their discomfort

    e. there needs to be more public awareness of Marah's syndrome

38. Ignatius II believed that gravity was not a force but actually the result of "falling demons" pulling on all objects. His friend Dot Matrix disagreed, and she set up an experiment to prove that the falling demons do not have anything to do with falling. She invoked the falling demons and dropped a ball from five feet in the air, timing how long it took to reach the ground. She then dispelled the falling demons and dropped the ball again, measuring exactly the same time. Ignatius argued that she had proven nothing since falling demons, once invoked, cannot be quickly expelled. *Which statement provides the best evidence to support Ignatius' argument, assuming the statement is true?*

    a. Excessive heaviness, often present in objects that have had the falling demons summoned into them, is often a cause of quicker acceleration toward the ground.

    b. Dot Matrix was actually an expert in demonology, and she was able to keep the falling demons from leaving despite appearing to dispel them.

    c. Falling demons are more common in places with substantial religious communities who are more likely to invoke them.

    d. Although gravity is a force common to all objects, the falling demons still manage to affect some objects.

    e. If the invoker waits at least twenty-four hours before dispelling the falling demons, the object is likely to take longer to reach the ground.

39. Citing the progress made in literacy since compulsory education was instituted in the United States, legislators have now proposed compulsory job education for young adults. Eighteen- to twenty-year-old mechanics, secretaries, salespeople, and all other workers not currently enrolled in schools will have to undergo at least five hours of class a week if the new legislation is instituted. Employers, who will have to pay for this education, argue that this is a one-size-fits-all solution that will not work well for some businesses. *Of the following statements, which casts the most doubt on the prudence of the legislative proposal?*

a. Reading needs to be taught in an academic setting, but not all job skills do. In some businesses, on-the-job training is sufficient without outside instruction.

b. The program will actually help businesses, which will no longer have to provide job training themselves.

c. The reason some workers are not sufficiently educated in how to perform their jobs is that many companies do not provide sufficient training.

d. Not being able to read is a much more serious problem than not being good at your job.

e. More investigation is needed concerning the number of people who don't have enough job training.

40. Between 1980 and 1985, the incarceration rate of the poorest 20% of Americans decreased from 70% of the total prison population to 60%. During the same period, however, the incarceration rate for the poorest 8% increased from 18% to 35%. *Which of the factors below helps to explain this discrepancy?*

a. Between 1980 and 1985, an estimated 20,000 more cops were put on the street.

b. Between 1980 and 1985, prosecution of crimes of desperation such as petty theft increased by more than 50%.

c. Between 1980 and 1985, many of the working poor were able to climb out of poverty.

d. Between 1980 and 1985, prosecution of white collar crime declined, leaving more rich criminals out of the justice system.

e. Between 1980 and 1985, the incarceration rate for Americans overall was below 1%.

41. The economic boom of the late 1950s affected the different states of a certain country in very different ways. Although the refrigerator factories of state Alpha and the television factories of state Beta both saw demand drastically increase during the boom, the border state of Alpha was able to quickly scale up production to meet the demand and so reap the rewards, while the inland state of Beta was not. *Of the possible explanations below, which best accounts for the fact that Beta was unable to benefit fully from the economic boom?*

    a. Beta manufactured televisions, which were far more cutting-edge consumer items than refrigerators in the 1950s.

    b. Alpha was able to draw on foreign workers from neighboring countries to work extra shifts in its factories, whereas Beta was nowhere near the border and could not as easily recruit new workers.

    c. Televisions are a luxury item, whereas refrigerators are a necessity. An economic boom naturally favors luxury items.

    d. Many neighboring countries also had factories that could produce refrigerators similar to those made in Alpha's factories.

    e. Because Beta had a diversified economy, it could do reasonably well, even with an inefficient manufacturing base.

# Answers and Explanations
## Quantitative
## Problem Solving

1. E: First perform the operations:

2 + 0.4 = 2.4

1 − 0.2 = 0.8

Next, solve the equation:     2.4 = x(0.8)

$x = 3$

2. C: The movie is now at the 90 + 12 = 102-minute mark. Therefore, $m$ minutes ago, it had reached the 102 − $m$ mark.

3. D: First calculate the area of the bull's-eye:

A = πr² = π(4/2)² = π2² = 4π

Then, let $x$ = the area of the target.

20 percent of $x$ = 4π

0.2x = 4π

x = 20π

4. C: First, find the decimal equivalent for $\frac{5}{8}$ by dividing. 5 ÷ 8 = 0.625. D is equal to $\frac{5}{8}$ and E is greater than $\frac{5}{8}$, so the answer must be A, B, or C. Divide to find the decimal equivalent of each.

A. $\frac{7}{10}$ = 0.70

B. $\frac{4}{5}$ = 0.80

C. $\frac{6}{11}$ = 0.5454...

Only C is less than 0.625.

5. E: After the first markup, the bread costs 1.2 times its original price of $x$, or $1.2x$. After the second markup, the bread costs 1.2 times the marked up price, or $1.2(1.2x) = 1.44x$. 1.44 is equivalent to a 44 percent markup.

6. B: The perpendicular bisector cuts a line into 90° angles.

7. B: If the volume halves every 2 days, it halves 5 times after 10 days. This halving action can be expressed as $(\frac{1}{2})(\frac{1}{2})(\frac{1}{2})(\frac{1}{2})(\frac{1}{2})$ or $(\frac{1}{2})^5$. Therefore, if the initial volume is $(10^6)$, then the volume will be $(\frac{1}{2})^5(10^6)$ after 10 days.

8. B: The total number of guests in attendance is $0.6(750) = 450$. If 46 percent of the attendees are male, then 54 percent are female. Therefore, the number of females in attendance is $0.54(450) = 243$.

9. C: The angles $a$, $b$, and $c$ form a straight line, so $a + b + c = 180$. Substituting 180 for $a + b + c$ in the proportion, we have:

$$\frac{b}{180} = \frac{3}{5}$$

By cross-multiplying, we can solve for $b$: $5b = 3(180)$ or $b = 108$.

10. D: Let $x$ equal the amount of the fourth order. Then using the formula Avg = (sum of values)/(# of values), the given information can be expressed in the following equation: $(75 + 40 + 107 + x)/4 = 80$. Cross-multiplying, we get $75 + 40 + 107 + x = 320$, or $x = 98$.

11. D: First, solve the second equation for $y$: $y = -2x - 5$. Next, substitute that expression for $y$ in the first equation:

$3(-2x - 5) - 2x = 9$

$-6x - 15 - 2x = 9$

$-8x = 24$

$x = -3$

Finally, substitute –3 for $x$ in either equation in order to solve for $y$:

$2(-3) + y = -5$

$-6 + y = -5$

$y = 1$


**12. C:** Using the Pythagorean Theorem, we first find AB.

$AB^2 + BC^2 = AC^2$

$AB^2 + 5^2 = 13^2$

$AB^2 + 25 = 169$

$AB^2 = 144$

$AB = 12$

Next, we draw a perpendicular bisector from C to AD, forming segment CE, which is the height of triangle ACD and is equal to segment AB. Thus, the height of the triangle is 12.

We know the base of triangle ACD, AD, equals 8. So, we use the area formula.

$A = \frac{1}{2}bh = \frac{1}{2}(8)(12) = 48$


**13. D: Justifications:**

First, convert 10 yards to inches: 1 yard = 36 inches, so 10 yards = 360 inches.

Next, convert the mixed fraction $6\frac{3}{4}$ to a decimal: 6.75.

Finally, divide: 360/6.75 = 53.3333...

So, the maximum number of strips that can be cut is 53.


**14. C:** Use the Distance Formula: distance = rate × time    AND    time = distance/rate.

   1. First half of trip: 1,500 = 400 × time, so time = $\frac{15}{4}$.

   2. Second half of trip: 1,500 = rate × distance/rate = rate × $\frac{1500}{r}$.

   3. Total trip: 3,000 = 500 × time, so total time = 6.

The total time of the trip is the sum of the times for the first 1,500 miles and the second 1,500 miles. So, $\frac{15}{4} + \frac{1500}{r} = 6$. Solving for $r$, we multiply both sides of the equation by $4r$ and get:

$15r + 6{,}000 = 24r$

$6{,}000 = 9r$

$r = 666\frac{2}{3}$.

15. B: The radius of circle O is one-fourth the diameter of circle P. The diameter is twice the radius, or $d = 2r$. So $r_o = \frac{1}{4}(2r_p) = \frac{1}{2}r_p$.

The circumference of circle P $= 2\pi\, r_p$.

The circumference of circle O $= 2\pi\, r_o = 2\pi\left(\frac{1}{2}r_p\right) = \pi\, r_p$.

The ratio of circle O's circumference to circle P's is $(\pi r_p)/(2\pi r_p) = \frac{1}{2}$.

16. D: Let F equal the total amount in the college fund. Then the amount spent on tuition, room and board, and books is $\frac{3}{8}F + \frac{1}{4}F + \frac{1}{5}F$. Finding the LCD, $\frac{3}{8}F + \frac{1}{4}F + \frac{1}{5}F = (15 + 10 + 8)F/40 = 33/40\ F$. The remainder of the fund is therefore $1 - 33F/40$, or $7F/40$. We are told $7F/40 = \$7{,}000$, so $F = \$40{,}000$.

17. D: If $x^2 + 3x - 18 = 0$, then $(x + 6)(x - 3) = 0$. So $x = -6$ or $3$. We are told $x < 0$, so $x$ must equal $-6$.

I. $(-6)^2 - 36 = 0$ True

II. $(-6)^2 - 2(-6) - 3 \neq 0$ False

III. $(-6)^2 + 5(-6) - 6 = 0$ True

18. E: Using the formula for volume $V = e^3$, where e represents the length of an edge of a cube, let the volume of cube B equal $e^3$ and so the volume of cube A is $\left(\frac{3}{4}e\right)^3 = \frac{27}{64}e^3$.

The ratio of the volume of cube B to the volume of cube A is $e^3 / \frac{27}{64}e^3 = \frac{64}{27}$.

19. B: We find the decimal equivalent of each fraction by dividing.

5/9 = 0.555..., 6/11 = 0.5454..., 1/2 = 0.50, 9/16 = 0.5625, and 3/5 = 0.60.

When we order these decimals from least to greatest, we find the second equivalent fraction to be 6/11.


20. E: Justifications:

For all large values of x, the value of $\frac{x}{1-2x}$ will be very close to the value of $\frac{x}{-2x} = -\frac{1}{2}$.


21. B: Using the formula for the perimeter of a rectangle, we know that P = 2*l* + 2*w*. Substituting the value given, we get 76 = 2*l* + 2*w* or 38 = *l* + *w*. We can now solve for *l*: 38 − *w* = *l*.

Using the formula for the area of a rectangle, we know that A = *lw*. Substituting the value given, we get 336 = *lw*.

If we substitute the 38 − *w* we found in the first step for *l*, we get (38−*w*)*w* = 336. Thus:

38*w* − *w*² = 336

0 = *w*² − 38*w* + 336

0 = (*w* − 14)(*w* − 24)

*w* = 14 or 24

The shorter of these two possibilities is 14.


22. C: If Anish was the 11th highest speller, 10 participants placed higher. If Anish was the 25th lowest speller, 24 participants placed lower. Therefore, the total number of participants was 10 + 24 + 1 (Anish) = 35


23. A: There are 4 members of the first set and 4 members of the second set, so there are 4(4) = 16 possible products for *cd*. *cd* is odd only when both *c* and *d* are odd. There are 2 odd numbers in the first set and two in the second set, so 2(2) = 4 products are odd and the probability *cd* is odd is 4/16 or 1/4.

24. A: We are given $l = 3w$, so $w = \frac{1}{3}l$. The diagonal is the hypotenuse of the triangle with sides $l$ and $w$, so we use the Pythagorean Theorem.

$$l^2 + w^2 = d^2 \qquad l^2 + (\tfrac{1}{3}l)^2 = d^2 \qquad l^2 + \tfrac{1}{9}l^2 = d^2 \qquad \tfrac{10}{9}l^2 = d^2$$

$$d = \sqrt{\tfrac{10}{9}}\, l = \tfrac{\sqrt{10}}{3}\, l$$

# Data Sufficiency

25. D: Justifications:

Since $\frac{q}{5} - \frac{r}{5} = \frac{1}{5}(q - r)$, we can cross-multiply (1) to get $q - r = 15$ and then substitute 15 into $\frac{1}{5}(q - r)$. $\frac{1}{5}(15) = 3$, so (1) alone is sufficient.

We can do the same substitution for (2). $\frac{1}{5}(15) = 3$, so (2) alone is also sufficient. In fact, both statements (1) and (2) are essentially the same. One could simply multiply both sides of equation (1) by 5 to obtain equation (2).

D. Therefore, the correct answer is D; EACH statement ALONE is sufficient

26. C: Justifications:

We are trying to find $y + z$. (1) tells us that $y = z + 16$. Substituting, we get $(z + 16) + z = 2z + 16$. This expression can vary in value, so (1) is not sufficient.

(2) tells us that $y + 10 = 2(z + 10)$ or $y + 10 = 2z + 20$. Thus, $y = 2z + 10$. This expression can also vary in value, so (2) is not sufficient.

Given (1) and (2): $y = z + 16$ and $y = 2z + 10$, we can solve the equations simultaneously to obtain values of y and z.

Therefore, the correct answer is C; BOTH statements TOGETHER are sufficient, but NEITHER statement ALONE is sufficient.

27. B: Justifications:

The volume of a rectangular solid is *lwh*.

(1) gives us *lw* = 40. Substituting that into the volume formula, we get V = 40*h*. This expression can vary in value, so (1) is not sufficient.

(2) gives us $\frac{1}{2}$ *lwh* = 30. Multiplying both sides by 2, we get *lwh* = 60. The volume is therefore 60 and (2) is sufficient.

Therefore, the correct answer is B; Statement (2) ALONE is sufficient, but statement (1) alone is not sufficient.

28. E: Justifications:

(1) does not give us the net proceeds total for the first day, so it is not sufficient.

(2) does not give us the net proceeds total for the second day, so it is not sufficient. Without the total net proceeds for either the first or the second day, we are unable to find the net proceeds for the third day.

Therefore, the correct answer is E; Statements (1) and (2) TOGETHER are not sufficient.

29. D: Justifications:

(1) Transposing like terms gives the equivalent equation –4 = 10x, or x = $-\frac{4}{10}$. So, (1) is sufficient.

(2) Cross-multiplying gives –10x = 4 or x = $-\frac{4}{10}$. So (2) is also sufficient.

Therefore the correct answer is D; EACH statement ALONE is sufficient.

30. A: Justifications:

(1) Using the Pythagorean Theorem, if $a^2 + b^2 = c^2$ then the triangle is a right triangle. $5^2 + 12^2 = 13^2$ or 25 + 144 = 169 is true, so (1) is sufficient.

(2) We know that $x + y + z = 180$. We are told that $x = 45$. Substituting, we get $45 + y + z = 180$, or $y + z = 135$. If either $y$ or $z$ is 90 then the triangle is a right triangle, but we are not given enough information to determine this. So (2) is not sufficient.

Therefore, the correct answer is A; Statement (1) ALONE is sufficient, but statement (2) alone is not sufficient.


31. B: Justifications:

If we let $d$, $r$, and $i$ be the number of Democrats, Republicans, and Independents surveyed respectively, then $d + r + i = 1,500$.


(1) We are told that 40 percent of the voters are Republicans, so $r = 0.40(1,500) = 600$. Plugging that into the equation $d + r + i = 1,500$, we get $d + 600 + i = 1,500$, or $d + i = 900$ and $i = 900 - d$. The value of this expression varies, so (1) is not sufficient.


(2) We are told $i = 0.25(d + r)$, or $4i = d + r$. By substituting $4i$ for $d + r$ in the original equation, we get $4i + i = 1,500$, or $i = 300$. So (2) is sufficient.


Therefore, the correct answer is B; Statement (2) ALONE is sufficient, but statement (1) alone is not sufficient.


32. A: Justifications:

First we find the midpoint of 10 and 25: $(10 + 25)/2 = 17.5$. So any number greater than 17.5 is closer to 25 and any number less than 17.5 is closer to 10.


(1) $25 - p < p - 10$

$35 < 2p$ or $17.5 < p$, so (1) is sufficient.


(2) We are told $p < 20$, but it could be, for example, 19 (closer to 25), or 11 (closer to 10). So (2) is not sufficient.

Therefore, the correct answer is A; Statement (1) ALONE is sufficient, but statement (2) alone is not sufficient.

33. D: Justifications:

(1) The formula for the area of a circle is $A = \pi r^2$ and the formula for the circumference of a circle is $C = 2\pi r$. So the ratio of A to C is $\frac{\pi r^2}{2\pi r} = \frac{r}{2}$. Setting this ratio equal to 2, we get $r = 4$, so (1) is sufficient.

(2) The formula for the area of a circle is $A = \pi r^2$. Setting this equal to $16\pi$, we get $16\pi = \pi r^2$, or $r^2 = 16$. So $r = 4$ or $-4$, but the radius must be positive. Thus, $r = 4$ and (2) is also sufficient.

Therefore, the correct answer is D; EACH statement ALONE is sufficient.

34. D: Justifications:

If we let i be the greatest of the consecutive integers, then the set of integers is $\{i - (m - 1) \text{ or } i - m + 1, ..., i - 3, i - 2, i - 1, i\}$.

(1) The range is the difference between the greatest and least members of the set, so $8 = i - (i - m + 1)$, which simplifies as $8 = m - 1$, or $m = 9$. And, we are given that $[(i - 9 + 1) + (i - 1) + (i - 2) ... + i]/9 = 7$, or $[(i - 9 + 1) + (i - 1) + (i - 2) ... + i] = 63$. A unique value of i can be determined so (1) is sufficient.

(2) Because the integers are consecutive, they form a data set that is symmetric about its average. So, the average of the integers is the average of the least and greatest numbers: $(3 + i) / 2 = 7$, or $3 + i = 14$, or $i = 11$. So (2) is sufficient.

Therefore, the correct answer is D; EACH statement ALONE is sufficient.

35. A: Justifications:

(1) If there are $x$ yards of black fabric then there are $1.5x$ yards of white fabric and $(3/2)(1.5)x$, or $2.25x$ yards of red fabric.

So $x + 1.5x + 2.25x = 19$ or $4.75x = 19$ or $x = 4$. So, the amount of white fabric can be determined: $1.5(4) = 6$ yards. Thus, (1) is sufficient.

(2) If the sum of the amounts of the white and black fabrics is $y$, then the amount of red fabric is $y - 1$. So $y + (y - 1) = 19$ or $2y = 20$, or $y = 10$. But we don't know how much of this quantity is black and how much is white. Thus, (2) is not sufficient.

Therefore, the correct answer is A; Statement (1) ALONE is sufficient, but statement (2) alone is not sufficient.

36. C: Justifications:

(1) The formula for circumference is $2\pi r$. Setting that equal to $6\pi$, we get $r = 3$, but the radius does not tell us anything about $x$. So (1) is not sufficient.

(2) The length of arc AB $= 2\pi$, but without knowing the circumference, we can't find $x$. So (2) is not sufficient.

Taking both (1) and (2) together, we know that AB $= 2\pi$ and C $= 6\pi$ and so arc AB is one-third the circumference. Thus, angle $x$ is one-third of the circle, or $(1/3)(360) = 120$.

Therefore, the correct answer is C; BOTH statements TOGETHER are sufficient, but NEITHER statement ALONE is sufficient.

37. B: Justifications:

(1) The even integers between 2 and 9 inclusive that are the square root of some integer are 2, 4, 6, and 8. So (1) is not sufficient.

(2) Of the integers 2 through 9, only 8 has a cube root that is an integer, so (2) is sufficient.

- 186 -

Therefore, the correct answer is B; Statement (2) ALONE is sufficient, but statement (1) alone is not sufficient.

# Verbal
# Reading Comprehension

1. B: In the first paragraph of the essay, the author characterizes amateurs as "an elite group within the music scene" and states that there are several "technological, demographic, and economic factors" that account for them doing better than professionals. The tone of the essay is documentary—the author doesn't make any judgments about whether this is a good development or a bad one. He simply states that amateurs are more successful relative to professionals than they have been before and goes on to examine the reasons for this.

2. D: The key is the phrase "directly support." The essay needs to come right out and say the correct answer, not imply that it is true. Paragraph 3 says that digital file sharing "robs the professionals of what has traditionally been one of their biggest sources of revenue." Paragraph 2 provides less direct evidence, saying that many clubs that were once able to pay professionals now can't. Professionals have lost most of their income from both small clubs and recordings.

3. B: The second sentence in the final paragraph is a giveaway. If the "amateurs are the only ones who can afford to buy new gear and fix broken equipment, keep their cars in working order to get to shows, and pay to promote their shows," then the professionals must not be able to do any of those things.

4. C: The essay as a whole discusses how the current musical scene negatively affects professional musicians while leaving amateurs unharmed. The second paragraph, for example, discusses how professionals are no longer able to make a living playing small venues and must "fight more desperately than ever for those few lucrative gigs." The final paragraph states that, because of the effect on their finances, professionals are unable to

maintain the gear and transportation they need to "keep the higher-paying gigs." It goes on to say that "a fairly skilled amateur . . . will be able to fake his way through most of what a professional does . . . to play professional shows." Therefore, professionals are falling behind amateurs at small venues (which professionals can't afford to play because of the lack of pay) and at professional gigs (where professionals can't play because they can't afford professional gear).

5. C: The third paragraph states that the Department of Homeland Security "argued that the new laws might actually limit protections for freedom of thought by . . . hampering the efforts of citizens to restrict their thought-processes to wholly legal topics." In other words, the laws would pose a legal problem for ordinary citizens by making it harder for them to precisely understand and obey the law.

6. A: The "review of thoughts" refers to the provision in the law that sets up a Civilian Thought Review Council with the power to legalize new thoughts. If that council "does not have the knowledge required to judge whether a thought is dangerous or not" as in choice A, a dangerous thought could be made legal, compromising national security.

None of the other choices has the potential to threaten security. Keeping threatening illegal thoughts that are no longer threatening, choice B, won't endanger security, since all threatening thoughts would still be illegal. Similarly, the amount of resources the civilian board needs, choice C, doesn't have any bearing on the impact of its decision. The government pressuring civilians not to legalize a thought, choice D, will not lead to dangerous risks, but rather to more conservative decisions. The veto power of the High Tribal Council, choice E, could actually be used to curtail anything dangerous the Civilian Thought Review Council does.

7. C: The fourth paragraph says "the president himself objected strongly to this, saying that the amendment would potentially expose huge numbers of government contacts and connections to public view unless the bureaucrats were able to show that each individual

secret was exempt from the law." Clearly, he feels that having to show that "each individual secret" is exempt is impractical.

8. C: Language change in multicultural areas is characterized as "drastic and rapid." These areas are contrasted with isolated communities. The implication is that languages change much more quickly in multicultural areas than isolated regions.

9. E: This question asks for the main purpose of the essay. The correct answer must not only refer to one part of the essay, but to the essay as a whole. Choice D is incorrect, since the author spends much of the essay talking about ways that language change can be predicted. Choices A, B, and C refer to things the author discusses in part of the essay, but only in part. The whole essay, however, discusses "how linguists study language change."

10. D: The first sentence of the paragraph is a giveaway (it often is). It states that "once . . . a language community is established, linguistic scholars can gather data from subcultures within that community." The paragraph then shows how they study those subcultures by observing and recording changes in speech of "young or marginalized subcultures" as a source of "early indicators of looming language shifts." The paragraph even examines some of the things linguists look for—phonological drift, for example—and discusses the way they catalog language change—"computer voice analysis."

11. A: The third paragraph says that "if the linguists posit a definition of a critical language shift. . . . [they can] predict the time it will take to evolve a completely new language."

12. C: The tricky thing about this question is that all the choices are true statements about things said in the essay. Only one, however, is the main idea. The best way to find it is to go to the first paragraph. In it, the author calls the ability to tell true and false statements apart "one of the main goals of every police officer." He goes further, calling this ability "the only way to punish the guilty, exonerate the innocent, and do the most possible good in preventing future crimes."

13. A: If there is one point that the author has repeated many times in this article, it is that police need to be able to investigate lies to conduct investigations. This is exactly the point explored in the explanation to question 33.

14. C: In paragraph 2, the author states that "smoke" lies "slow down an investigation."

## Sentence Correction

15. C: The question contains an error of agreement. "a tangible experience . . . that are called" should be "a tangible experience . . . that is called".

16. C: The "and it" is an awkward way of joining the two clauses. Does "it" refer to enrolling or to out-of-state schools? The "thereby" in choice C connects the ideas much more nicely. By the act of enrolling in out-of-state schools, students grow apart from their friends.

17. A: There are two things going on in the answer choices. First, the word "evidently" is being moved around. As the word works perfectly well where it begins, there is no need to move it—a clue that choice A is probably correct. More important is the change of "are believed" to "were believed." Although the servants were buried in the past, the belief about their burial—that it occurred nearly 4,000 years ago—occurs in the present. The servants are currently believed—presumably by the Egyptologists—to have been buried nearly 4,000 years ago.

18. B: Since Robert Anton Wilson is being contrasted directly to Hakim Bey, his name has to directly follow the first comma. We can therefore rule out D and E right off the bat. Notice, however, that the original sentence doesn't make sense. The phrase "felt how late 20th-century technology not as" seems awkward and ungrammatical. Sentence C corrects this error, but leaves the "and" at the end. Since we are trying to draw a contrast between Hakim Bey's view of late 20th-century technology as "an inherently alienating force" and Robert Anton Wilson's view of it as "something that could potentially liberate people," we need to use a "but" to draw the contrast.

19. D: The statement "at the least as many as 80 or more other ones had not been given any" is painfully awkward and clearly wrong. The phrase "at least as many" implies that there could be more. Therefore, the phrase "at least as many . . . or more" is redundant. Choice D succinctly expresses the idea that at least 80 passengers were not given flotation devices.

20. E: This question is about parallel structure. If fighting "was" a popular sport in the past, then it "is" in the present.

21. D: The original sentence contains incorrect pronoun reference. It implies that "Johnny Rotten's first number 1 song" was "born John Joseph Lydon." The correct answer should show that it was Johnny Rotten who was born as John Joseph Lydon.

22. B: This question requires parallel structure. The phrase "as the music is played" means "at the same time." It should be contrasted with "in a digital simulation" meaning "at another time after the music is played."

23. E: The sentence contains an error of agreement. The Discordian Society is a collective group, and therefore takes the pronoun "it" and not "they." In addition, "they did and will keep continuing" is an extremely awkward construction.

24. C: The subject "Kyoto protocols" is plural, so the singular "is" does not agree with it. Choices C, D, and E correct this error. Choice E has the awkward possessives "20th century's" and "climate change's." In choice D, the verb phrases "have only been slowing" and "rather than stopped" are not parallel.

25. C: The word "all" does not agree with the verb "takes." Choice C corrects this error without making the sentence excessively convoluted as in choices D and E.

26. B: The subject complement "still using . . . from Shakespeare" has to be followed by the subject, "21st-century poets." Both choices B and E do this, but B is a simpler, less awkward sentence.

27. B: The phrase "have force to compete" should strike you as odd when you hear it, because the verb "force" does not take the auxiliary verb "have." Choice B corrects this problem while leaving the correct "to compete" in its original form.

28. A: There is nothing wrong with the original sentence. All of the other choices either complicate the sentence or make it incorrect.

29. A: The original sentence represented by choice A, works fine. The verb phrase "works as an interrogation" is parallel to "does as a response." Both are also in the same tense, and the sentence is easy to read and understand.

30. A: The original sentence, represented by choice A, is the clearest version. The conjunction "so" joins the phrases "the rarity of musical all-ages venues" and "the absence of public transportation," creating parallel structure. All of the other choices make the sentence more convoluted and more difficult to understand.

## Critical Reasoning

31. C: The question asks us to reinforce the conclusion that deceptive television commercials could cause consumers to be tricked into making a poorer health choice. For this to be true, we need to know that consumers actually believe what the ad says.

32. D: The correct answer will contradict the senator's argument that legalization will reduce crime. Choices A and C address the rate of drug use, not the crime rate. Choice B talks about the budget. Choice E talks about legal alternatives to illegal drugs. Only choice D argues that more crime might be committed as a result of legalization.

33. The robot was thinking about crushing humans but in a passive recharging state. When the chip was removed, the robot began crushing humans without leaving the recharging state. This obviously implies that it was acting out a dream in the recharging state. If the chip removed were stopping commands from getting to the robot's body, then without it the robot will act out its evil robot dreams.

34. C: The modern theory states that the Lothars, the Hill People, and other cultures influenced each other, and that modern Mucky Muck shows the influence of more than one society. Therefore, we are looking for evidence of cultural cross-pollination. Choice A doesn't say that the cultures influenced each other, only that they both came from Central Europe. Choice B shows that the two peoples looked similar, but that doesn't mean that they had similar cultures or even a lot of contact—they may have evolved similar physical traits because they occupied the same environment. Choice D shows the two cultures diverging, not influencing each other. Choice E shows a difference between the two cultures but does not show them influencing each other. Only choice C shows cultural cross-influence. If a Mucky Muck myth incorporates a Hill People hero and a Lothar god, presumably the two cultures influenced each other to create the myth.

35. E: There are two possible causes for the increase in mutations: radiation and a higher population of thrill-seekers. The original statement argues that thrill-seekers are more prone to mutations, and therefore the rise in their population is the cause of the rise in mutations. If the factor that causes thrill-seekers to be prone to mutation is the radiation, it undermines the argument.

36. D: The question poses a problem (bankruptcy) and a cause (the promise of bailouts leading to high-risk loans) and asks for a solution. The solution should stop the bailouts as a way to stop the risky loans and, in turn, prevent insolvency. Choice A stops current high-risk loan programs from expanding, but it doesn't stop them from existing, nor does it stop companies from making new ones. Choice B is irrelevant—we already know that risky loans lead to bankruptcy. Choice C might help and might not, but it doesn't directly address the cause. Choice E has the same problem as choice C. Only choice D attempts to do away

with high-risk loans by both buying back current ones and removing bailouts, the cause of future ones.

37. A: The author says that victims of Marah's disease "appear" to be comfortable but "beneath it all" are in pain. He says that they are "inaccurately" diagnosed as low on the pain scale. This shows that the pain scale is not an accurate way to measure Marah's disease.

38. E: We are not looking for an answer that supports the existence of falling demons in general, but one that supports the specific statement of Ignatius that "falling demons, once invoked, cannot be quickly expelled." Choice E provides evidence that falling demons can be dispelled 24 hours later, indicating that the results of Dot's initial experiment may have been the result of her not waiting long enough to dispel the demons.

39. A: The proposal draws an analogy between improving literacy through compulsory education and improving work performance through compulsory training outside work. We are asked to undermine this argument. Choice A shows that illiteracy and lack of job skills are not the same sort of problems. Whereas teaching literacy requires an educational program, job skills can often simply be taught on the job.

40. B: While poor Americans were being incarcerated at a lower rate, the poorest Americans were being incarcerated more. Since the poorest are the most likely to commit "crimes of desperation" as a means to feed their families or take care of basic needs, it makes sense that increased prosecution would target them, while leaving the slightly less-poor unaffected.

41. B: We are asked to account for the fact that two states with similar industries are affected to much different degrees by an economic boom. We know that Alpha, which is located on the border, is able to scale up production much more quickly than Beta, which is an inland state. The location is our clue. A more ready supply of foreign workers is a plausible explanation for why Alpha might be able to scale up production more quickly.

# Practice Test #2

## Practice Questions
## Analytical Writing Assessment

### Analysis of an issue

This writing task is designed to test your ability to present a position on an issue effectively and persuasively. Your task is to analyze the issue presented, considering various perspectives, and to develop your own position on the issue. In scoring your issue essay, readers will consider how effectively you: recognize and deal with the complexities and implications of the issue; organize, develop, and express your ideas; support your ideas with reasons and examples; control the elements of standard written English. You are given 30 minutes to write the response. You must not write on any other subject than the one expressed in the prompt. You are allowed to accept, reject, or qualify the statement made by the prompt, though you must be sure to support whatever position you take with reasons and examples from your experience, observation, reading, and/or academic studies. You should take a few minutes to plan your response before typing.

*Issue:* The federal government has long struggled with the issue of income tax. Many people feel that government programs require the collection of an income tax, and that it makes sense to collect more tax money from the wealthier members of society. Other people declare that is unfair to penalize individuals for being successful, and suggest that the same amount of income tax be applied to all citizens. These people further suggest that overtaxing the wealthiest members of society actually has a deleterious effect on the economy for everyone, because it discourages investment and the creation of new jobs.

### Analysis of an argument

This writing task is designed to test your critical reasoning skills as well as your writing skills. Your task is to critique the stated argument in terms of its logical soundness and in terms of the strength of the evidence offered in support of the argument. In scoring your argument essay, the reader will consider how effectively you: identify and analyze the key elements of the argument; organize, develop, and express your critique; support your ideas with reasons and examples; control the elements of standard written English.

You are not being asked to agree or disagree with any of the statements in the argument. You should only consider the argument's line of reasoning. Specifically, you should consider: questionable assumptions underlying the argument; the extent to which the evidence presented supports the conclusion of the argument; what additional evidence would help to strengthen or refute the argument; and what additional information if any would help you to evaluate the argument's conclusion.

*Argument:* Over the past few years, baseball officials have come to the realization that it is impossible to entirely eradicate performance-enhancing drugs. Despite stringent testing measures, many players continue to use amphetamines, steroids, and other banned substances to improve their performance on the diamond. In light of this failure, some players have demanded that the commissioner of baseball simply allow all players to make use of these substances under medical supervision. According to these players, allowing performance-enhancing drugs will eliminate cheating and ensure that training regimens are safe.

# Quantitative
# Problem Solving

1. If $a = 3$ and $b = -2$, what is the value of $a^2 + 3ab - b^2$?

    a. 5

    b. 13

    c. -4

    d. -20

    e. 13

2. 34 is what percent of 80?

    a. 34%

    b. 40%

    c. 42.5%

    d. 44.5%

    e. 52%

3. Jack and Kevin play in a basketball game. If the ratio of points scored by Jack to points scored by Kevin is 4 to 3, which of the following could NOT be the total number of points scored by the two boys?

    a. 7

    b. 14

    c. 16

    d. 28

    e. 35

4. Factor the following expression: $x^2 + x - 12$

    a. $(x - 4)(x + 4)$

    b. $(x - 2)(x + 6)$

    c. $(x + 6)(x - 2)$

    d. $(x - 4)(x + 3)$

    e. $(x + 4)(x - 3)$

5. The average of six numbers is 4. If the average of two of those numbers is 2, what is the average of the other four numbers?

    1,3

    a. 5

    b. 6

    c. 7

    d. 8

    e. 9

6. What is the next-highest prime number after 67?

    a. 68

    b. 69

    c. 71

    d. 73

    e. 76

7. Solve: 0.25 x 0.03 =

    a. 75

    b. 0.075

    c. 0.75

    d. 0.0075

    e. 7.5

8. Dean's Department Store reduces the price of a $30 shirt by 20%, but later raises it again by 20% of the sale price. What is the final price of the shirt?

   a. $24.40

   b. $32

   c. $30

   d. $28.80

   e. $26.60

9. How many 3-inch segments can a 4.5-yard line be divided into?

   a. 15

   b. 45

   c. 54

   d. 64

   e. 84

10. Sheila, Janice, and Karen, working together at the same rate, can complete a job in 3 1/3 days. Working at the same rate, how much of the job could Janice and Karen do in one day?

   a. 1/5

   b. 1/4

   c. 1/3

   d. 1/9

   e. 1/8

11. Dave can deliver four newspapers every minute. At this rate, how many newspapers can he deliver in 2 hours?

   a. 80

   b. 160

   c. 320

   d. 400

   e. 480

12. $4^6 \div 2^8 =$

 a. 2

 b. 8

 (c.) 16

 d. 32

 e. 64

*Handwritten work:*

$$\frac{4 \times 4 \times 4 \times 4 \times 4 \times 4}{2 \times 2 \times 2 \times 2 \times 2 \times 2 \times 2 \times 2}$$

13. If $a = 4$, $b = 3$, and $c = 1$, then $\dfrac{a(b-c)}{b(a+b+c)} =$

 a. 4/13

 (b.) 1/3

 c. 1/4

 d. 1/6

 e. 2/7

*Handwritten work:*

$$\frac{4(3-1)}{3(4+3+1)} = \frac{8}{24} = \frac{1}{3}$$

14. What is 20% of $\dfrac{12}{5}$, expressed as a percentage?

 (a.) 48%

 b. 65%

 c. 72%

 d. 76%

 e. 84%

*Handwritten work:*

$$\frac{20}{100} \times \frac{12}{5} = \frac{48}{100}$$

15. Archie's gas tank is 1/3 full. If Archie adds 3 gallons of gas to the tank, it will be ½ full. What is the capacity in gallons of Archie's tank?

 a. 28

 b. 12

 c. 20

 d. 16

 (e.) 18

*Handwritten work:*

$$\frac{1}{2} - \frac{1}{3} = \frac{3-2}{6} = \frac{1}{6}$$

16. Given the triangle shown in the figure, what is the length of the side B?

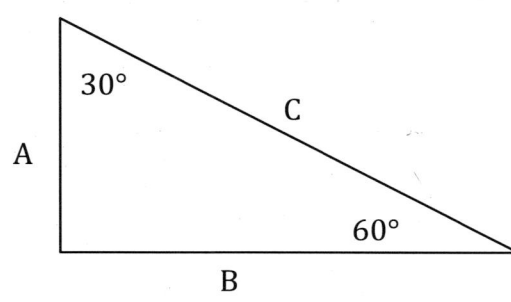

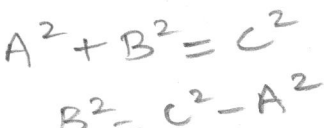

$$A^2 + B^2 = C^2$$
$$B^2 = C^2 - A^2$$

a. $C/2$

b. $A/2$

c. $(A+C)/2$

d. $2A$

e. $2C$

17. If the two lines $2x + y = 0$ and $y = 3$ are plotted on a typical $xy$ coordinate grid, at which point will they intersect?

a. -1.5, 3

b. 1.5, 3

c. -1.5, 0

d. 4,1

e. 4.5, 1

18. What is the surface area, in square inches, of a cube if the length of one side is 3 inches?

a. 9

b. 27

c. 54

d. 18

e. 21

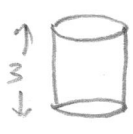

19. Which of the following values is closest to the diameter of a circle with an area of 314 square inches?

$A = 314 \ in^2 = \pi r^2$

a. 20 inches

b. 10 inches

c. 100 inches

d. 31.4 inches

e. 2 $\pi$ inches

20. Two angles of a triangle measure 15 and 70 degrees, respectively. What is the size of the third angle?

a. 90 degrees

b. 80 degrees

c. 75 degrees.

d. 125 degrees

e. 95 degrees

21. The triangle shown in the figure has angles A, B, and C, and sides *a, b,* and *c*. If *a* = 14 cm and *b* = 12 cm, and if angle $\angle B = 35$ degrees, what is angle $\angle A$ ?

a. 35 degrees

b. 42 degrees

c. 64 degrees

d. 18 degrees

e. 28 degrees

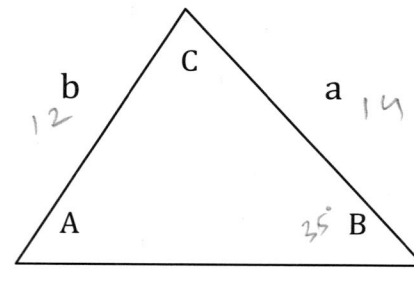

- 202 -

22. The town of Fram will build a water storage tank on a hill overlooking the town. The tank will be a right circular cylinder of radius $R$ and height $H$. The plot of ground selected for the installation is large enough to accommodate a circular tank 60 feet in diameter. The planning commission wants the tank to hold 1,000,000 cubic feet of water, and they intend to use the full area available. Which of the following is the minimum acceptable height?

    a. 655 ft

    b. 455 ft

    c. 355 ft

    d. 255 ft

    e. 155 ft

23. Given the equation $\dfrac{3}{y-5} = \dfrac{15}{y+4}$, what is the value of $y$?

    a. 45

    b. 54

    c. $\dfrac{29}{4}$

    d. $\dfrac{4}{29}$

    e. $\dfrac{4}{45}$

$$3y + 12 = 15y - 75$$

$$12y = 87$$

$$y = \frac{87}{12} = \frac{29}{4}$$

# Data sufficiency

This Data Sufficiency problem consists of a question and two statements, labeled (1) and (2), in which certain data are given. You have to decide whether the data given in the statements are sufficient for answering the question, using only the data given in the statements and your knowledge of mathematics and everyday facts (such as the number of days in July or the meaning of counterclockwise).

F. Statement (1) ALONE is sufficient, but statement (2) is not sufficient.
G. Statement (2) ALONE is sufficient, but statement (1) is not sufficient.
H. BOTH statements TOGETHER are sufficient, but NEITHER statement ALONE is sufficient.
I. EACH statement ALONE is sufficient.
J. Statements (1) and (2) TOGETHER are NOT sufficient.

24. Does Jonathan get paid more than Deborah?

(1) Alice gets paid more than Deborah.

(2) Jonathan makes less money than Alice.

a.          b.          c.          d.          e.

25. Is the integer $a$ less than the integer $b$?

(1) $a^3 < b^3$

(2) $a^2 < b^2$

a.          b.          c.          d.          e.

26. Is the perimeter of a given rectangle greater than 8 inches?

(1) The two shorter sides of the rectangle are 2 inches long.

(2) The length of the rectangle is 2 inches greater than the width of the

a.          b.          c.          d.          e.

27. Is $a$ an integer?

(1) $a > 0$

(2) $4^2 + 3^2 = a^2$

a.          b.          c.          d.          e.

28. What is the value of the integer *P*?

(1) *P* is an integer multiple of 2, 4, and 5.

(2) $40 < P < 70$

a.          b.          c.          d.          e.


29. Brian is dividing 50 marbles into 3 groups. How many marbles are in the largest of the three groups?

(1) The sum of the two smaller groups of marbles is equal to the largest group of marbles.

(2) The smallest group contains 6 marbles.

a.          b.          c.          d.          e.


30. Is *b* a positive number?

(1) $1,452(b) > 0$

(2) $-b < 0$

a.          b.          c.          d.          e.


31. Is *x* greater than *y*?

(1) $x > 2y$

(2) $x - y > 0$

a.          b.          c.          d.          e.


32. What is the average test score of Angela, Barry, Carl, Dennis, and Edward?

(1) The average of the test scores of Barry, Carl, and Edward is 87.

(2) The average of the test scores of Angela and Dennis is 84.

a.          b.          c.          d.          e.


33. If *y* is an integer, is it an odd number?

(1) $y^3 \geq 0$

(2) *y* is either an odd number or a negative number

a.          b.          c.          d.          e.

34. Is Set C closed under subtraction?

(1) Set A is a subset of Set C.

(2) Set A is not closed under subtraction.

a.                b.                c.                d.                (e.)


35. In Triangle ABC, is $\overline{AB}$ longer than $\overline{AC}$?

(1) $\overline{AC}$ is opposite angle B.

(2) $\overline{BC}$ is longer than $\overline{AC}$.

(a.)                b.                c.                d.                (e.)


36. Is Triangle DEF a right triangle?

(1) The measure of angle D is 45 degrees.

(2) The side lengths of Triangle DEF measure 12 units, 16 units, and 20 units.

a.                (b.)                (c.)                d.                e.


37. Is $\overline{AB}$ perpendicular to $\overline{CD}$?

(1) The slope of $\overline{AB}$ is the negative reciprocal of the slope of $\overline{CD}$.

(2) $\overline{AB}$ and $\overline{CD}$ intersect at four right angles.

a.                b.                c.                (d.)                e.

# Verbal Ability
# Reading Comprehension

*Questions 1 – 3 pertain to the following passage:*

In the United States, where we have more land than people, it is not at all difficult for persons in good health to make money. In this comparatively new field there are so many avenues of success open, so many vocations which are not crowded, that any person of either sex who is willing, at least for the time being, to engage in any respectable occupation that offers, may find lucrative employment.

Those who really desire to attain an independence, have only to set their minds upon it, and adopt the proper means, as they do in regard to any other object which they wish to accomplish, and the thing is easily done. But however easy it may be found to make money, I have no doubt many of my hearers will agree it is the most difficult thing in the world to keep it. The road to wealth is, as Dr. Franklin truly says, "as plain as the road to the mill." It consists simply in expending less than we earn; that seems to be a very simple problem. Mr. Micawber, one of those happy creations of the genial Dickens, puts the case in a strong light when he says that to have annual income of twenty pounds per annum, and spend twenty pounds and sixpence, is to be the most miserable of men; whereas, to have an income of only twenty pounds, and spend but nineteen pounds and sixpence is to be the happiest of mortals.

Many of my readers may say, "we understand this: this is economy, and we know economy is wealth; we know we can't eat our cake and keep it also." Yet I beg to say that perhaps more cases of failure arise from mistakes on this point than almost any other. The fact is, many people think they understand economy when they really do not.

1. Which of the following statements best expresses the main idea of the passage?

    a. Getting a job is easier now than it ever has been before

    b. Earning money is much less difficult than managing it properly

    c. Dr. Franklin advocated getting a job in a mill

    d. Spending money is the greatest temptation in the world

    e. There is no way to predict changes in the economy

2. What would this author's attitude likely be to a person unable to find employment?

    a. descriptive

    b. conciliatory

    c. ingenuous

    d. incredulous

    e. exculpatory

3. According to the author, what is more difficult than making money?

    a. getting a job

    b. traveling to a mill

    c. reading Dickens

    d. understanding the economy

    e. managing money

*Questions 4 – 7 pertain to the following passage:*

We all know the drill: the consequences of urban sprawl, American's long work hours, and devotion to television and the internet are doing nothing good for American communities.

A new study by sociologists at Duke University and the University of Arizona adds more grist to this mill, noting that Americans in 2004 had smaller networks of people with whom they talk about matters important to them than they did in 1985. (*Social Isolation in America: Changes in Core Discussion Networks Over Two Decades*, American Sociological Review, June 2006.) In

1985, Americans had three confidants, in 2004, we averaged two. The number of Americans who had no one with whom to talk about important matters almost doubled in 2004 to over 25%. Increasingly, most confidants are family: in 2004, 80% of people talked only to family about important matters and about 9% people depended totally on their spouse.

This decrease in confidants is part (a result) of the same trend that's leaving fewer people knowing their neighbors or participating in social clubs or public affairs than in the past (phenomena noted in the book <u>Better Together: Restoring the American Community</u> by Robert Putnam and Lewis Feldstein). We know a lot of people, but not necessarily very well.

Left to our own devices and cultural trends then, we seem to be moving in an unpleasant direction. Communities are formed ad hoc, around specific shared individual interests. This wouldn't be bad, of course, except that those communities seem to exist only within the constraints of those shared interests, and don't develop into close and meaningful relationships. The transient and specific nature of many of our relationships today can keep us socially busy without building the lasting relationships and communities that we want.

So what do we do about it if we want to change things? Harvard University's School of Government put together 150 ways to increase what they call "social capital" (the value of our social networks). Among their suggestions are: support local merchants; audition for community theater or volunteer to usher; participate in political campaigns; start or join a carpool; eat breakfast at a local gathering spot on Saturdays; and stop and make sure the person on the side of the highway is OK.

4. According to the author, which of the following was true in 2004:

    a. The average American had three confidants and 9% of people depended totally on their spouse for discussion of important matters

    b. The average American had two confidants, and 80% of people discussed important matters only with their spouses

    c. The average American had two confidants, and 9% of people discussed important matters only with family members

    d. The average American had two confidants, and 80% of people discussed important matters only with family members

    e. The average American had three confidants, and 80% of people discussed important matters only with family members

5. The author argues that the transient nature of many of today's relationships is problematic because:

    a. we don't share specific interests

    b. we don't know many people

    c. it prevents us building lasting relationships and communities

    d. we have too much social capital

    e. we talk to too many people about private matters

6. Which of the following are some of the causes to which the author attributes problems in American communities?

    a. too much homework and devotion to television

    b. devotion to television and decline of sports team membership

    c. long work hours and too much homework

    d. urban sprawl and decline of sports team membership

    e. urban sprawl and long work hours

7. Which of the following is not something the author states was suggested by Harvard University as a way to increase social capital:

    a. eat breakfast at a local gathering spot

    b. join a bowling team

    c. support local merchants

    d. join a carpool

    e. audition for community theater

*Questions 8 – 11 pertain to the following passage:*

George Washington Carver was always interested in plants. When he was a child, he was known as the "plant doctor." He had a secret garden where he grew all kinds of plants. People would ask him for advice when they had sick plants. Sometimes he'd take their plants to his garden and nurse them back to health.

Later, when he was teaching at Tuskegee Institute, he put his plant skills to good use. Many people in the South had been growing only cotton on their land. Cotton plants use most of the nutrients in the soil. (Nutrients provide nourishment to plants.) So the soil becomes "worn out" after a few years. Eventually, cotton will no longer grow on this land.

This was especially bad for poor African American farmers, who relied on selling cotton to support themselves. Carver was dedicated to helping those farmers, so he came up with a plan.

Carver knew that certain plants put nutrients back into the soil. One of those plants is the peanut! Peanuts are also a source of protein.

Carver thought that if those farmers planted peanuts, the plants would help restore their soil, provide food for their animals, and provide protein for their families--quite a plant! In 1896 peanuts were not even recognized as a crop in the United States, but Carver would help change that.

Carver told farmers to rotate their crops: plant cotton one year, then the next year plant peanuts and other soil-restoring plants, like peas and sweet potatoes. It worked! The peanut plants grew and produced lots of peanuts. The plants added enough nutrients to the soil so cotton grew the next year.

8. Why was George Washington Carver known as the "plant doctor"?

   a. He studied medicine in college

   b. He grew peanuts on sick soil

   c. He was a plant pathologist

   d. He could nurse sick plants back to health

   e. He knew plants could put nutrients back into the soil

9. How is this passage structured?

   a. cause and effect

   b. problem and solution

   c. chronological order

   d. compare and contrast

   e. proposition and support

10. According to the passage, what problem were cotton farmers facing?

   a. They needed food for their animals

   b. Peanuts were not recognized as a crop in the United States

   c. They were growing too much cotton

   d. Tuskegee Institute needed more teachers

   e. The cotton had stripped the land of its nutrients

11. This passage is mainly about?

    a. how George Washington Carver invented the cotton gin

    b. how George Washington Carver became a teacher at the Tuskegee Institute

    c. how George Washington Carver helped farmers improve their crop production

    d. why George Washington Carver studied plants

    e. *how George Washington Carver made peanuts a recognized crop in the United States*

*Questions 12 and 13 pertain to the following passage:*

From 1892 to 1954, over twelve million immigrants entered the United States through the portal of Ellis Island, a small island in New York Harbor. Ellis Island is located in the upper bay just off the New Jersey coast, within the shadow of the Statue of Liberty. Through the years, this gateway to the new world was enlarged from its original 3.3 acres to 27.5 acres by landfill supposedly obtained from the ballast of ships, excess earth from the construction of the New York City subway system and elsewhere. Before being designated as the site of one of the first Federal immigration station by President Benjamin Harrison in 1890, Ellis Island had a varied history. The local Indian tribes had called it "Kioshk" or Gull Island. Due to its rich and abundant oyster beds and plentiful and profitable shad runs, it was known as Oyster Island for many generations during the Dutch and English colonial periods. By the time Samuel Ellis became the island's private owner in the 1770's, the island had been called Kioshk, Oyster, Dyre, Bucking and Anderson's Island. In this way, Ellis Island developed from a sandy island that barely rose above the high tide mark, into a hanging site for pirates, a harbor fort, ammunition and ordinance depot named Fort Gibson, and finally into an immigration station.

12. Which of the following is true about Ellis Island?

    I. It houses the Statue of Liberty

    II. The local Indian tribes called it Oyster Island

    III. It was expanded using dirt from the construction of the subway system

a. I only

b. I and II only

c. II and III only

d. III only

e. I, II, and III


13. The style of this passage is most like that found in a(n)

a. immigrant's diary

b. business letter

c. history textbook

d. persuasive essay

e. short story

# Sentence Correction

These questions present a sentence, all or part of which is underlined. Beneath each sentence you will find five ways of phrasing the underlined part. The first of these repeats the original; the other four are different. If you think the original is best, choose the first answer; otherwise, choose one of the other answers.

These questions test correctness and effectiveness of expression. In choosing your answer, follow the requirements of standard written English; that is, pay attention to grammar, choice of words, and sentence construction. Choose the answer that produces the most effective sentence; this answer should be clear and exact, without awkwardness, ambiguity, redundancy, or grammatical error.

14. If he stops to consider the ramifications of this decision, it is probable that he will rethink his original decision a while longer.

    a. it is probable that he will rethink his original decision.

    b. he will rethink his original decision over again.

    c. he probably will rethink his original decision.

    d. he will most likely rethink his original decision for a bit.

    e. he probably will rethink his decision a while longer.

15. "When you get older," she said "you will no doubt understand what I mean."

    a. older," she said "you will no doubt

    b. older" she said "you will no doubt

    c. older," she said, "you will no doubt

    d. older," she said "you will not

    e. older", she said, "you will no doubt

16. <u>Dr. Anderson strolled past the nurses, examining a bottle of pills.</u>

    a. Dr. Anderson strolled past the nurses, examining a bottle of pills.

    b. Dr. Anderson strolled past the nurses examining a bottle of pills.

    c. Dr. Anderson strolled past, the nurses examining a bottle of pills.

    d. Examining a bottle of pills Dr. Anderson strolled past the nurses.

    e. Examining a bottle of pills, Dr. Anderson strolled past the nurses.


17. Karl and Henry <u>raced to the reservoir, climbed the ladder, and then they dove into</u> the cool water.

    a. raced to the reservoir, climbed the ladder, and then they dove into

    b. first raced to the reservoir, climbed the ladder, and then they dove into

    c. raced to the reservoir, they climbed the ladder, and then they dove into

    d. raced to the reservoir; climbed the ladder; and then they dove into

    e. raced to the reservoir, climbed the ladder, and dove into


18. Did either <u>Tracy or Vanessa realize that her decision would be</u> so momentous?

    a. Tracy or Vanessa realize that her decision would be

    b. Tracy or Vanessa realize that each of their decision was

    c. Tracy or Vanessa realize that her or her decision would be

    d. Tracy or Vanessa realize that their decision would be

    e. Tracy or Vanessa realize that their decision was


19. Despite their lucky escape, <u>Jason and his brother could not hardly enjoy themselves</u>.

    a. Jason and his brother could not hardly enjoy themselves

    b. Jason and his brother could not enjoy themselves

    c. Jason and Jason's brother could not hardly enjoy themselves

    d. Jason and his brother could not enjoy them

    e. Jason and his brother could hardly enjoy them

20. Stew recipes call <u>for rosemary, parsley, thyme, and these sort of herbs.</u>

    a. for rosemary, parsley, thyme, and these sort of herbs.

    b. for: rosemary; parsley; thyme; and these sort of herbs.

    c. for rosemary, parsley, thyme, and these sorts of herbs.

    d. for rosemary, parsley, thyme, and this sorts of herbs.

    e. for rosemary, parsley, thyme, and these sorts of herb.


21. Mr. King, <u>an individual of considerable influence, created a personal fortune and gave back</u> to the community.

    a. an individual of considerable influence, created a personal fortune and gave back

    b. an individual of considerable influence, he created a personal fortune and gave back

    c. an individual of considerable influence created a personal fortune and gave back

    d. an individual of considerable influence, created a personal fortune and gave it back

    e. an individual of considerable influence, created a personal fortune and then he gave it back


22. <u>She is the person whose opinion matters the most.</u>

    a. She is the person whose opinion matters the most.

    b. She is the person to whom opinion matters the most.

    c. She is the person who matters the most, in my opinion.

    d. She is the person for whom opinion matters the most.

    e. She is the person which has her opinion matter the most.


23. When are the Federal government, the State and the city going to realize <u>that they cannot raise its rates and taxes</u> year after year?

    a. that they cannot raise its rates and taxes

    b. that they cannot raise it's rates and taxes

    c. that they can not raise its rates and taxes

    d. that rates and taxes can not be raised by them

    e. that they cannot raise their rates and taxes

24. Since she moved into her own place, Janet <u>has been doing</u> her own cooking.

    a. has been doing

    b. does

    c. did

    d. is doing

    e. will do

25. To help install the software, <u>instructions provided by the manufacturer.</u>

    a. instruction provided by the manufacturer.

    b. instruction manuals provided by the manufacturer.

    c. manufacturer-provided instructions.

    d. instructions were provided by the manufacturer.

    e. instructions was provided by the manufacturer.

26. A daily routine of physical exercise is not only good for one's health, <u>and also improves one's mental outlook.</u>

    a. and also improves one's mental outlook.

    b. but also improves one's mental outlook.

    c. as it also improves one's mental outlook.

    d. and improves one's mental outlook, too.

    e. and would foster an improved mental outlook, as well.

27. King Lear is one of Shakespeare's greatest <u>plays it explores the nature of human suffering and kinship.</u>

    a. plays it explores the nature of human suffering and kinship.

    b. plays as it explores the nature of human suffering and kinship.

    c. plays who explores the nature of human suffering and kinship.

    d. plays; it explores the nature of human suffering and kinship.

    e. plays when it explores the nature of human suffering and kinship.

# Critical reasoning

28. The latest movie by a certain director gets bad reviews before it opens in theatres. Consequently, very few people go to the movie and the director is given much less money to make his next movie, which is also unsuccessful. *What can be inferred from this scenario?*

    a. This director makes terrible movies

    b. The general public does not pay attention to movie reviews

    c. The movie reviewers were right about the first movie

    d. Movie reviewers exert influence on the movie quality

    e. The director will not make another movie

29. The most important determinant of success in life is education. Even children from broken or dysfunctional homes tend to establish themselves as solid citizens so long as they obtain a high school education. On the other hand, children who fail to earn a high school diploma are much less likely to avoid prison, welfare, or divorce. *Which of the following statements most effectively strengthens the above argument?*

    a. A recent study demonstrated a link between education and lifetime earnings

    b. Most federal prisoners receive a high school diploma while incarcerated

    c. Research indicates that college graduates from abusive homes are more likely to be arrested

    d. Individuals with heart problems are more likely to have postgraduate education

    e. Children from functional homes are more likely to attend preschool

30. (1) All *A* are *B*.

(2) Some *B* are *C*.

*Which of the following is true?*

    a. All *A* are *C*

    b. No *A* are *C*

    c. Some *A* are *C*

    d. No *C* are *A*

    e. None of the above

31. Shakespeare is the greatest writer of all time. This is because he wrote the greatest plays, and the greatest writer is the one who composes the greatest works. *Which of the following statements most effectively challenges the reasoning above?*

    a. This argument disproves its own premise

    b. This argument uses ambiguous language

    c. This argument assumes what it claims to prove

    d. This argument introduces irrelevant evidence

    e. This argument fails to make a clear claim

32. In the 2000 local election, only 28% of individuals between the ages of 18 and 25 voted. In the 2004 local election, however, candidates made more of an effort to appeal to these younger voters, so turnout was slightly higher at 39%. *Which of the following pieces of information weakens the above argument?*

    a. The candidates for city council were ages 55, 72, and 64

    b. The turnout among voters between the ages of 35 and 44 was 42% in 2004

    c. Turnout among African-Americans between 18 and 25 decreased from 2000 to 2004

    d. The polls stayed open later on Election Day in 2000

    e. In 2004, a referendum on lowering the legal age for purchasing alcohol to 18 was on the ballot

33. Members of Congress should not be paid. After all, members of the school board receive no payment, and are therefore not beholden to any particular group. *Which of the following facts most significantly weakens the above argument?*

    a. Members of Congress can also serve on the school board

    b. Being in Congress is a full-time job, while school board members have time to pursue other occupations

    c. Congress only is in session during part of the year

    d. Members of Congress typically have been successful in their prior professional lives

    e. Members of Congress are not allowed to show favoritism to any particular group

34. All German cars are safe. Dale drives a German car, so his car is safe. *Which of the following arguments contains logic that closely resembles that of the preceding argument?*

    a. The newest cars often get better gas mileage. Helen has a new car, which must get better gas mileage

    b. A few of the candidates for governor are women. Dr. Lopez is a woman

    c. No brands of natural peanut butter contain preservatives. The peanut butter in Dave's cabinet contains preservatives

    d. Every shark has a tailfin. The hammerhead is a kind of shark and therefore has a tailfin

    e. Some days of the week are Saturdays and Sundays. Today is neither Saturday nor Sunday


35. The Tigers football team usually loses when they score fewer than 30 points. In their game against the Wildcats, they scored 24 points.

*Which of the following statements would logically complete the argument with the above premises?*

    a. The Tigers lost to the Wildcats.

    b. The Wildcats are the best football team in the league.

    c. The Wildcats probably lost to the Tigers.

    d. The Tigers are not a very good football team.

    e. The Tigers probably lost to the Wildcats.

36. Dr. Jacobson stood up at the recent town hall meeting and declared that building a new shopping center at the corner of George and Vidalia Streets would be a bad move. He cited transportation department statistics indicating that the intersection would become overloaded with traffic, and would be very dangerous for motorists and pedestrians alike. The mayor dismissed Dr. Jacobson's opinion, on the grounds that the proposed shopping center is within a block of Dr. Jacobson's practice. *Why is the mayor's argument weak?*

    a. He does not challenge Dr. Jacobson's argument, but merely challenges him personally

    b. He does not acknowledge the location of his own office

    c. He fails to recognize that Dr. Jacobson would probably welcome a new shopping center near his practice

    d. He does not support his view with statistics from the transportation department

    e. He doesn't realize that Dr. Jacobson is about to retire


37. Islam spread to Europe during the medieval period, bringing scientific and technological insights. The Muslim emphasis on knowledge and learning can be traced to an emphasis on both in the Qur'an [Koran], the holy book of Islam. Because of this emphasis, scholars preserved some of the Greek and Roman texts that were lost to the rest of Europe. The writings of Aristotle, among others, were saved by Muslim translators. Islam scholars modified a Hindu number system. Their modification became the more commonly used Arabic system, which replaced Roman numerals. They also developed algebra. Muslim contributions also include inventing the astrolabe, a device for telling time that also helped sailors to navigate. In medicine, Muslim doctors cleaned wounds with antiseptics. They closed the wounds with gut and silk sutures. They also used sedatives. *Based on the information above, which of the following conclusions is likely true?*

    a. People of Muslim faith were braver than others when facing surgery

    b. Fewer Muslim patients died of wound infections than did their European counterparts

    c. The silk market expanded because of the Muslim use of silk sutures

    d. Math classes would be easier without Muslim influence

    e. No one would read Aristotle today had the Muslims not saved the translations

38. Mother Jones, who was a labor activist, wrote the following about children working in cotton mills in Alabama: "Little girls and boys, barefooted, walked up and down between the endless rows of spindles, reaching thin little hands into the machinery to repair snapped threads. They crawled under machinery to oil it. They replaced spindles all day long; all night through...six-year-olds with faces of sixty did an eight-hour shift for ten cents a day; the machines, built in the North, were built low for the hands of little children."

*Which of the following do you predict occurred after this was published?*

    a. More children signed up to work in the factories

    b. Cotton factories in the South closed

    c. Laws were passed to prevent child labor

    d. The pay scale for these children was increased

    e. Night shift work ended


39. In 1781, a county court in Massachusetts heard the case Brom & Bett v. Ashley. What was unusual about the case was that the plaintiffs were both enslaved by John Ashley's family. They had walked out and appealed to a lawyer for help after Mrs. Ashley tried to hit Mum Bett's sister. Mum Bett, whose real name was Elizabeth Freeman, claimed that if all people were free and equal, as she had heard while serving at the Ashley table, slaves too were equal. The court agreed, basing their decision on the Massachusetts constitution of the previous year. The decision, affirmed in subsequent cases, led to the abolishing of slavery in that state.

*Which of the following statements is most accurate?*

    a. Mrs. Ashley was probably just having a bad day when she tried to strike another person

    b. Elizabeth Freeman's actions helped to gain women the right to vote

    c. White people in Southern states applauded the court's decision

    d. The ideals of the American Revolution reached farther than the founders may have intended

    e. All slaveholders in Massachusetts rushed to free their servants

40. When the euro was introduced in January 2002, a single euro was valued at 88 cents in United States currency. In the summer of 2008, at one point it required $1.60 U.S. to buy 1 euro. In late October 2008, the euro fell to its lowest level against the dollar in two years. *Which of the following statements represents an accurate conclusion?*

    a. The world in 2008 was headed for another Great Depression

    b. The dollar regained strength after significant devaluing against the euro

    c. The euro remains the world's strongest currency

    d. Investors need to keep buying stocks

    e. Globalization is a very bad idea


41. A recent Newsweek poll found that for the first time, a majority of Americans now believe that gay and lesbian couples deserve legal recognition. Fifty-five percent of the poll's respondents stated they support legally sanctioned unions. The poll also indicated that there was increased backing for inheritance and other property rights, and that 39 percent support legalizing gay marriage.

*Which one of the following, if true, most weakens the assertion of increased support for gay unions among the American people?*

    a. The poll firm used by Newsweek to conduct the survey is owned and operated by a company not aligned with any political organizations

    b. All polling was conducted through random telephone calls to people across the nation

    c. Respondents queried by Newsweek chose which poll questions to answer

    d. Other news magazines were conducting a similar poll during the same period that Newsweek was

# Answers and Explanations
## Quantitative
## *Problem-Solving*

1. B: Simply substitute the given values for *a* and *b* and perform the required operations.

2. C: This problem is solved by finding *x* in this equation: $34/80 = x/100$.

3. C: Every possible combination of scores is a multiple of 7, since the two terms of the ratio have a sum of seven.

4. E: To solve this problem, work backwards. That is, perform FOIL on each answer choice until you derive the original expression.

5. A: A set of six numbers with an average of 4 must have a collective sum of 24. The two numbers that average 2 will add up to 4, so the remaining numbers must add up to 20. The average of these four numbers can be calculated: $20/4 = 5$.

6. C: Prime numbers are those that are only evenly divisible by one and themselves.

7. D: Simple Multiplication.

8. D: Multiply 30 by 0.2 and subtract this from the original price of the shirt to find the sale price: $24. Then multiply 24 by 0.2 and add the product to the sale price to find the final price.

9. C: There are 12 inches in a foot and 3 feet in a yard. Four and a half yards is equal to 162 inches. To determine the number of 3-inche segments, divide 162 by 3.

10. A: If it takes 3 people 3 1/3 days to do the job, then it would take one person 10 days: $3 \times 3\frac{1}{3} = 10$. Thus, it would take 2 people 5 days, and one day of work for two people would complete 1/5 of the job.

11. E: There are 60 minutes in an hour, so Dave can deliver 240 newspapers every hour. In 2 hours, then, he can deliver 480 papers.

12. C: Since 4 is the same as $2^2$, $4^6 = 2^{12}$. When dividing exponents with the same base, simply subtract the exponent in the denominator from the exponent in the numerator.

13. B: Substitute the given values and solve. Resolve the parenthetical operations first.

14. A: Convert 20% to the fraction 1/5, then multiply by 12/5. The resulting fraction, 12/25, must have both numerator and denominator multiplied by 4 to become a percentage.

15. E: This problem can be solved with the following equation, in which $x$ = the total capacity of the tank: $\frac{1}{2}x = \frac{1}{3}x + 3$.

16. A: This is a right triangle, since the two angles shown add up to 90 degrees, and the remaining angle must therefore be 90 degrees. For a right triangle, the length of a side is related to the hypotenuse by the sine of the opposite angle. Thus $B = C\sin(30°)$ and since the sine of a 30-degree angle is 0.5, $B = C/2$.

17. A: Since the second line, $y = 3$, is a vertical, the intersection must occur at a point where $y = 3$. If $x = 1.5$, the equation describing the line is satisfied: $(2 \times [-1.5] + 3) = 0$

18. C: The surface of a cube is obtained by multiplying the area of each face by 6, since there are 6 faces. The area of each face is the square of the length of one edge.

Therefore, $A = 6 \times 3^2 = 6 \times 9 = 54$. Answers A, B, D, and E are incorrect since the surface area is a unique value.

19. A: The area $A$ of a circle is given by $A = \pi \times r^2$, where $r$ is the radius. Since $\pi$ is approximately 3.14, we can solve for $r = \sqrt{\dfrac{A}{\pi}} = \sqrt{\dfrac{314}{3.14}} = \sqrt{100} = 10$. Now, the diameter $d$ is twice the radius, or $d = 2 \times 10 = 20$.

B. 10 is the value of the radius, not the diameter. C, D, and E are all wrong as they do not equal 20.

20. E: The sum of angles in a triangle equals 180 degrees. Therefore solve for the remaining angle as 180 − (15 + 70) = 95 degrees. Since this value is unique, all other answers are incorrect.

21. B: This answer may be determined using the Law of Sines, which relates the sides of a triangle and their opposing angles as follows:

Thus we have $\sin A = a \times \dfrac{\sin B}{b} = 14 \times \dfrac{\sin(35)}{12} = 14 \times \dfrac{0.57}{12} = 0.67$, and

$\sin^{-1}(0.67) = 42$ Degrees.

Since this value is unique, all other answers are incorrect.

22. C: The volume of a right circular cylinder is equal to its height multiplied by the area of its base, $A$. Since the base is circular, $A = \pi R^2$, where $R$, the radius, is half the diameter, or 30 feet. Therefore,

$V = H \times \pi R^2$

Solving for $H$,

$H = \dfrac{V}{\pi R^2} = \dfrac{1{,}000{,}000}{\pi \times 30^2} = \dfrac{1{,}000{,}000}{\pi \times 900} = 353.7 \, \text{Ft}$

A and B are both greater than 355, so they do not represent the minimum acceptable height.

D and E are both too low to hold the required volume.

23. C: Rearranging the equation gives
$3(x + 4) = 15(x - 5)$, which is equivalent to
$15x - 3x = 12 + 75$, or
$12x = 87$, and solving for $x$,
$$x = \frac{87}{12} = \frac{29}{4}.$$

Since this value is unique, all the other answers are incorrect.

# Data Sufficiency

24. E: The two statements establish only that Alice is paid more than both Jonathan and Deborah; they do not indicate which of these latter two is paid more.

25. A: Since the cubes of $a$ and $b$ will retain the original sign (whether positive or negative), it will be possible to assess the relative sizes of $a$ and $b$.

26. A: If the two shorter sides add up to 4 inches in length, the two longer sides must be greater than 4 inches, meaning that the perimeter will be greater than 8 inches.

27. B: The first statement only establishes that $a$ is a positive number; it does not require that $a$ is an integer.

28. C: 60 is the only integer between 40 and 70 that is a multiple of 2, 4, and 5.

29. A: The first statement establishes that the larger group constitutes half of the total amount of marbles, which means it must be equal to 25 marbles.

30. D: For (1), the fact that a positive number multiplied by $b$ has a positive product establishes that $b$ is a positive number. For (2), any positive number with a negative sign placed in front of it will become negative, indicating that $b$ is a positive number.

31. B: It would be possible for $x$ and $y$ to be negative numbers and still satisfy the conditions of (1), but it then would be impossible to satisfy (2).

32. C: As long as the sum of all five test scores can be calculated, it will be possible to calculate the average score.

33. C: In order for (1) to be true, $y$ must be either positive or zero. Therefore, according to the terms of (2), $y$ must be odd.

34. E: The two statements explain that Set A is a subset of Set C, with Set A not being closed under subtraction. These facts do not indicate whether or not Set C is closed under subtraction. For example, the set of natural numbers could represent Set A. In this case, Set A is not closed under subtraction (as the second statement indicates). If Set C were the set of whole numbers, with Set A being a subset of this set, Set C would not be closed under subtraction. However, if Set C were the set of real numbers, with Set A again being a subset of this set, Set C would be closed under subtraction. Since the specifics of Set C are not given, the posed question cannot be answered, using the information in the two statements.

35. E: The statements simply indicate the placement of the vertices of the triangle and the fact that $\overline{BC}$ is longer than $\overline{AC}$. It cannot be determined, from the given information, whether or not $\overline{AB}$ is longer than $\overline{AC}$. In order to make such a deduction, the statements would need to indicate the angle measures of each angle.

36. B: A right triangle has side lengths that adhere to the Pythagorean Theorem, which states: $a^2 + b^2 = c^2$. Statement (1) could possibly describe a 45-45-90 right triangle, but this isn't explicitly stated. Such a triangle could be 45-60-105. The given information only depicts one angle of the triangle to have a measure of 45 degrees. Statement (2) indicates

that the triangle has side lengths, in accordance with the Pythagorean Theorem, revealing the Pythagorean Triples of 12, 16, and 20: $12^2 + 16^2 = 20^2$ or $400 = 400$.

37. D: Perpendicular lines have negative reciprocal slopes. Thus, Statement (1) is sufficient. Statement (2) indicates intersect to form four right angles. Perpendicular lines intersect to form four right angles. Thus, either statement is sufficient.

## Verbal Ability
## Reading Comprehension

1. B: The author asserts both that earning money is increasingly easy and that managing money is difficult.

2. D: The author seems to believe that there are plenty of lucrative jobs for everyone.

3. E: The author insists that many people who have no trouble earning money waste it through lavish spending.

4. D: This information is all given in the second paragraph.

5. C: In the fourth paragraph, the author states that the transient nature of relationships based solely on shared interests is keeping us "socially busy without building the lasting relationships and communities that we want."

6. E: The author lists urban sprawl, long work hours, and devotion to television and the internet as causes of problems for American communities.

7. B: This is the only one of the answer choices that is not listed in the fourth paragraph as suggestions put forth by the Harvard University study.

8. D: The first paragraph gives the information to correctly answer this question

9. B: This passage in arranged by problem and solution. The author states a problem that the cotton farmers were having: "Eventually, cotton will no longer grow on this land." The author then presents a solution: "Carver told farmers to rotate their crops: plant cotton one year, then the next year plant peanuts and other soil-restoring plants, like peas and sweet potatoes. It worked! The peanut plants grew and produced lots of peanuts."

10. E: The second paragraph discusses the problem the cotton farmers were facing. The cotton crops had depleted the nutrients from the soil.

11. C: Answer choice (C) best summarizes what this passage is mainly about. Choices (A), (B), and (C) are not even discussed in this passage. Paragraph 5 does discuss choice (E), but it is not the main focus of the passage.

12. D: The only true statement about Ellis Island is statement III: The island was expanded using dirt excavated from the construction of the New York City subway system. Statement I is false. According to Paragraph 1, Ellis Island is "within the shadow" of the Statue of Liberty. This means that it is close to the Statue of Liberty, but does not house the Statue of Liberty. Statement II is also false. Paragraph 2 states that the local Indian tribes had called it "Kioshk" or Gull Island, not Oyster Island.

13. C: The author's style is giving facts and details, much like the style used in a history textbook. An immigrant's diary would be written in first-person and most likely give thoughts and feelings about the experience at Ellis Island. A business letter would have a date, salutation, and closing. A persuasive essay would use persuasive techniques to persuade the reader to adopt a particular argument or position, and a short story would be written to entertain, not inform.

## Sentence Correction

14. C: The original sentence is redundant and wordy.

15. C: The syntax of the original sentence is fine, but a comma after *said* but before the open-quotation mark is required.

16. E: In the original sentence, the modifier is placed too far away from the word it modifies.

17. E: The verb structure should be consistent in a sentence with parallel structures.

18. A: The singular pronoun *her* is appropriate since the antecedents are joined by *or*. Also, the subjunctive verb form is required to indicate something indefinite.

19. B: The combination of *hardly* and *not* constitutes a double negative.

20. C: The plural demonstrative adjective *these* should be used with the plural noun *sorts*.

21. A: This sentence contains a number of parallel structures that must be treated consistently.

22. A: In this sentence, *whose* is the appropriate possessive pronoun to modify *opinion*.

23. E: The subject of the sentence comprises three items (the federal government, the state and the city) and is therefore plural. The sentence discusses raising the rates and taxes of all three.

24. A: The past progressive form indicates that Janet began doing something in the past, and continues to do so today.

25. D: The original lacks a verb, as do choices B and C. Choice E mismatches a plural subject and singular verb.

26. B: The expression "not only…but also" is used to compare two conditions that are mutually reinforcing.

27. D: The original is a run-on sentence. Choice D correctly separates two related independent clauses with a semi-colon. Choices B and E change the meaning, and choice C incorrectly uses the pronoun "who" for the inanimate "play."

## Critical Reasoning

28. D: The negative reviews led to the poor quality of the second movie.

29. A: This evidence would support the assertions of the given argument.

30. E: There is no way of determining whether any, some, or none of $A$ are $C$.

31. C: This is an example of circular reasoning, in which the proof depends on assumptions which themselves have not been proven.

32. E: It seems likely that this referendum could influence many young people to vote.

33. B: Drawing an analogy between being a member of Congress and serving on the school board is highly dubious.

34. D: The logic of this argument can be expressed as follows: All $A$ are $B$. $C$ is $A$, therefore $C$ is $B$.

35. E: There is no way to be certain that the Tigers lost, though it seems likely.

36. A: The mayor is essentially using an *ad hominem* argument, in which the character of the opponent rather than the merits of his reasoning is attacked.

37. B: By using antiseptics, Muslim doctors prevented the infection that often led to loss of limbs or life among Europeans. Antiseptics kept infections down. The other responses are opinion or not supported by the paragraph. We have no way of comparing the bravery of

Muslim people with those of other faiths when facing surgery, so number 1 can be eliminated. Likewise, number 3 is incorrect; there would not be sufficient rise in silk use for sutures to account for an expanded silk market. Number 4 is an opinion, not a fact. It is not clear that the Muslims were the only people to have translations of the works of Aristotle, nor does the passage suggest such.

38. C: Mother Jones was agitating for laws protecting child workers, and legislators finally responded to her appeal and that of others. None of the other statements would logically follow. The words would not have been an inducement to children to work in factories, so response 1 is incorrect. Answer 2 is also not right; the South continued to be a major textile region. Increasing pay for child labor was not the solution to the problem; thus the fourth response is incorrect. The final answer is also not true; running mills at night when it was cooler was profitable.

39. D: Many of the founders were also slaveholders, even though they believed the practice was wrong. Response 1 is an assumption that cannot be supported. The second answer is false; Freeman's actions had no effect on women's suffrage though it did have an impact on slavery. White Southerners, the majority of whom were sympathetic to slavery, were unlikely to applaud the decision of the court; the third answer is incorrect. Response 5 suggests a broader response to the ruling than actually can be determined from the passage.

40. B: Although the nation faced recession, the U.S. dollar made a comeback in world currency during the fall of 2008. Response 1 cannot be concluded from the information given, which focuses solely on the dollar and euro rather than on the entire world. Response 3 is incorrect as well; the euro fell in 2008 against the dollar. The wisdom of buying stocks cannot be concluded from the information given; therefore, option 4 is not viable. The final option is a statement of opinion having nothing to do with the strength or weakness of the dollar.

41. C: In order to assure a statistically valid result, the sample size must be statistically valid and free of bias. Having a politically neutral organization in charge of polling is standard practice and avoids influencing the questions or the pollers, so such a condition would not weaken the central assertion, which eliminates Statement A. Random phone calling avoids selecting respondents from specific demographics and geographic areas, which also minimizes bias, so Statement B is also unsuitable. The fact of other polls being conducted in the same period has no effect on the poll in question, as they are independent events; thus, Statement D is invalid as well. Only Statement C, where the respondents' bias affects the questions answered, could provide a valid argument against the poll's objectivity; thus, C is correct.

# Practice Test #3

## Practice Questions
## Analytical Writing Assessment

### Analysis of an issue

This writing task is designed to test your ability to present a position on an issue effectively and persuasively. Your task is to analyze the issue presented, considering various perspectives, and to develop your own position on the issue. In scoring your issue essay, readers will consider how effectively you: recognize and deal with the complexities and implications of the issue; organize, develop, and express your ideas; support your ideas with reasons and examples; control the elements of standard written English. You are given 30 minutes to write the response. You must not write on any other subject than the one expressed in the prompt. You are allowed to accept, reject, or qualify the statement made by the prompt, though you must be sure to support whatever position you take with reasons and examples from your experience, observation, reading, and/or academic studies. You should take a few minutes to plan your response before typing.

*Issue:* There is at present a heated debate over the role of the United States in foreign affairs. Some experts argue that the cost and unintended consequences of American intervention are so great that the United States should simply mind its own business. Others assert that America's economic and political power necessitate foreign intervention, both to protect American interests and human rights. Another group derides these opposing views as condescending to the people of other countries, and suggests that the United States consult with foreign countries before becoming involved in their affairs.

### Analysis of an argument

This writing task is designed to test your critical reasoning skills as well as your writing skills. Your task is to critique the stated argument in terms of its logical soundness and in terms of the strength of the evidence offered in support of the argument. In scoring your argument essay, the reader will consider how effectively you: identify and analyze the key elements of the argument; organize, develop, and express your critique; support your ideas with reasons and examples; control the elements of standard written English.

You are not being asked to agree or disagree with any of the statements in the argument. You should only consider the argument's line of reasoning. Specifically, you should consider: questionable assumptions underlying the argument; the extent to which the evidence presented supports the conclusion of the argument; what additional evidence would help to strengthen or refute the argument; and what additional information if any would help you to evaluate the argument's conclusion.

*Argument:* When drivers visit a state office to renew their licensure, they are not tested on the road or on the basic signs and procedures of driving. A new safety commission has declared that in order to reduce accidents on the road, drivers should be required to pass a comprehensive driving test every time they seek to renew their driver's license. They also argue that individuals over the age of 60 should be forced to provide permission from a doctor in order to maintain their licensure.

# Quantitative
# Problem-Solving

*Solve these problems and indicate the best of the answer choices given. All numbers used are real numbers.*

1. In the figure, pictured below, the distance from *A* to *D* is 48. The distance from *A* to *B* is equal to the distance from *B* to *C*. If the distance from *C* to *D* is twice the distance of *A* to *B*, how far apart are *B* and *D*?

    a. 12

    b. 16

    c. 24

    d. 26

    e. 36

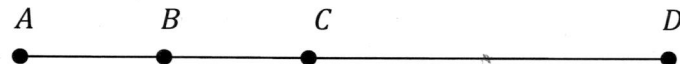

2. Which of the following is NOT less than .33?

    a. 4/15

    b. 13/45

    c. 26/81

    d. 8/27

    e. 4/9

3. If $a - 16 = 8b + 6$, what does $a + 3$ equal?

    a. b + 3

    b. 8b + 9

    c. 8b + 22

    d. 8b + 25

    e. 25

$$a - 16 = 8b + 6$$

$$a + 3 = 8b + 6 + 19$$

$$= 8b + 25$$

4. In the figure, pictured below, angles *b* and *d* are equal. What is the degree measure of angle *d*?

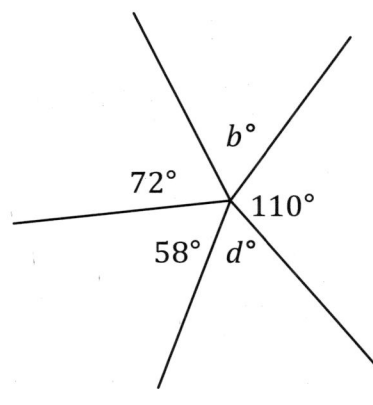

72°

*b*°

110°

58° *d*°

110
72
58
─────
240

a. 240°

b. 120°

c. 80°

d. 60°

e. 30°

5. Janice weighs *x* pounds. Elaina weighs 23 pounds more than Janice. June weighs 14 pounds more than Janice. In terms of *x*, what is the sum of their weights minus 25 pounds?

a. 3x + 37

b. 3x + 12

c. x + 12

d. 3x - 25

e. x = 4

J = x pounds

E = J + 23
or (x + 23)

June = (J + 14)
= (x + 14)

= x + x + 23 + x + 14 - 25

= 3x + 12

6. A bag contains 14 blue, 6 red, 12 green and 8 purple buttons. 25 buttons are removed from the bag randomly. How many of the removed buttons were red if the chance of drawing a red button from the bag is now ¹/₃?

  a. 0

  b. 1

  c. 3

  d. 5

  e. 6

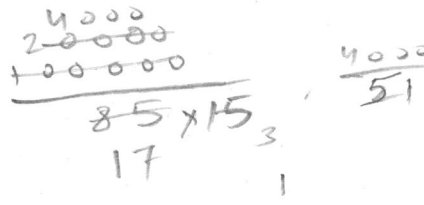

7. A washing machine makes 85 revolutions per minute on the spin cycle. If the washing machine spends 15 minutes on the spin cycle per wash, about how many washes will it take to reach 100,000 revolutions (rounded to the nearest whole number)?

  a. 1,275

  b. 1,175

  c. 100

  d. 78

  e. 35

8. There are 80 mg / 0.8 ml in Acetaminophen Concentrated Infant Drops. If the proper dosage for a four year old child is 240 mg, how many milliliters should the child receive?

  a. 0.8 ml

  b. 1.6 ml

  c. 2.4 ml

  d. 3.2 ml

  e. 5.2 ml

9. Solve the following equation: $(y + 1)(y + 2)(y + 3)$

   a. y2 + 3y + 2

   b. 3y2 + 6y + 3

   c. 2y2 + 11y

   d. y3 + 6y2 + 11y + 6

   e. 8y3 + 6y + 8

10. What is the area of the parallelogram in the figure, pictured below?

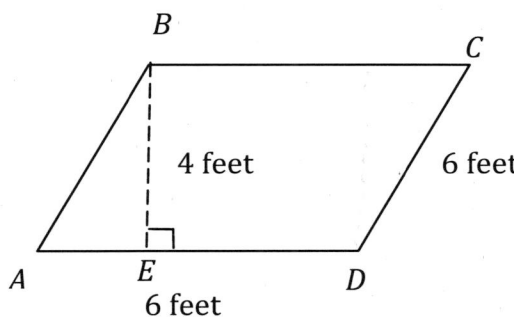

   a. 10 square feet

   b. 12 square feet

   c. 16 square feet

   d. 24 square feet

   e. 36 square feet

11. 50 students are enrolled in both English and Math. 90 students are enrolled in either English or Math. If 25 students are enrolled in English, but not Math, how many students are enrolled in Math but not English?

   a. 15

   b. 25

   c. 50

   d. 65

   e. 90

   E + M = 50

   E/M = 90

   E = 25

12. If a savings account earns 3.75% simple interest, how much interest will a deposit of $2,500 earn in one month?

    a. $93.75

    b. $666.67

    c. $2,503.75

    d. $2,593.75

    e. $9,375.00

$$2500 \times \frac{375}{100} = \frac{9375}{100}$$

13. In the figure, pictured below, $AD = 5$ and $AB = 12$, what is the length of $AC$ (not shown)?

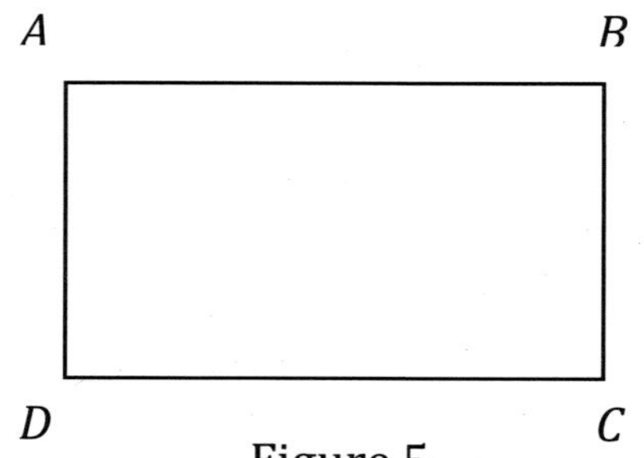

Figure 5

$$5^2 + 12^2 = AC^2$$
$$25 + 144 = AC^2$$
$$AC^2 = 169$$
$$AC = 13$$

    a. 10

    b. 13

    c. 17

    d. 60

    e. 169

14. Convert 12.5% to a fraction.

    a. 1/3

    b. 1/8

    c. 3/8

    d. 5/8

    e. 7/8

$$\frac{12.5}{100} =$$

15. Rick scores 95%, 68%, 86%, 83%, 64%, 92%, and 79% on his math tests over the semester. When calculating students' semester averages, Rick's teacher disregards each student's highest and lowest score. What is Rick's average test score?

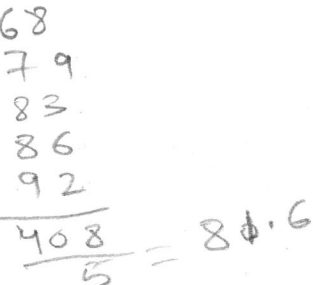

   a. 57.71%

   b. 75.5%

   c. 80.8%

   d. 81%

   e. 81.6%

16. Five dice are rolled together one time. What is the probability of rolling five 6s?

   a. 1/30

   b. 5/6

   c. 1/1,000

   d. 1/7,776

17. Simplify the following equation: $4(6 - 3)^2 - (-2)$

   a. 34

   b. 38

   c. 42

   d. 48

   e. 62

18. In the number 6,502,104.9738, what digit is in the thousandths place?

   a. 3

   b. 5

   c. 6

   d. 8

   e. 9

19. A square and an equilateral triangle have the same perimeter. If one side of the triangle measures 4 inches, how long is one side of the square?

a. 10

b. 8

c. 6

d. 4

e. 3

20. Which of the following fractions, when entered into the triangle, makes the statement true?

$$^3/_8 < \Delta < {}^{13}/_{24}$$

a. 7/8

b. 5/8

c. 5/12

d. 1/3

e. 1/4

21. Using the chart below, which equation describes the relationship between $x$ and $y$?

| $x$ | $y$ |
|---|---|
| 2 | 6 |
| 3 | 9 |
| 4 | 12 |
| 5 | 15 |

a. x = 3y

b. y = 3x

c. y = 1/3x

d. x/y = 3

e. y/x = 3

22. What is the product of four squared and six?

    a. 22
    b. 28
    c. 55
    d. 96
    e. 106

23. Solve the following equation: $(y + 2)(y + 3)(y + 4)$

    a. $y^2 + 3y + 2$
    b. $3y^2 + 6y + 3$
    c. $y^3 + 9y^2 + 26y + 24$
    d. $8y^3 + 6y + 8$
    e. $y^3 + 6y^2 + 11y + 6$

# Data-Sufficiency

This Data Sufficiency problem consists of a question and two statements, labeled (1) and (2), in which certain data are given. You have to decide whether the data given in the statements are sufficient for answering the question, using only the data given in the statements and your knowledge of mathematics and everyday facts (such as the number of days in July or the meaning of counterclockwise).

   a. Statement (1) ALONE is sufficient, but statement (2) is not sufficient

   b. Statement (2) ALONE is sufficient, but statement (1) is not sufficient

   c. BOTH statements TOGETHER are sufficient, but NEITHER statement ALONE is sufficient

   d. EACH statement ALONE is sufficient

   e. Statements (1) and (2) TOGETHER are NOT sufficient

24. Is the integer, $a$, greater than the integer, $c$?

(1) The integer, $c$, is less than the integer, $b$

(2) The integer, $a$, is greater than the integer, $b$

a.              b.              c.              d.              e.

25. What is the sum of the first 100 natural numbers?

(1) There are 50 pairs of numbers, for which a sum can be determined for each pair.

(2) The sum of each pair is 101.

a.              b.              c.              d.              e.

26. Given the sequences produced by the functions, $a_n = 2^n$ and $a_n = 2^{n+1}$, which sequence has a larger value for the $11^{th}$ term?

(1) n is a real number

(2) n is a positive integer

a.              b.              c.              d.              e.

27. Does Alexander finish more miles than Bruce?

(1) Bruce finishes fewer miles than Eric.

(2) Eric finishes fewer miles than Alexander.

a.                b.                (c.)                d.                e.

28. Given the same value for the first term, does infinite geometric series A converge to a

larger number than geometric series B?

(1) The common ratio in the infinite geometric series A is smaller than the common ratio in

the infinite geometric series B.

(2) The difference between the common ratio and 1 in series A is larger than the difference

between the common ratio and 1 in series B.

a.                b.                c.                (d.)                e.

29. Does $y$ vary directly with $x$?

(1) The $y$-intercept of the linear equation, relating $x$ and $y$, is 0.

(2) There is a constant rate of change in the value of $y$ for each subsequent $x$-value.

(a.)                b.                c.                d.                e.

30. Is Triangle ABC similar to Triangle DEF?

(1) The corresponding side lengths of Triangles ABC and DEF are proportional.

(2) The corresponding angles of Triangles ABC and DEF are congruent.

a.                b.                c.                (d.)                e.

31. Is line AB parallel to line CD?

(1) A transversal, intersecting the two lines, forms congruent corresponding angles.

(2) A transversal, intersecting the two lines, forms congruent alternate interior angles.

a.                b.                c.                (d.)                e.

32. How many positive integers less than 100 are prime?

(1) There are 48 positive multiples of 2, less than 100.

(2) There are 50 odd, positive integers, less than 100.

a.        b.        c.        d.        **(e.)**

33. Is Relation A also a function?

(1) Relation A forms a parabola, when graphed.

(2) Each $y$-value in Relation A is mapped to a unique $x$-value.

**(a.)**        b.        c.        d.        e.

34. Is the range of a data set less than the mode of a data set?

(1) The median is greater than the mode.

(2) The range is less than the median.

a.        b.        **(c.)**        d.        **(e.)**

35. Is the value of the $n$th term of arithmetic sequence A greater than the value of the nth term of arithmetic sequence B?

(1) The value of the initial term of arithmetic sequence A is less than the value of the initial term of arithmetic sequence B.

(2) The difference in value in subsequent terms for arithmetic sequence A is greater than the difference in value in subsequent terms for arithmetic sequence B.

a.        b.        c.        d.        **(e.)**

36. What is the tangent of angle A?

(1) The cosine of angle A is $\frac{4}{5}$.

(2) The sine of angle A is $\frac{3}{5}$.

a.        b.        **(c.)**        d.        e.

37. Is the sum of the first *n*, even numbers, an even integer?

(1) The rate of change between subsequent even numbers is even.

(2) The rate of change in the sum of the first *n*, even numbers, is even.

a.          b.          c.          d.          e.

# Verbal Ability
# Reading Comprehension

*Questions 1 -3 pertain to the following passage:*

Peanut allergy is the most prevalent food allergy in the United States, affecting around one and a half million people, and it is potentially on the rise in children in the United States. While thought to be the most common cause of food-related death, deaths from food allergies are very rare. The allergy typically begins at a very young age and remains present for life for most people. Approximately one-fifth to one-quarter of children with a peanut allergy, however, outgrow it. Treatment involves careful avoidance of peanuts or any food that may contain peanut pieces or oils. For some sufferers, exposure to even the smallest amount of peanut product can trigger a serious reaction.

Symptoms of peanut allergy can include skin reactions, itching around the mouth, digestive problems, shortness of breath, and runny or stuffy nose. The most severe peanut allergies can result in anaphylaxis, which requires immediate treatment with epinephrine. Up to one-third of people with peanut allergies have severe reactions. Without treatment, anaphylactic shock can result in death due to obstruction of the airway, or heart failure. Signs of anaphylaxis include constriction of airways and difficulty breathing, shock, a rapid pulse, and dizziness or lightheadedness.

As of yet, there is no treatment to prevent or cure allergic reactions to peanuts. In May of 2008, however, Duke University Medical Center food allergy experts announced that they expect to offer a treatment for peanut allergies within five years.

Scientists do not know for sure why peanut proteins induce allergic reactions, nor do they know why some people develop peanut allergies while others do not. There is a strong genetic component to allergies: if one of a child's parents has an allergy, the child has an almost 50% chance of developing an allergy. If both parents have an allergy, the odds increase to about 70%.

Someone suffering from a peanut allergy needs to be cautious about the foods he or she eats and the products he or she puts on his or her skin. Common foods that should be checked for peanut content are ground nuts, cereals, granola, grain breads, energy bars, and salad dressings. Store prepared cookies, pastries, and frozen desserts like ice cream can also contain peanuts. Additionally, many cuisines use peanuts in cooking – watch for peanut content in African, Chinese, Indonesian, Mexican, Thai, and Vietnamese dishes.

Parents of children with peanut allergies should notify key people (child care providers, school personnel, etc.) that their child has a peanut allergy, explain peanut allergy symptoms to them, make sure that the child's epinephrine auto injector is always available, write an action plan of care for their child when he or she has an allergic reaction to peanuts, have their child wear a medical alert bracelet or necklace, and discourage their child from sharing foods.

1. Which allergy does the article state is thought to be the most common cause of food-related death?

a. Peanut

b. Tree nut

c. Bee sting

d. Poison oak

e. Shellfish

2. It can be inferred from the passage that children with peanut allergies should be discouraged from sharing food because:

a. Peanut allergies can be contagious

b. People suffering from peanut allergies are more susceptible to bad hygiene

c. Many foods contain peanut content and it is important to be very careful when you don't know what you're eating

d. Scientists don't know why some people develop peanut allergies

e. There is no treatment yet to prevent peanut allergies

3. Which of the following does the passage not state is a sign of anaphylaxis?

a. constriction of airways

b. shock

c. a rapid pulse

d. dizziness

e. running or stuffy nose

*Questions 4 – 6 pertain to the following passage:*

Daylight Saving Time (DST) is the practice of changing clocks so that afternoons have more daylight and mornings have less. Clocks are adjusted forward one hour in the spring and one hour backward in the fall. The main purpose of the change is to make better use of daylight.

DST began with the goal of conservation. Benjamin Franklin suggested it as a method of saving on candles. It was used during both World Wars to save energy for military needs. Although DST's potential to save energy was a primary reason behind its implementation, research into its effects on energy conservation are contradictory and unclear.

Beneficiaries of DST include all activities that can benefit from more sunlight after working hours, such as shopping and sports. A 1984 issue of *Fortune* magazine estimated that a seven-week extension of DST would yield an additional $30 million for 7-Eleven stores. Public safety may be increased by the use of DST: some research suggests that traffic fatalities may be reduced when there is additional afternoon sunlight.

On the other hand, DST complicates timekeeping and some computer systems. Tools with built-in time-keeping functions such as medical devices can be affected negatively. Agricultural and evening entertainment interests have historically opposed DST.

DST can affect health, both positively and negatively. It provides more afternoon sunlight in which to get exercise. It also impacts sunlight exposure; this is good for getting vitamin D, but bad in that it can increase skin cancer risk. DST may also disrupt sleep.

Today, daylight saving time has been adopted by more than one billion people in about 70 countries. DST is generally not observed in countries near the equator because sunrise times do not vary much there. Asia and Africa do not generally observe it. Some countries, such as Brazil, observe it only in some regions.

DST can lead to peculiar situations. One of these occurred in November, 2007 when a woman in North Carolina gave birth to one twin at 1:32 a.m. and, 34 minutes later, to the second twin. Because of DST and the time change at 2:00 a.m., the second twin was officially born at 1:06, 26 minutes earlier than her brother.

4. According to the passage, what is the main purpose of DST?

 a. To increase public safety

 b. To benefit retail businesses

 c. To make better use of daylight

 d. To promote good health

 e. To save on candles

5. Which of the following is not mentioned in the passage as a negative effect of DST?

 a. Energy conservation

 b. Complications with time keeping

 c. Complications with computer systems

 d. Increased skin cancer risk

 e. Sleep disruption

6. The article states that DST involves:

 a. Adjusting clocks forward one hour in the spring and the fall

 b. Adjusting clocks backward one hour in the spring and the fall

 c. Adjusting clocks forward in the fall and backward in the spring

 d. Adjusting clocks forward in the spring and backward in the fall

 e. None of the above

*Questions 7 – 9 pertain to the following passage:*

> Judicial review, the power of courts to determine the legality of governmental acts, usually refers to the authority of judges to decide a law's constitutionality. Although state courts exercised judicial review prior to the ratification of the Constitution, the doctrine is most often traced to the landmark U.S. Supreme Court decision *Marbury* v. *Madison* (1803), which struck down an act of Congress as unconstitutional. In a now classic opinion, Chief Justice John Marshall found the power of judicial review implied in the Constitution's status as "the supreme Law of the Land" prevailing over ordinary laws.
>
> Both federal and state courts have exercised judicial review. Federal courts review federal and state acts to ensure their conformity to the Constitution and the supremacy of federal over state law; state courts review laws to

ensure their conformity to the U.S. Constitution and their own state constitutions. The power of judicial review can be exercised by any court in which a constitutional issue arises.

Judicial review gained added importance in the late nineteenth and early twentieth century's, as courts passed judgment on laws regulating corporate behavior and working conditions. In these years, the Supreme Court repeatedly struck down laws regulating wages, hours of labor, and safety standards. This is often called the *Lochner* Era, after *Lochner* v. *New York*, a 1905 decision ruling a New York maximum-hours law unconstitutional on the grounds that it violated the Fourteenth Amendment. During this period, the Supreme Court invalidated no fewer than 228 state laws.

Justice Oliver Wendell Holmes Jr., dissenting from many of these decisions, urged judges to defer to legislatures. In the later 1930's, the Supreme Court adopted the Holmes approach-partly in response to the threat of President Franklin Delano Roosevelt's "court packing" plan of 1937. Deferring to legislative judgment, the Supreme Court thereafter upheld virtually all laws regulating business and property rights, including laws similar to those invalidated during the *Lochner* Era.

Under the chief justiceship of Earl Warren (1953-1969) and beyond, however, the Court moved toward striking down law restricting personal rights and liberties guaranteed by the Bill of Rights, particularly measures limiting freedom of expression, freedom or religion, the right of criminal defendants, equal treatment of the sexes, and the rights of minorities to equal protection of the law. In another extension of judicial review, the Court read new rights into the Constitution, notably the right of privacy (including abortion rights) and invalidated laws restricting those rights. Many other countries including Germany, Italy, France, and Japan, adopted the principle of judicial review after World War II, making constitutional law one the more important recent American exports.

7. Which of the following statements about judicial review does the passage best support?
   a. States should defer to the Federal Government when interpreting the Constitution
   b. Judicial Review was started due to the Lochner Era
   c. The Constitution overrides state law in some cases
   d. The Courts do not have the power to regulate business
   e. Judicial Review was founded by Earl Warren Chief Justice of the Supreme Court

8. From the passage, it can be inferred ordinary laws created by lawmakers must be within the framework of the Constitution. Which of the following sentences supports this claim the best?

a. Although state courts exercised....

b. Both federal and state courts....

c. Judicial review gained added importance...

d. During this period, the Supreme...

e. Deferring to legislature judgment....

9. Which of the following words best characterizes the content of the passage?

a. historical

b. transcription

c. prospective

d. figurative

e. demonstrative

*Questions 10 – 13 pertain to the following passage:*

Theodore Roosevelt first implied the term "muckrakers" to a group of journalists and writers who had exposed corruption in business and government in the early twentieth century. Roosevelt intended the term, borrowed from John Bunyan's *Pilgrim's Progress*, to be somewhat pejorative, but the muckrakers were very influential for a time and provided strong impetus to the ongoing Progressive Era reform movement.

Around 1902, a number of prominent magazines including *McClure's*, *Collier's*, *Cosmopolitan*, *Everybody's* and the *Arena*, began featuring crusading exposes or "muckraking" articles. Some of these pieces were later expanded into full length books. Among the best-known were Ida Tarbell's *History of the Standard Oil Company* (1902); Lincoln Steffen's *The Shame of the Cities* (1904), documenting corruption in municipal government; Samuel Hopkins Adams's *The Great American Fraud* (1906), lambasting the patent-medicine industry; and Ray Stannard Baker's *Following the Color Line* (1908), a pioneering expose of American racism.

A few muckrakers made their case in works of fiction. Upton Sinclair's *The Jungle* (1906), a fictionalized account of the Chicago meatpacking industry, was the best known of the genre, but David Graham Phillips was perhaps the most prolific of the muckraking novelists. Among his numerous works were *Lightfingered Gentry* (1907), on the insurance industry; *Susan Lenox; Her Fall and Rise* (1908) published in 1917), on prostitution; and many others.

The muckraking spirit also influenced some of the major novelists of the time, although usually in less tractarian form. Frank *Norris's The Octopus* (1901) and *The Pit* (1903); Theodore Dreiser's *The Financier* (1912) and *The Titan* (1914); and Jack London's *Iron Heel* (1908) all address the social consequences of unregulated capitalist expansion.

After about 1912, the muckraking movement abated. The public tired of the exposes, some of which seem sensationalized and overly sordid. But muckraking already had exerted a major impact on the reform movement and would influence the policies of President Woodrow Wilson. Indeed, Ray Standard Baker became an aide to Wilson and later edited a six-volume collection of Wilson's public papers (1926-1927). Assuming many different forms, the muckraking impulse continued to influence American journalism as the twentieth century wore on.

10. Which of the following statements about Muckrakers does the passage best support?

    a. Muckrakers were viewed as criminologists during the early 1900s

    b. Muckrakers were exposing corruption during the Progressive Era

    c. Muckrakers were used by politicians during the 1900s to downplay social reforms

    d. The Muckrakers continued to have success following 1912

    e. Muckrakers had a background in detective operations and a passion for exposing the truth


11. From the passage, it can be inferred the muckrakers fueled the Progressive Era. Which of the following sentences supports this claim the best?

    a. After about 1912...

    b. A few muckrakers made...

    c. The muckraking spirit...

    d. Roosevelt intended the...

    e. Around 1902, a number...

12. Which of the following words best characterizes the content of the passage?

    a. cooperative

    b. degrading

    c. revealing

    d. conventional

    e. operational


13. Which of the following did not contribute to the rise of the mudrackers?

    a. The Octopus

    b. Journalists

    c. The Jungle

    d. The Pit

    e. Pilgrim's Progress

# Sentence Correction

These questions present a sentence, all or part of which is underlined. Beneath each sentence you will find five ways of phrasing the underlined part. The first of these repeats the original; the other four are different. If you think the original is best, choose the first answer; otherwise, choose one of the other answers.

These questions test correctness and effectiveness of expression. In choosing your answer, follow the requirements of standard written English; that is, pay attention to grammar, choice of words, and sentence construction. Choose the answer that produces the most effective sentence; this answer should be clear and exact, without awkwardness, ambiguity, redundancy, or grammatical error.

14. Given the price of going to a movie, a ticket usually costs around $10, more and more people are renting films to watch at home.
    a. a ticket usually costs
    b. which is usually
    c. which usually costs
    d. which can be usually
    e. a ticket costs

15. Composers of modern popular music can feature syncopated rhythms, multiple-part harmonies, and used electronic instrument orchestration.
    a. and used electronic instrument orchestration.
    b. and they use electronic instrument orchestration.
    c. and orchestration using electronic instruments.
    d. as well as using electronic instrument orchestration.
    e. with electronic instrument orchestration.

16. As the price of gasoline increased during the past ten years, American car manufacturers should have realized that a drop in the demand for gas-guzzling vehicles <u>was likely and would probably happen</u>.

    a. was likely and would probably happen.

    b. was likely and would probably happen in the future.

    c. would be likely and would probably happen soon.

    d. was a likely thing.

    e. was likely.

17. As more and more of the younger generation moves to Tokyo to find work, <u>the remaining population of Japan's rural towns gets older and older</u>.

    a. the remaining population of Japan's rural towns gets older and older.

    b. the average population of Japan's rural towns gets older and older.

    c. the population of Japan's rural towns continues to get older.

    d. the population remaining in Japan's rural towns gets older and older.

    e. the remaining population of Japan's rural towns gets older.

18. When the team got off the plane, <u>they were met by a throng of adoring fans</u>.

    a. they were met by a throng of adoring fans.

    b. they were met by many adoring fans,

    c. it was met by a throng of adoring fans.

    d. they encountered a throng of adoring fans.

    e. it meets a throng of adoring fans.

19. One of Shakespeare's favorite forms was the sonnet, <u>it is a fourteen line poem</u> written in iambic pentameter.

    a. it is a fourteen line poem

    b. a fourteen-line poem

    c. it is a fourteen-line poem

    d. these were fourteen-line poems

    e. it was a fourteen line poem

20. Home music production equipment has become so <u>sophisticated, and</u> amateur musicians can produce recordings that are competitive with the output of professional studios.

    a. sophisticated, and

    b. sophisticated, also

    c. sophisticated that

    d. sophisticated consequently

    e. sophisticated wherefore

21. Since people who drive while intoxicated are responsible for many injuries and deaths, <u>severely punished</u> is what they deserve.

    a. severely punished

    b. severe punishment

    c. severely punishment

    d. severeness of punishment

    e. severity in punishment

22. Tobacco use is still very high in China, where public health officials are urging the public to stop <u>smoking which has been linked to lung cancer</u>.

    a. smoking which has been linked to lung cancer.

    b. smoking because it has been linked to lung cancer.

    c. smoking on account of its being linked to lung cancer.

    d. smoking, which has been linked to lung cancer.

    e. smoking when it has been linked to lung cancer.

23. Even professional chefs disagree <u>about what is the best way to</u> cook a steak.

    a. about what is the best way to

    b. about, what is the best way to

    c. about how to

    d. about what the best way is to

    e. about the best way to

24. Across the country there are hundreds of thousands, if not millions, <u>of potentially affected families</u> by the distress of this industry.

    a. of potentially affected families

    b. of potential families affected

    c. of families potentially affected

    d. of families affected potentially

    e. of affected families


25. A ski holiday can be ruined either because of warm weather, <u>but also because</u> someone is injured in a fall.

    a. but also because

    b. but also owing to

    c. or the cause is

    d. or because of

    e. but possible because


26. Drug therapies are replacing a lot of <u>medicines as we used to know it.</u>

    a. medicines as we used to know it.

    b. medicine as we used to know it.

    c. medicines as we used to know.

    d. therapies as we used to know it.

    e. other therapies as we used to know it.


27. If you teach a child to read, <u>he or her will</u> be able to pass a literacy test.

    a. he or her will

    b. they will

    c. it will

    d. he will

    e. he or she will

# Critical Reasoning

28. A recent Newsweek poll found that for the first time, a majority of Americans now believe that gay and lesbian couples deserve legal recognition. Fifty-five percent of the poll's respondents stated they support legally sanctioned unions. The poll also indicated that there was increased backing for inheritance and other property rights, and that 39 percent support legalizing gay marriage. *The statements above most strongly support which of the following assertions?*

    a. The gay population of the United States is higher than it was.

    b. Acceptance of gays and lesbians is higher in the United States than it was.

    c. Marriage proponents have persuaded a larger set of the population to partake.

    d. The gay population of the United States is lower than it was.


29. Radio listener: Van Morrison and Nick Lowe started their music careers only a few years apart, but while both men have released numerous albums, their levels of fame and renown are wildly different. Morrison has had a long career in the popular eye, and has made many millions of dollars, as well as having had critical acclaim. Lowe has also made money, but substantially less than Morrison. Lowe is a respected songwriter, but hasn't had more than a couple of popular hits. Because of their differing levels of fame, Morrison is clearly the better musician. *This argument assumes which of the following?*

    a. There are only two relevant performers that can be compared

    b. Popular music covers country and classical arrangements

    c. Readers are familiar with a wide range of popular performers

    d. Quality of musicianship and popular appeal are directly related

30. No one in the trauma unit that Dr. James belongs to can work more than one shift in the emergency room per any given work week. For the next week, all the shifts available to work are non-emergency room shifts. Thus, it is untrue that Dr. James can work any emergency room shift in the next week. *Which one of the following conditions, if true, most directly weakens the argument concerning Dr. James working in the emergency room?*

    a. The shifts are scheduled and set only a few days in advance

    b. The shifts still available were overtime shifts, and have no relation to regularly scheduled shifts

    c. Dr. James has privileges at a different nearby hospital

    d. The trauma unit is affiliated with a mobile medical clinic

31. Infidelity can have a number of psychological effects on the partner committing the infidelity. Aside from the various factors that led to the act, one of the more common side effects has to do with the perception of trust. Often, the effort of keeping an illicit relationship from the other partner is extremely stressful, with the straying party having to resort to more and more elaborate tactics to keep the infidelity secret. As the pressure mounts, and the unfaithful party reflects on their own behavior, the cheating party will often reinterpret the other partner's behavior through the prism of the cheater's own duplicity, leading to _____. *Which of the following phrases most logically completes the argument?*

    a. increasing distrust and, ironically, suspicion that the other party is cheating

    b. a desire to lay down strict rules regarding communication

    c. isolating the other party through silence and rejection of affection

    d. erratic behavior and occasional fits of excessive attention or affection

32. The ability of an organism to adapt to environmental change is strictly controlled by how well it fits into the environment prior to the change, which is directly related to time spent in that ecology. If an environment is stable over long periods of time, as was seen during the lengthy period between the Triassic and Cretaceous eras, the lifeforms that appear and flourish in that environment are so specialized to the climate and ecological system that any sudden change, even if relatively insignificant, can result in species extinction. The rise of mammals after the Cretaceous-Tertiary extinction event and the subsequent fall of dinosaurs is simply the best-known example.

*What assumption is made in the argument as stated that, if incorrect, could weaken the argument's logic?*

    a. The extinction event was a geological phenomenon

    b. Mammals developed some time after dinosaurs appeared

    c. The earth's climate stabilized into a subtropical system

    d. Dinosaurs first appeared in the pre-Triassic era


33. An engineering manager reports that the latest revision of the company's product, a rotational ring used as part of the spindle assembly for high-revolution hard drives, is ready for production, barely within the stated deadline for ramping up production. Test results show that the ring performs above the 99% operational function standard within the narrow range of temperature and revolution laid out in the official product specifications. However, further analysis shows the failure rate rose dramatically when tested outside that well-defined range in temperatures and revolution rates that are common for those devices, falling to a 92% operational function standard. The manager states that because the product functions within stated tolerances inside the specified ranges, the product is ready to manufacture, and that modifications can wait for future revisions.

*The reasoning in the manager's argument is flawed because the argument:*

    a. Bases a liability analysis on time factors only

    b. Follows a narrowly defined interpretation of the warranty

    c. Assumes customers will primarily use the product in optimal conditions

    d. Is predicated on a timeframe that may not occur

34. In virtually all species of cockroach, the nervous and respiratory systems are heavily decentralized. Laboratory experiments have repeatedly demonstrated that cockroaches can be decapitated completely, yet continue to survive for up to several weeks before dying of lack of food or water. This demonstrates the relative superiority of cockroaches over virtually all other insect species, since hardly any other species has demonstrated such ability to survive after being introduced to extreme damage or environmental conditions. *Which of the following statements, if true, most seriously weakens the cockroach argument?*

    a. Cockroaches are found in the widest environmental ranges of any insect species

    b. The estimated cockroach population has increased dramatically since modern cities appeared

    c. More bird species prey on cockroaches than any other insect species

    d. The lethal dose for common household chemicals is far lower for cockroaches than most other insect species

35. A poll of employees at Widgets, Inc. concluded that employee satisfaction levels were among the five highest-ranked companies in the United States. Poll data was gathered by representatives from human resources quizzing employees in private meetings about their satisfaction levels with their jobs, and the company as a whole, and then computing the results based on a predetermined index. A recruiter with a national staffing firm has argued with the results, claiming that the percentages listed do not match with surveys of former and present employees placed with the company. *The recruiter can most properly criticize the reasoning by which the poll reached its result on what basis?*

    a. The index used to measure satisfaction was not compiled to the same objectives and specifications as other companies

    b. The poll was not conducted by an objective party, and may have skewed the results

    c. Former employees were not included in the polling sample

    d. Polling was not conducted electronically, making tampering more likely

36. Teenage couch potato: My folks are always telling me to sit back from the TV set; they say my eyes will go bad if I sit too close to the screen. Our TV is a an older set with one of those tubes, and I read that the refresh rate on older TVs is the part that eyes have trouble focusing on, which is why computer screens on TV are always so hard to see. Flat-panel plasma TVs don't have that problem, since they have much higher resolution and refresh much faster, so instead of always sitting back so far, buying a flat-panel plasma TV will take care of any focus issues my eyes might have. *Which of the following best states the flaw in this argument's reasoning?*

    a. Refresh rates do not have an effect on the ability to read an image

    b. Simply moving back from the TV is a simpler and less expensive solution

    c. Flat-panel plasma TVs have a similar effect on the eyes, despite their higher performance standards

    d. The teenager does not have any vision issues


37. All college students who play video games develop increased hand-eye coordination. All college students who major in the biological sciences make excellent doctors and surgeons. Everyone in Riley's study group, including Riley, is majoring in the biological sciences, and all of them except Riley play video games. Therefore, everyone in Riley's study group will make excellent surgeons. *What assumption is made in the above argument that is not explicitly supported in the argument's text?*

    a. Riley and her study group peers intend to be surgeons

    b. Riley and her study group peers started as biological science majors

    c. Riley and her study group peers are college students

    d. Riley and her study group peers are good at video games

38. Librarian: Every year, there are a handful of challenges from parents angry that Harper Lee's *To Kill A Mockingbird* is available for children to check out. For the last several years, the challenges have always been over the racially charged material and the "liberal" nature of Atticus Finch; although the library board has consistently ruled in favor of the book, the challenges keep coming every year. However, the movie version, which is also available for children to check out, has never been challenged once, despite the fidelity of the adaptation to the novel. *The reasoning in the librarian's argument is flawed because:*

   a. It assumes that parents are aware that the movie is also available for children to check out

   b. It fails to note whether other novels with similar thematic elements are also being challenged.

   c. It ignores the possibility that challenges are being issued for non-textual issues

   d. It assumes that the text and movie versions are being checked out at similar rates

39. The latest report from The Tabletop Stock Report indicates that Widgets, Inc. remains a sound long-term investment and is a good buy for casual investors, despite some mixed profit reports. However, the publisher of The Tabletop Stock Report is a minority owner of a small investment firm, which owns several hundred thousand shares of Widgets, Inc. Thus, since there is clearly reason to doubt the conclusions drawn, Widgets, Inc. is obviously a poor candidate for investment. *The reasoning in this argument is most vulnerable to criticism on what grounds?*

   a. The argument equates an apparent bias as evidence that the Tabletop Stock Report's claims are false

   b. The argument draws a conclusion based solely on a statistically insignificant sample of the Tabletop Stock Report's articles

   c. The argument fails to take into account the possibility that the publisher may have just as much financial motivation to create negative publicity for Widgets

   d. The argument fails to provide evidence that Widgets, Inc. stock is not a good buy

40. All teenagers who play Dungeons and Dragons are excellent students. All teenagers who play World of Warcraft are indifferent students. Everyone in Mark's circle of teenage friends play both Dungeons and Dragons and World of Warcraft. Therefore, all of Mark's friends are students with performance scores in the mid-range. *Which of the following arguments most exemplifies the flawed reasoning used in the argument above?*

  a. All Grand Theft Auto players who practice rigorously score well in the game. But some players who do not practice rigorously also do well in the game. Jim practices moderately; therefore, Jim's scores are in the mid-range

  b. Every programmer knows Java. Every system analyst learns Visio. Susanne started working at Widgets as a programmer, and then was promoted to systems analyst. Therefore, Susanne knows Java and Visio

  c. All green Amazonian banana spiders are poisonous to humans. All blue Amazonian tree spiders are non-poisonous to humans. A new species of Amazonian spider was discovered that is a hybrid of the green Amazonian banana spider and the blue Amazonian tree spider. Thus, the new species is moderately poisonous to humans

  d. Every worker at Widgets lives in Pennsylvania. Every worker at Doodads lives in New Jersey. Alex has relatives that work at Widgets and relatives that work at Doodads. Thus, Alex has relatives in Pennsylvania and New Jersey

41. When a relationship ends, it is often emotionally similar to losing a loved one. The abrupt end of a relationship can create strong sensations of loss and depression among partners who were not aware of the impending end. Just as people who have lost someone to death may go through the common five-stage process of grieving, people whose relationship has abruptly ended may _____. *Which of the following phrases most logically completes the argument?*

  a. experience a fear of their own suitability as a romantic partner

  b. go through a grieving period for their relationship

  c. focus on the positive aspects of the past relationship

  d. withdraw from romantic pursuits completely

# Answers and Explanations
## Quantitative
## Problem-Solving

1. E: Segment $AD = 48$. Because the length of $CD$ is 2 times the length of $AB$, let $AB = x$ and let $CD = 2x$. Since $AB = BC$, let $BC = x$ also. The total length of $AD = AB + BC + CD = x + x + 2x = 4x = 48$. Thus, $x = 12$ and $BC + CD = x + 2x = 3x = 3 \times 12 = 36$.

2. E: .33 is equal to roughly $^1/_3$, so find which choice is NOT less (i.e. greater) than $^1/_3$. Since the "3" in the denominator of $^1/_3$ is a factor of the denominators of all the answer choices, you can compare the fractions with relative ease.

3. D: Isolate $a$: $a = 8b + 6 + 16$. Thus, $a = 8b + 22$. Next add 3 to both side of the equation: $a + 3 = 8b + 22 + 3 = 8b + 25$.

4. D: Angles around a point add up to 360 degrees. Add the degrees of the given angles: $72° + 110° + 58° = 240°$. Then subtract from $360° - 240° = 120°$. Remember to divide $120°$ in half, since the question is asking for the degree measure of one angle, angle $d$.

5. B: Translate this word problem into a mathematical equation. Let Janice's weight $= x$. Let Elaina's weight $= x + 23$. Let June's weight $= x + 14$. Add their weights together and subtract 25 pounds:

$= x + x + 23 + x + 14 - 25$

$= 3x + 37 - 25$

$= 3x + 12$

6. B: Add the 14 blue, 6 red, 12 green and 8 purple buttons to get a total of 40 buttons. If 25 buttons are removed, there are 15 buttons remaining in the bag. If the chance of drawing a red button is now $^1/_3$, divide 15 into thirds to get 5 red buttons remaining in the bag. The original total of red buttons was 6; so $6 - 5 = 1$: one red button was removed, choice (B).

- 269 -

7. D: First, determine how many revolutions the washer makes in one wash by multiplying 85 X 15 = 1,275. Then divide 100,000 by 1,275 to determine how many washes it will take to reach 100,000 revolutions 100,000 ÷ 1,275 = 78.431373. Round this number to 78, the nearest whole number.

You may not be able to determine the precise answer, but you may be able to solve at least to the tenths decimal place and see that the answer is roughly 78.

8. C: Divide the mg the child should receive by the number of mg in 0.8 ml to determine how many 0.8 ml doses the child should receive: 240 ÷ 80 = 3. Multiply the number of doses by 0.8 to determine how many ml the child should receive: 3 X 0.8 = 2.4 ml

9. D: This equation is asking you to multiply three algebraic expressions. When multiplying more than two expressions, multiply any two expressions (using the FOIL method), then multiply the result by the third expression. Start by multiplying:

$(y + 1)(y + 2) = (y \times y) + (y \times 2) + (1 \times y) + (1 \times 2)$

$= y^2 + 2y + y + 2$

$= y^2 + 3y + 2$

Then multiply the result by the third expression:

$(y^2 + 3y + 2)(y + 3) = (y^2 + 3y + 2)(y) + (y^2 + 3y + 2)(3)$

$= (y^3 + 3y^2 + 2y) + (3y^2 + 9y + 6)$

$= y^3 + 3y^2 + 2y + 3y^2 + 9y + 6$

$= y^3 + 3y^2 + 3y^2 + 9y + 2y + 6$

$= y^3 + 6y^2 + 11y + 6$

10. D: The area of a parallelogram is base X height or $A = bh$, where $b$ is the length of a side and $h$ is the length of an altitude to that side. In this problem, $A = 6 \times 4$; $A = 24$. Remember, use the length of BE, not the length of CD for the height.

11. A: There are a total of 90 students that take Math, English, or both. You must avoid counting the same students twice, and you may find it helpful to create a Venn diagram or some sort of chart to keep the different types of students separate.

Total students                                      90

Students taking both courses:          -50

Students taking just English:            <u>-25</u>

Students taking just Math:                 15

12. A: To find the interest earned, multiply the interest rate by the deposit amount. Because this account uses simple interest, you do not need to worry about compounding the interest. Remember to convert the interest rate to a percentage.

$0.0375 \times 2{,}500 = 93.75$.

Choice (D) might be a tempting answer, since it is the deposit amount added to the interest earned, but the question asks how much interest will be earned, not the total amount of the deposit after earning interest.

13. B: Use the Pythagorean Theorem to solve this problem: $a^2 + b^2 = c^2$ where c is the hypotenuse while $a$ and $b$ are the legs of the triangle.
$5^2 + 12^2 = c^2$
$25 + 144 = 169$
$\sqrt{169} = 13$.

14. B: A percentage is changed into a fraction by first converting the percentage into a decimal, and then changing the decimal to a fraction.

To convert a percentage into a decimal, divide the percentage by 100 by moving the decimal point two places to the left:

$12.5\% = .125$

To convert this decimal into a fraction, the numbers to the right of the decimal point become the numerator. Because the last decimal place is the thousandths place, the numerator of the faction is 1000. Reduce the fraction to the lowest terms:

$^{125}/_{1000} = ^1/_8$

Remember that you can reduce the fraction into progressively lower terms until you find the most reduced fraction (ex: $^{25}/_{200}$ → $^{5}/_{40}$ → $^{1}/_{8}$).

15. E: The average of a group of terms is the sum of the terms divided by the number of terms. In this problem, the teacher disregards Rick's highest and lowest scores, so do not use 95% or 64% in your calculation. Add the remaining scores: 68 + 86 + 83 + 92 + 79 = 408

Divide by the number of scores: 408 ÷ 5 = 81.6.

16. E: Use the formula for probability to solve this problem:

Probability =

<u>Number of Desirable Outcomes</u>

Number of Possible Outcomes

Because there are effectively multiple events – the roll of each die is its own event – you must multiply all the possible outcomes for each die. Thus, to determine the number of possible outcomes, multiply the number of sides on dice exponentially by the number dice: $6^5$ = (6 x 6 x 6 x 6 x 6) = 7,776

There is one desirable outcome: rolling all sixes. Probability = $^{1}/_{7,776}$

17. B: Remember to use the order of operations when simplifying this equation. The acronym *PEMDAS* will help you remember the correct order: Parenthesis, Exponentiation, Multiplication/Division, Addition/Subtraction.

$4(6 - 3)^2 - (-2)$

First, simplify the parentheses: $4 \times 3^2 - (-2)$

Next, simplify the exponent: 4 x 9 – (-2)

Then multiply: 36 – (-2)

Finally, subtract: 36 – (-2) = 36 + 2 = 38

The PEMDAS method is used to simplify multiple equations in this practice test.

18. A: You can eliminate choices (B) and (C) since they are to the left of the decimal point. This problem asks for the number in the thousandths place, and the "ths" indicate digits to the right of the decimal point. Of those digits:

- 9 is in the tenths place
- 7 is in the hundredths place
- 3 is in the thousandths place
- 8 is in the ten thousandths place

19. E: An equilateral triangle has three sides of equal length. If each side is 4 inches long, the perimeter of the triangle is 12 inches. A square has four sides of equal length. Since its perimeter also must equal 12 inches, divide 12 by 4: $12 \div 4 = 3$

20. C: Find the common denominator of $^3/_8$ and $^{13}/_{24}$.

$^3/_8 \times {}^3/_3 = {}^9/_{24}$

$^{13}/_{24} \times {}^1/_1 = {}^{13}/_{24}$

The value in the triangle must be greater than $^9/_{24}$ and less than $^{13}/_{24}$. Choice (C), $^5/_{12}$, when expressed as the equivalent fraction $^{10}/_{24}$, is correct.

21. B: The chart indicates that each $x$ value must be tripled to equal the corresponding $y$ value, so $y = 3x$. One way you can determine this is by plugging corresponding pairs of $x$ and $y$ into the answer choices.

22. D: Turn the word problem into an equation. Remember that product means multiplication:

$4^2 \times 6 = 96$.

23. C: This equation is asking you to multiply three algebraic expressions. When multiplying more than two expressions, multiply any two expressions, (using the FOIL method) then multiply the result by the third expression. Start by multiplying:

$(y + 2)(y + 3) = (y \times y) + (y \times 3) + (2 \times y) + (2 \times 3)$

$= y^2 + 3y + 2y + 6$

$= y^2 + 5y + 6$

Then multiply the result by the third expression:

$(y^2 + 5y + 6)(y + 4) = (y^2 + 5y + 6)(y) + (y^2 + 5y + 6)(4)$

$= (y^3 + 5y^2 + 6y) + (4y^2 + 20y + 24)$

$= y^3 + 5y^2 + 6y + 4y^2 + 20y + 24$

$= y^3 + 9y^2 + 26y + 24$

## Data Sufficiency

24. C: The relationship described in (1) can be written as: $c < b$. The relationship described in (2) can be written as: $b < a$. If $c < b$ and $b < a$, then $c < a$, by the transitive property.

25. C: The sum of the first 100 natural numbers can be determined by finding the product of the number of pairs of numbers and the sum of each pair. Thus, the sum is equal to $50 \cdot 101$, or 5,050.

26. D: For any real number or positive integer, the sequence, $a_n = 2^{n+1}$, will have a larger value for the 11th term, since the exponent of n, has 1 added to it. The exponent on the base will always be larger in this sequence than in the other sequence, resulting in a larger value of each term.

27. C: The relationship described in (1) can be written as: $b < e$, where $b$ represents the number of miles Bruce finishes and $e$ represents the number of miles Eric finishes. The relationship described in (2) can be written as: $e < a$, where $e$ represents the number of miles Eric finishes and $a$ represents the number of miles Alexander finishes. If $b < e$ and $e < a$, then $b < a$, by the transitive property. Thus, Bruce finishes fewer miles than Alexander.

28. D: Either statement (1) or statement (2) reveal that infinite geometric series A will converge to a smaller number than infinite geometric series B, given the same value for the first term. The reasoning rests with the fact that the smaller ratio for infinite geometric series A will result in a larger difference in the denominator, thus resulting in division by a

larger number, which produces a smaller quotient. For example, suppose each series starts with the first value of 2. A common ratio of $\frac{1}{3}$ shows a convergence of the series to the number, 3. Note $S = \frac{a}{1-r}$, where $a$ represents the value of the first term and $r$ represents the common ratio. Thus, the convergence can be written as: $S = \frac{2}{1-\frac{1}{3}}$, which equals 3. A common ratio of $\frac{1}{2}$ shows a convergence of the series to the number, 4; $\frac{2}{1-\frac{1}{2}} = 4$.

29. A: When $y$ varies directly with $x$, the relationship is proportional, meaning the graph of the relationship passes through the origin, $(0, 0)$, indicating a $y$-intercept of 0. In other words, no constant amount is added to or subtracted from the term, containing the slope of the line. Statement (2) simply implies that the relationship is linear, with the constant rate of change noted. However, not all linear relationships are proportional. Such lines have $y$-intercepts, other than $(0, 0)$. Note. Not all linear relationships are proportional, but all proportional relationships are linear.

30. D: By definition, two triangles are similar if corresponding side lengths are proportional or if corresponding angles are congruent.

31. D: By definition, two lines are parallel, if a transversal, intersecting the lines, forms congruent corresponding angles or congruent alternate interior angles.

32. E: Statement (1) only eliminates composite numbers that are multiples of 2. Statement (2) is not helpful, since odd numbers can be either prime or composite.

33. A: A parabola is a function because each $x$-value is mapped to one and only one $y$-value. A vertical line, passing through the graph, will only intersect the parabola at one point. Statement (2) indicates an inverse function. The inverse of a relation can be a function, when the relation itself is not a function. A function maps each $x$-value to a unique $y$-value, whereas an inverse function maps each $y$-value to a unique $x$-value. For example, given the relation, $R = \{(1,3), (1,5), (2,7)\}$, the relation is not a function, since 1 is mapped to 3 and 5.

However, the inverse of the relation is a function, since each $y$-value is mapped to a unique $x$-value.

34. E: These statements simply reveal that the median is greater than both the mode and the range. There isn't any information given, relating the mode and the range.

35. E: The formula for finding the $n$th term of an arithmetic sequence is: $a_n = a_1 + (n-1)d$, where $a_n$ represents the value of the $n$th term, $a_1$ represents the value of the first term, $n$ represents the nth term number, and $d$ represents the common difference between the terms. Let the equation for arithmetic sequence A be: $a_n = a_1 + (n-1)d_a$ and let the equation for arithmetic sequence B be: $b_n = b_1 + (n-1)d_b$. The two statements explain that arithmetic sequence A will have a smaller value for the first term $(a_1 < b_1)$ and a larger common difference $(d_a > d_b)$. Substituting $n = 1$, the value of arithmetic sequence A will be less than B. Substituting $n = 2$, the value of arithmetic sequence A is $a_1 + d_a$, and the value of arithmetic sequence B is $b_1 + d_b$. Since no information is provided on whether the first term is greater or less than the difference for each sequence, it cannot be determined whether sequence A or B is greater in this scenario.

36. C: While it might be tempting to pick D since $\tan\left(sin^{-1}\frac{3}{5}\right)$ and $\tan\left(cos^{-1}\frac{4}{5}\right)$ are the same most of the time (when angle A is between 0 and 90°, for instance), both statements are necessary to know for certain that $\tan A = \frac{3}{4}$ and not $-\frac{3}{4}$.

The tangent of angle A can be represented by the ratio, $\frac{opposite}{adjacent}$. The sine of angle A can be represented by the ratio, $\frac{opposite}{hypotenuse}$. The cosine of angle A can be represented by the ratio, $\frac{adjacent}{hypotenuse}$. Since the cosine of angle A is $\frac{4}{5}$, the adjacent length is 4, and the hypotenuse length is 5. Since the sine of angle A is $\frac{3}{5}$, the opposite length is 3, and the hypotenuse length is 5, as previously determined. Thus, the tangent is $\frac{3}{4}$.

37. D: Considering the even numbers, starting with 0, the sequence can be written: 0, 2, 4, 6, .... Statement (1) indicates that the rate of change between subsequent even integers is even. This statement indicates that each subsequent term will change by an even value, indicating that each subsequent sum will also change by an even value, thus indicating an even sum. Statement (2) actually states that the rate of change in each subsequent sum is even, thus allowing the previous deduction to be made.

# Verbal Ability
## Reading Comprehension

1. A: The second sentence of the first paragraph states that peanut allergy is the most common cause of food-related death.

2. C: The passage implies that it is not always easy to know which foods have traces of peanuts in them and that it's important to make sure you know what you're eating. This is hard or impossible if you share someone else's food.

3. E: Paragraph two gives examples of symptoms of peanut allergies and, more specifically, examples of symptoms of anaphylaxis. A running or stuffy nose is given as a symptom of the former, but not of the latter.

4. C: The first paragraph states that the main purpose of DST it to make better use of daylight.

5. A: Energy conservation is discussed as a possible benefit of DST, not a negative effect of it.

6. D: The first paragraph states that DST involves setting clocks forward one hour in the spring and one hour backward in the fall.

7. C: This is discussed in second paragraph. None of the other statements are supported by the passage.

8. A: This sentence discusses an instance where a federal law was struck down because it was deemed to be unconstitutional.

9. A: The passage would be best described as historical. It gives an account of the history of judicial review in America.

10. B: The first paragraph talks about the muckrakers operating during the Progressive Era, and the rest of the passage discusses the specific corruption and societal ills that they brought to light.

11. D: This sentence states that the muckrakers "provided strong impetus to the ongoing Progressive Era reform movement."

12. C: The passage would be best characterized by the word "revealing." The theme of the muckrakers was to reveal things to the public that were previously kept hidden behind closed doors.

13. E: Pilgrim's Progress was the book from which the term "muckraker" was taken, but the book itself did not contribute to the success of the muckrakers.

## Sentence Correction

14. B: The pronoun "which" refers to the price. The original and choice E are run-on sentences. In choice C, "cost" is redundant with "price," and choice D is awkwardly phrased.

15. C: This answer establishes a list separated by series commas. The original changes the verb tense in mid-sentence, choices B and D are awkwardly phrased, and choice E changes the meaning slightly and is not appropriate following a comma.

16. E: The original is redundant, since "likely" and "would probably happen" mean the same thing. The same holds for choices B and C. Choice D is awkward and less succinct than the preferred choice E.

17. B: This answer specifies that it is the average population age that is increasing. All of the other choices simply indicate that the people in these towns are getting older, not that the average age is changing.

18. C: The pronoun "it" matches the word "team" for which it stands, and which is singular, not plural.

19. B: This answer simply defines the word "sonnet" in a dependent clause.

20. C: The dependent clause shows a consequence of the condition described in the first clause, and is not separated by a comma when introduced by a correlative conjunction ("so...that").

21. B: The noun "punishment" is modified by the adjective "severe."

22. D: The absence of the comma in the original version suggests that only some smoking has been linked to lung cancer, and that it is only that smoking which nutritionists are urging the public to stop. The comma makes it clear that all smoking is linked to cancer. Choice E is similar to the original. Choice B requires a comma to separate the independent clause. Choice C is awkwardly phrased.

23. E: This answer is far more succinct than choice D. The original version is slang usage. Choice C does not explicitly state that the disagreement is about the best practice.

24. C: This answer links the verb "affected" to the cause of the effect, i.e., the distress of the industry, for maximum clarity.

25. D: This answer makes use of the correlative conjunction "either...or" to link two equivalent portions of a sentence. Note that "either...also", "either...owing to", and "either...but" do not make sense.

26. B: The pronoun "it" used at the end of the sentence must refer to a singular noun. The word "medicine" in Choice B refers to the practice of medicine, and is singular. Note that there are many other ways to fix this sentence by replacing "it" with "them", for example, but they are not offered as choices.

27. E: Note that "he" and "she" are both subjects of the verb "to be able", and so must be in the subjective case. The objective "her" is suited to be the object of a verb.

## Critical Reasoning

28. B: Based on the statements in the paragraph above, the poll was specifically focused on the question of legal unions and/or marriages for the gay and lesbian population. Since the statements reflect no information or speculation about the percentage of gays and lesbians among the general population, both Statements A and D can be rejected out of hand, as there is no information or inference to draw on. Also, since the statements specifically reflect respondents' opinions on a specific population with regards to marriage, there is no general information from which to draw an overall opinion of marriage itself, which eliminates Statement C from consideration. Only the assertion in Statement B can reasonably be drawn from the statements in the question; thus, B is correct.

29. D: The assumptions of the argument are implicit in the statements used, so those statements must be examined in order to extract its assumptions. Although there are only two performers cited, the comparison being made is explicitly made only between the two listed; since there is no basis to assume the argument was constructed to apply to any other performers, Statement A can be rejected. There is no discussion of musical types in the argument, so no assumptions can be made about what genres are considered popular,

which disqualifies Statement B. As the argument is constructed, it applies only to the two cited directly in the statements, and requires no prior knowledge of music or these musicians; thus, Statement C is irrelevant. Only Statement D, which is indirectly stated in the conclusion and implied throughout, is relevant here; thus, D is correct.

30. B: In order for the argument to be weakened or refuted, there must be a condition or qualification that contradicts the conclusion without altering the statements given. With this in mind, Statement A is irrelevant, because the scheduling of the shifts does not affect who is assigned to which ones or the rules governing them. Since one specific emergency room is being discussed in the argument, the shifts Dr. James could work at a different emergency room have no bearing on the shifts being discussed, so Statement C is invalid. For identical reasons, Statement D is also invalid, as the mobile clinic is outside the scope of the argument. Only Statement B, which opens the possibility that the shifts discussed are separate from regularly scheduled shifts and thus Dr. James could already be scheduled for an emergency room shift, addresses the question, making B correct.

31. A: Since the argument is based on the perception of trust within a relationship, the completing phrase should reference the linchpin of the argument directly. Although issues of communication are implied to be a factor, there is no direct citing of this, nor is there any inferred reference, so Statement B is not suitable here. Both Statements C and D do not address the issue of trust perception, only potential side effects of this, which fails to logically complete the argument or support the main assertion; thus, both statements can be rejected. Only Statement A refers back to the central pillar of the argument and follows logically with the conclusion's first half; thus, A is the correct answer.

32. B: Since the thesis of the argument is that a direct relationship can be drawn between adaptability and time spent in an ecosystem, any assumption that would address time and/or adaptability could greatly affect the argument if wrong. Statement A can be discarded immediately, because it addresses the possible cause of the extinction event; all that matters here is that there was an extinction event, not its cause. Similarly, Statement C can be rejected, as it only concerns climate, not adaptability or time. While a weak

connection is made with the idea of time in Statement D, it is irrelevant because the extinction event, not time itself, was the agent of change; thus, Statement D can be rejected. Only Statement B addresses the unspoken assumption that mammals came along later and thus were less finely tuned to the environment, making them more adaptable; thus, B is correct.

33. C: Although there are several real-world factors that must be considered in a business environment, the manager's argument is based on a small subset of these factors, which must be considered in the context of the larger issues. Statement A, while initially weakly implied, is invalid because the manager has not explicitly weighed liability factors, choosing to focus solely on deadline issues. Since warranty issues are generated by customer usage, and the product has not been manufactured yet, Statement B is invalid. Time is the primary issue to the manager, which creates a connection to Statement D, but since the manager is deciding based on a defined deadline, the inference is too weak to use in this context. Only Statement C, which presupposes a practical limitation in product usage that the original conditions contradict, adequately answers the question, making C correct.

34. D: Since the point of the cockroach argument is to demonstrate their superiority through hardiness, the statement that best weakens that argument would downplay or disprove that quality. Statement A, since it argues for the adaptability of cockroaches, would support the cockroach argument, so it is invalid in this context. Similarly, Statement B would imply biological success, which supports the original argument. As a result, Statement B is also invalid in this context. Statement C is invalid because it refers to the larger role of cockroaches in the ecosystem, specifically the predator/prey relationship, and has no bearing on the relationship to other insects and the relative hardiness therein. Only Statement D, which would indicate a greater weakness in human habitation than other insect species, would contradict the cockroach argument's main conclusion if true, making D correct.

35. B: Since an analysis of the poll's veracity can only be based on the information given, any issues must be identifiable from that information. Since it is only known that a

predetermined index was used, and not what that index measured or how, there is no way to properly analyze that index's utility in this context, so Statement A is invalid here. The company poll was intended to measure employee satisfaction, so former employees would not be a valid sample population in any case, making Statement C also inapplicable. Finally, there is no mention of how the poll answers were recorded, so any speculation on that aspect is irrelevant to the argument, thereby eliminating Statement D. Only Statement B, which rightfully questions the objectivity of a company-administered poll, is relevant grounds for criticism, making B correct.

36. B: Statement A can be discarded out of hand, since the rate of refresh has a definite and noticeable effect on how an image is perceived (as cited in the argument); thus, A is patently false and is irrelevant to the argument. Statement C can also be rejected for similar reasons; due to differing mechanisms and higher technology, the capabilities of flat-panel plasma TVs are much different than older technology, and as cited in the argument, the statement in C is contradicted by the supporting statements. While Statement D is arguably true, since the argument is designed to help stave off such issues, it has no bearing on the argument's reasoning, and so can be rejected. Statement B, however, directly contradicts the conclusion by pointing out a reasonable and simpler alternative, so in this context, B is the correct answer.

37. C: The argument as written is intended to argue that the students mentioned will make excellent surgeons, but not that they must, or even intend to pursue that path. Additionally, the argument states that such students make excellent doctors and surgeons, which thus opens the possibility of not being a surgeon; thus, Statement A can be rejected. Statement B is invalid, because the argument states only that they are biological science majors, which has no bearing on their initial majors. Since the argument explicitly states that Riley does not play video games, the question of whether or not she is good is unanswerable, which makes Statement D inapplicable. However, while the first supporting statements reference college students, the argument does not explicitly state that Riley and her peers themselves are college students; thus, C is correct.

38. A: As the argument states, the challenges are over the fact that the novel is available to check out by children, so the other statements in the argument must be evaluated in that light. Since the challenges are specifically against one novel, the similarity to other novels that are available, if such novels exist, are irrelevant in this case, so Statement B can be rejected. The argument gives specific reasons for the general challenges to the novel, so any other possibility for the challenges is also irrelevant, which invalidates Statement C. Finally, since the challenges are directed toward the novel's availability with no reference to its actual circulation among children, Statement D has no bearing on the argument. Only Statement A, which refers a possible and reasonable reason behind the lack of challenges to the film version, is relevant in this context, making A correct.

39. A: There is an implied conflict of interest criticism inherent in the argument and also an implication that the report's conclusions are false. Option B is not a valid answer, because it refers to statistical evidence which does not exist in the argument. There is no "statistically insignificant sample" submitted in the argument, so this assertion cannot be evaluated. Option C is not valid for much the same reason; the argument may not be valid for any number of reasons, but it can only be criticized for elements which are present. While the statement expressed in Option C is true, the speculations are not addressed in the presentation of the argument. Nor is there a discussion of implied motivation. Option D is not valid, because the existence of evidence is not in question, only the validity of the argument. Only Option A addresses the argument as presented, and thus, only Option A is valid.

40. C: The flawed argument of the original statement makes two statements about two separate groups of individuals, and draws an unsupported conclusion about both of the groups. Option A is not a good choice because it does not follow the logical sequence of the original statement. Neither is the conclusion consistent with the original paragraph's conclusion. Options B and D are also ruled out based on the argument structure. Option B is ruled out because it has a logical argument structure with a correct conclusion, unlike the original paragraph, where the conclusion is flawed or erroneous. Option D is ruled out for the same reason; enough information is given in the statement to make a correct

conclusion. Only Option C follows the original structure of the argument, and in so doing, duplicates the flawed logic therein. Thus, Option C is correct.

41. B: The argument outlined in the paragraph explicitly draws a parallel between losing a relationship and losing a loved one. Therefore, logic would demand a conclusion in line with the argument's terms. While each of the options listed can be seen as reasonable consequences of the end of a romantic relationship, only Option B points to the parallels between the end of a relationship and the death of a loved one. The five-stage grieving process is compared to the sense of loss felt in grieving for an abruptly ended relationship. The other options focus on individual reactions to a situation, which are outside the scope and intent of the argument. There is no metaphorical linkage. Thus, only Option B is correct.

# Special Report: How to Overcome Your Fear of Math

If this article started by saying "Math," many of us would feel a shiver crawl up our spines, just by reading that simple word. Images of torturous years in those crippling desks of the math classes can become so vivid to our consciousness that we can almost smell those musty textbooks, and see the smudges of the #2 pencils on our fingers.

If you are still a student, feeling the impact of these sometimes overwhelming classroom sensations, you are not alone if you get anxious at just the thought of taking that compulsory math course. Does your heart beat just that much faster when you have to split the bill for lunch among your friends with a group of your friends? Do you truly believe that you simply don't have the brain for math? Certainly you're good at other things, but math just simply isn't one of them? Have you ever avoided activities, or other school courses because they appear to involve mathematics, with which you're simply not comfortable?

If any one or more of these "symptoms" can be applied to you, you could very well be suffering from a very real condition called "Math Anxiety."

It's not at all uncommon for people to think that they have some sort of math disability or allergy, when in actuality, their block is a direct result of the way in which they were taught math!

In the late 1950's with the dawning of the space age, New Math - a new "fuzzy math" reform that focuses on higher-order thinking, conceptual understanding and solving problems - took the country by storm. It's now becoming ever more clear that teachers were not supplied with the correct, practical and effective way in which they should be teaching new math so that students will understand the methods comfortably. So is it any wonder that so many students struggled so deeply, when their teachers were required to change their entire math systems without the foundation of proper training? Even if you have not been personally, directly affected by that precise event, its impact is still as rampant as ever.

Basically, the math teachers of today are either the teachers who began teaching the new math in the first place (without proper training) or they are the students of the math teachers who taught new math without proper training. Therefore, unless they had a unique, exceptional teacher, their primary, consistent examples of teaching math have been teachers using methods that are not conducive to the general understanding of the entire class. This explains why your discomfort (or fear) of math is not at all rare.

It is very clear why being called up to the chalk board to solve a math problem is such a common example of a terrifying situation for students - and it has very little to do with a fear of being in front of the class. Most of us have had a minimum of one humiliating experience while standing with chalk dusted fingers, with the eyes of every math student piercing through us. These are the images that haunt us all the way through adulthood. But it does not mean that we cannot learn math. It just means that we could be developing a solid case of math anxiety.

But what exactly is math anxiety? It's an very strong emotional sensation of anxiety, panic, or fear that people feel when they think about or must apply their ability to understand mathematics. Sufferers of math anxiety frequently believe that they are incapable of doing activities or taking classes that involve math skills. In fact, some people with math anxiety have developed such a fear that it has become a phobia; aptly named math phobia.

The incidence of math anxiety, especially among college students, but also among high school students, has risen considerably over the last 10 years, and currently this increase shows no signs of slowing down. Frequently students will even chose their college majors and programs based specifically on how little math will be compulsory for the completion of the degree.

The prevalence of math anxiety has become so dramatic on college campuses that many of these schools have special counseling programs that are designed to assist math anxious students to deal with their discomfort and their math problems.

Math anxiety itself is not an intellectual problem, as many people have been lead to believe; it is, in fact, an emotional problem that stems from improper math teaching techniques that have slowly built and reinforced these feelings. However, math anxiety can result in an intellectual problem when its symptoms interfere with a person's ability to learn and understand math.

The fear of math can cause a sort of "glitch" in the brain that can cause an otherwise clever person to stumble over even the simplest of math problems. A study by Dr. Mark H. Ashcraft of Cleveland State University in Ohio showed that college students who usually perform well, but who suffer from math anxiety, will suffer from fleeting lapses in their working memory when they are asked to perform even the most basic mental arithmetic. These same issues regarding memory were not present in the same students when they were required to answer questions that did not involve numbers. This very clearly demonstrated that the memory phenomenon is quite specific to only math.

So what exactly is it that causes this inhibiting math anxiety? Unfortunately it is not as simple as one answer, since math anxiety doesn't have one specific cause. Frequently math anxiety can result of a student's either negative experience or embarrassment with math or a math teacher in previous years.

These circumstances can prompt the student to believe that he or she is somehow deficient in his or her math abilities. This belief will consistently lead to a poor performance in math tests and courses in general, leading only to confirm the beliefs of the student's inability. This particular phenomenon is referred to as the "self-fulfilling prophecy" by the psychological community. Math anxiety will result in poor performance, rather than it being the other way around.

Dr. Ashcraft stated that math anxiety is a "It's a learned, almost phobic, reaction to math," and that it is not only people prone to anxiety, fear, or panic who can develop math anxiety. The image alone of doing math problems can send the blood pressure and heart rate to race, even in the calmest person.

The study by Dr. Ashcraft and his colleague Elizabeth P. Kirk, discovered that students who suffered from math anxiety were frequently stumped by issues of even the most basic math rules, such as "carrying over" a number, when performing a sum, or "borrowing" from a number when doing a subtraction. Lapses such as this occurred only on working memory questions involving numbers.

To explain the problem with memory, Ashcraft states that when math anxiety begins to take its effect, the sufferer experiences a rush of thoughts, leaving little room for the focus required to perform even the simplest of math problems. He stated that "you're draining away the energy you need for solving the problem by worrying about it."

The outcome is a "vicious cycle," for students who are sufferers of math anxiety. As math anxiety is developed, the fear it promotes stands in the way of learning, leading to a decrease in self-confidence in the ability to perform even simple arithmetic.

A large portion of the problem lies in the ways in which math is taught to students today. In the US, students are frequently taught the rules of math, but rarely will they learn why a specific approach to a math problems work. Should students be provided with a foundation of "deeper understanding" of math, it may prevent the development of phobias.

Another study that was published in the Journal of Experimental Psychology by Dr. Jamie Campbell and Dr. Qilin Xue of the University of Saskatchewan in Saskatoon, Canada, reflected the same concepts. The researchers in this study looked at university students who were educated in Canada and China, discovering that the Chinese students could generally outperform the Canadian-educated students when it came to solving complex math problems involving procedural knowledge - the ability to know how to solve a math problem, instead of simply having ideas memorized.

A portion of this result seemed to be due to the use of calculators within both elementary and secondary schools; while Canadians frequently used them, the Chinese students did not.

However, calculators were not the only issue. Since Chinese-educated students also outperformed Canadian-educated students in complex math, it is suggested that cultural factors may also have an impact. However, the short-cut of using the calculator may hinder the development of the problem solving skills that are key to performing well in math.

Though it is critical that students develop such fine math skills, it is easier said than done. It would involve an overhaul of the training among all elementary and secondary educators, changing the education major in every college.

## Math Myths

One problem that contributes to the progression of math anxiety, is the belief of many math myths. These erroneous math beliefs include the following:

Men are better in math than women - however, research has failed to demonstrate that there is any difference in math ability between the sexes.
There is a single best way to solve a math problem - however, the majority of math problems can be solved in a number of different ways. By saying that there is only one way to solve a math problem, the thinking and creative skills of the student are held back.

Some people have a math mind, and others do not - in truth, the majority of people have much more potential for their math capabilities than they believe of themselves.
It is a bad thing to count by using your fingers - counting by using fingers has actually shown that an understanding of arithmetic has been established.

People who are skilled in math can do problems quickly in their heads - in actuality, even math professors will review their example problems before they teach them in their classes.

The anxieties formed by these myths can frequently be perpetuated by a range of mind games that students seem to play with themselves. These math mind games include the following beliefs:

I don't perform math fast enough - actually everyone has a different rate at which he or she can learn. The speed of the solving of math problems is not important as long as the student can solve it.

I don't have the mind for math - this belief can inhibit a student's belief in him or herself, and will therefore interfere with the student's real ability to learn math.

I got the correct answer, but it was done the wrong way - there is no single best way to complete a math problem. By believing this, a student's creativity and overall understanding of math is hindered.

If I can get the correct answer, then it is too simple - students who suffer from math anxiety frequently belittle their own abilities when it comes to their math capabilities.
Math is unrelated to my "real" life - by freeing themselves of the fear of math, math anxiety sufferers are only limiting their choices and freedoms for the rest of their life.

Fortunately, there are many ways to help those who suffer from math anxiety. Since math anxiety is a learned, psychological response to doing or thinking about math, that interferes with the sufferer's ability to understand and perform math, it is not at all a reflection of the sufferer's true math skills and abilities.

# Helpful Strategies

Many strategies and therapies have been developed to help students to overcome their math anxious responses. Some of these helpful strategies include the following:

Reviewing and learning basic arithmetic principles, techniques and methods. Frequently math anxiety is a result of the experience of many students with early negative situations, and these students have never truly developed a strong base in basic arithmetic, especially in the case of multiplication and fractions. Since math is a discipline that is built on an accumulative foundation, where the concepts are built upon gradually from simpler concepts, a student who has not achieved a solid basis in arithmetic will experience difficulty in learning higher order math. Taking a remedial math course, or a short math course that focuses on arithmetic can often make a considerable difference in reducing the anxious response that math anxiety sufferers have with math.

Becoming aware of any thoughts, actions and feelings that are related to math and responses to math. Math anxiety has a different effect on different students. Therefore it is very important to become familiar with any reactions that the math anxiety sufferer may have about him/herself and the situation when math has been encountered. If the sufferer becomes aware of any irrational or unrealistic thoughts, it's possible to better concentrate on replacing these thoughts with more positive and realistic ones.

Find help! Math anxiety, as we've mentioned, is a learned response, that is reinforced repeatedly over a period of time, and is therefore not something that can be eliminated instantaneously. Students can more effectively reduce their anxious responses with the help of many different services that are readily available. Seeking the assistance of a psychologist or counselor, especially one with a specialty in math anxiety, can assist the sufferer in performing an analysis of his/her psychological response to math, as well as learning anxiety management skills, and developing effective coping strategies. Other great tools are tutors, classes that teach better abilities to take better notes in math class, and other math learning aids.

Learning the mathematic vocabulary will instantly provide a better chance for understanding new concepts. One major issue among students is the lack of understanding of the terms and vocabulary that are common jargon within math classes. Typically math classes will utilize words in a completely different way from the way in which they are utilized in all other subjects. Students easily mistake their lack of understanding the math terms with their mathematical abilities.

Learning anxiety reducing techniques and methods for anxiety management. Anxiety greatly interferes with a student's ability to concentrate, think clearly, pay attention, and remember new concepts. When these same students can learn to relax, using anxiety management techniques, the student can regain his or her ability to control his or her emotional and physical symptoms of anxiety that interfere with the capabilities of mental processing.

Working on creating a positive overall attitude about mathematics. Looking at math with a positive attitude will reduce anxiety through the building of a positive attitude.

Learning to self-talk in a positive way. Pep talking oneself through a positive self talk can greatly assist in overcoming beliefs in math myths or the mind games that may be played. Positive self-talking is an effective way to replace the negative thoughts - the ones that create the anxiety. Even if the sufferer doesn't believe the statements at first, it plants a positive seed in the subconscious, and allows a positive outlook to grow.

Beyond this, students should learn effective math class, note taking and studying techniques. Typically, the math anxious students will avoid asking questions to save themselves from embarrassment. They will sit in the back of classrooms, and refrain from seeking assistance from the professor. Moreover, they will put off studying for math until the very last moment, since it causes them such substantial discomfort. Alone, or a combination of these negative behaviors work only to reduce the anxiety of the students, but in reality, they are actually building a substantially more intense anxiety.

There are many different positive behaviors that can be adopted by math anxious students, so that they can learn to better perform within their math classes.

Sit near the front of the class. This way, there will be fewer distractions, and there will be more of a sensation of being a part of the topic of discussion.
If any questions arise, ASK! If one student has a question, then there are certain to be others who have the same question but are too nervous to ask - perhaps because they have not yet learned how to deal with their own math anxiety.

Seek extra help from the professor after class or during office hours.

Prepare, prepare, prepare - read textbook material before the class, do the homework and work out any problems available within the textbook. Math skills are developed through practice and repetition, so the more practice and repetition, the better the math skills.

Review the material once again after class, to repeat it another time, and to reinforce the new concepts that were learned.

Beyond these tactics that can be taken by the students themselves, teachers and parents need to know that they can also have a large impact on the reduction of math anxiety within students.

As parents and teachers, there is a natural desire to help students to learn and understand how they will one day utilize different math techniques within their everyday lives. But when the student or teacher displays the symptoms of a person who has had nightmarish memories regarding math, where hesitations then develop in the instruction of students, these fears are automatically picked up by the students and commonly adopted as their own.

However, it is possible for teachers and parents to move beyond their own fears to better educate students by overcoming their own hesitations and learning to enjoy math.

Begin by adopting the outlook that math is a beautiful, imaginative or living thing. Of course, we normally think of mathematics as numbers that can be added or subtracted, multiplied or divided, but that is simply the beginning of it.

By thinking of math as something fun and imaginative, parents and teachers can teach children different ways to manipulate numbers, for example in balancing a checkbook. Parents rarely tell their children that math is everywhere around us; in nature, art, and even architecture. Usually, this is because they were never shown these relatively simple connections. But that pattern can break very simply through the participation of parents and teachers.

The beauty and hidden wonders of mathematics can easily be emphasized through a focus that can open the eyes of students to the incredible mathematical patterns that arise everywhere within the natural world. Observations and discussions can be made into things as fascinating as spider webs, leaf patterns, sunflowers and even coastlines. This makes math not only beautiful, but also inspiring and (dare we say) fun!

## Pappas Method

For parents and teachers to assist their students in discovering the true wonders of mathematics, the techniques of Theoni Pappas can easily be applied, as per her popular and celebrated book "Fractals, Googols and Other Mathematical Tales." Pappas used to be a math phobia sufferer and created a fascinating step-by-step program for parents and teachers to use in order to teach students the joy of math.

Her simple, constructive step-by-step program goes as follows:

Don't let your fear of math come across to your kids - Parents must be careful not to perpetuate the mathematical myth - that math is only for specially talented "math types." Strive not to make comments like; "they don't like math" or "I have never been good at math." When children overhear comments like these from their primary role models they begin to dread math before even considering a chance of experiencing its wonders. It is important to encourage your children to read and explore the rich world of mathematics, and to practice mathematics without imparting negative biases.

Don't immediately associate math with computation (counting) - It is very important to realize that math is not just numbers and computations, but a realm of exciting ideas that touch every part of our lives -from making a telephone call to how the hair grows on someone's head. Take your children outside and point out real objects that display math concepts. For example, show them the symmetry of a leaf or angles on a building. Take a close look at the spirals in a spider web or intricate patterns of a snowflake.

Help your child understand why math is important - Math improves problem solving, increases competency and should be applied in different ways. It's the same as reading. You can learn the basics of reading without ever enjoying a novel. But, where's the excitement in that? With math, you could stop with the basics. But why when there is so much more to be gained by a fuller Understanding? Life is so much more enriching when we go beyond the basics. Stretch your children's minds to become involved in mathematics in ways that will not only be practical but also enhance their lives.

Make math as "hands on" as possible - Mathematicians participate in mathematics. To really experience math encourage your child to dig in and tackle problems in creative ways. Help them learn how to manipulate numbers using concrete references they understand as well as things they can see or touch. Look for patterns everywhere, explore shapes and symmetries. How many octagons do you see each day on the way to the grocery store? Play math puzzles and games and then encourage your child to try to invent their own. And, whenever possible, help your child realize a mathematical conclusion with real and tangible results. For example, measure out a full glass of juice with a measuring cup and then ask your child to drink half. Measure what is left. Does it measure half of a cup?

Read books that make math exciting:

Fractals, Googols and Other Mathematical Tales introduces an animated cat who explains fractals, tangrams and other mathematical concepts you've probably never heard of to children in terms they can understand. This book can double as a great text book by using one story per lesson.

A Wrinkle in Time is a well-loved classic, combining fantasy and science.

The Joy of Mathematics helps adults explore the beauty of mathematics that is all around.

The Math Curse is an amusing book for 4-8 year olds.

The Gnarly Gnews is a free, humorous bi-monthly newsletter on mathematics.

The Phantom Tollbooth is an Alice in Wonderland-style adventure into the worlds of words and numbers.

Use the internet to help your child explore the fascinating world of mathematics.

Web Math provides a powerful set of math-solvers that gives you instant answers to the stickiest problems.

Math League has challenging math materials and contests for fourth grade and above.

Silver Burdett Ginn Mathematics offers Internet-based math activities for grades K-6.

The Gallery of Interactive Geometry is full of fascinating, interactive geometry activities.


Math is very much like a language of its own.  And like any second language, it will get rusty if it is not practiced enough.  For that reason, students should always be looking into new ways to keep understanding and brushing up on their math skills, to be certain that foundations do not crumble, inhibiting the learning of new levels of math.

There are many different books, services and websites that have been developed to take the fear out of math, and to help even the most uncertain student develop self confidence in his or her math capabilities.


There is no reason for math or math classes to be a frightening experience, nor should it drive a student crazy, making them believe that they simply don't have the "math brain" that is needed to solve certain problems.


There are friendly ways to tackle such problems and it's all a matter of dispelling myths and creating a solid math foundation.

Concentrate on re-learning the basics and feeling better about yourself in math, and you'll find that the math brain you've always wanted, was there all along.

# Special Report: Analyzing a Potential Scholarship/Fellowship

When analyzing a potential scholarship a student should identify the following information:

- Name of the scholarship
- Sponsor
- Sponsor e-mail or mailing address (phone number)
- Contact person
- Deadline
- Field of study required
- Value
- Rules of the application
- Required information for the scholarship packet
- Breakdown of emphasis on grades/leadership/athletics

## Internet scholarship/fellowship search companies

Many internet scholarship search companies are designed to separate students and their money. Often a front end fee is required focusing on the potential upside of the transaction, however many times that front end charge is never returned to the student. Some of these companies have been set up to scam unsuspecting students out of millions of dollars. In addition, prosecution of these companies is often complicated and a drawn out process. Many students simply give up trying to get their money back, and the scam artists win big.

# Sample Application Checklist

- 1. Official college and high school transcripts with the seal of the school
- Recommendation letters
- Resume may be required
- Official score report of test required (GRE, MCAT, GMAT)
- List of work experience
- List of volunteer work
- Proof of awards and commendations
- List of references
- Payment of application fee in correct form
- Re-check due date of application

# Potential Scholarships/Fellowships Available

- Religious groups
- Racial groups
- Community organizations
- Athletic organizations
- Parent's employment
- Veteran's groups
- Unions
- Lion's club
- Key club
- Parent-teacher organizations
- Specialty clubs
- Hospitals
- Library
- American Legion

- Chamber of Commerce
- Banks
- Private Foundations
- Civic Groups
- Fire and Police Departments

## FAFSA

Free Application for Federal Student Aid – completed upon start of graduate program if graduate program is receiving federal dollars.  If the program is not receiving federal dollars, low interest federal loans and grants may not be available at that school.

Run a trial test of the FAFSA (www.finaid.org/calculators/) – play with the various factors to determine your estimated financial aid. The potential reward on the investment of your time could be quite exceptional.

Free scholarship searches with:

www.fastweb.com

www.fastaid.com/scholarships

## Potential Reference Web-sites

www.Gradschools.com

www.Lawschool.com

www.StudentDoctor.com

www.EssayEdge.com

www.asgs.org  (Thesis assistance)

www.cgsnet.org  (Graduate education articles)

www.ilrg.com (Website that focuses on law)

# Admission Committee Review

Your application for graduate school will probably end up being scored according to letters of recommendation, academic achievements, interview results, and essay results. It is quite possible that a group of 4-10 reviewers will pour over your information to determine if you are an appropriate selection for graduate school. Moreover, it is possible that your application will be assigned a number of points based upon the above criteria. In addition, a cut-off number will probably be established. Depending on where your value falls in relationship to the cut-off number you may or may not be accepted to graduate school. It is absolutely critical that each aspect of the application generates the highest number of possible points to create admission to graduate school.

# Special Report: What is Test Anxiety and How to Overcome It?

The very nature of tests caters to some level of anxiety, nervousness or tension, just as we feel for any important event that occurs in our lives. A little bit of anxiety or nervousness can be a good thing. It helps us with motivation, and makes achievement just that much sweeter. However, too much anxiety can be a problem; especially if it hinders our ability to function and perform.

"Test anxiety," is the term that refers to the emotional reactions that some test-takers experience when faced with a test or exam. Having a fear of testing and exams is based upon a rational fear, since the test-taker's performance can shape the course of an academic career. Nevertheless, experiencing excessive fear of examinations will only interfere with the test-takers ability to perform and his/her chances to be successful.

There are a large variety of causes that can contribute to the development and sensation of test anxiety. These include, but are not limited to lack of performance and worrying about issues surrounding the test.

## Lack of Preparation

Lack of preparation can be identified by the following behaviors or situations:

- Not scheduling enough time to study, and therefore cramming the night before the test or exam
- Managing time poorly, to create the sensation that there is not enough time to do everything
- Failing to organize the text information in advance, so that the study material consists of the entire text and not simply the pertinent information
- Poor overall studying habits

Worrying, on the other hand, can be related to both the test-taker and many other factors around him/her that will be affected by the results of the test. These include worrying about:

- Previous performances on similar exams, or exams in general
- How friends and other students are achieving
- The negative consequences that will result from a poor grade or failure

There are three primary elements to test anxiety: physical components, which involve the same typical bodily reactions as those to acute anxiety (to be discussed below); emotional factors, which have to do with fear or panic; and mental or cognitive issues, which concern attention spans and memory abilities.

## Physical Signals

There are many different symptoms of test anxiety, and these are not limited to mental and emotional strain. Frequently there are a range of physical signals that will let a test taker know that he/she is suffering from test anxiety. These bodily changes can include the following:

- Perspiring
- Sweaty palms
- Wet, trembling hands
- Nausea
- Dry mouth
- A knot in the stomach
- Headache
- Faintness
- Muscle tension
- Aching shoulders, back and neck

- Rapid heart beat
- Feeling too hot/cold

To recognize the sensation of test anxiety, a test-taker should monitor him/herself for the following sensations:

- The physical distress symptoms as listed above
- Emotional sensitivity, expressing emotional feelings such as the need to cry or laugh too much, or a sensation of anger or helplessness
- A decreased ability to think, causing the test-taker to blank out or have racing thoughts that are hard to organize or control.

Though most students will feel some level of anxiety when faced with a test or exam, the majority can cope with that anxiety and maintain it at a manageable level. However, those who cannot are faced with a very real and very serious condition, which can and should be controlled for the immeasurable benefit of this sufferer.

Naturally, these sensations lead to negative results for the testing experience. The most common effects of test anxiety have to do with nervousness and mental blocking.

## Nervousness

Nervousness can appear in several different levels:

- The test-taker's difficulty, or even inability to read and understand the questions on the test
- The difficulty or inability to organize thoughts to a coherent form
- The difficulty or inability to recall key words and concepts relating to the testing questions (especially essays)
- The receipt of poor grades on a test, though the test material was well known by the test taker

Conversely, a person may also experience mental blocking, which involves:

- Blanking out on test questions
- Only remembering the correct answers to the questions when the test has already finished

Fortunately for test anxiety sufferers, beating these feelings, to a large degree, has to do with proper preparation. When a test taker has a feeling of preparedness, then anxiety will be dramatically lessened.

The first step to resolving anxiety issues is to distinguish which of the two types of anxiety are being suffered. If the anxiety is a direct result of a lack of preparation, this should be considered a normal reaction, and the anxiety level (as opposed to the test results) shouldn't be anything to worry about. However, if, when adequately prepared, the test-taker still panics, blanks out, or seems to overreact, this is not a fully rational reaction. While this can be considered normal too, there are many ways to combat and overcome these effects.

Remember that anxiety cannot be entirely eliminated; however, there are ways to minimize it, to make the anxiety easier to manage. Preparation is one of the best ways to minimize test anxiety. Therefore the following techniques are wise in order to best fight off any anxiety that may want to build.

To begin with, try to avoid cramming before a test, whenever it is possible. By trying to memorize an entire term's worth of information in one day, you'll be shocking your system, and not giving yourself a very good chance to absorb the information. This is an easy path to anxiety, so for those who suffer from test anxiety, cramming should not even be considered an option.

Instead of cramming, work throughout the semester to combine all of the material which is presented throughout the semester, and work on it gradually as the course goes by, making sure to master the main concepts first, leaving minor details for a week or so before the test.

To study for the upcoming exam, be sure to pose questions that may be on the examination, to gauge the ability to answer them by integrating the ideas from your texts, notes and lectures, as well as any supplementary readings.

If it is truly impossible to cover all of the information that was covered in that particular term, concentrate on the most important portions, that can be covered very well. Learn these concepts as best as possible, so that when the test comes, a goal can be made to use these concepts as presentations of your knowledge.

In addition to study habits, changes in attitude are critical to beating a struggle with test anxiety. In fact, an improvement of the perspective over the entire test-taking experience can actually help a test taker to enjoy studying and therefore improve the overall experience. Be certain not to overemphasize the significance of the grade - know that the result of the test is neither a reflection of self worth, nor is it a measure of intelligence; one grade will not predict a person's future success.

To improve an overall testing outlook, the following steps should be tried:

Keeping in mind that the most reasonable expectation for taking a test is to expect to try to demonstrate as much of what you know as you possibly can.
Reminding ourselves that a test is only one test; this is not the only one, and there will be others.
The thought of thinking of oneself in an irrational, all-or-nothing term should be avoided at all costs.

A reward should be designated for after the test, so there's something to look forward to. Whether it is going to a movie, going out to eat, or simply visiting friends, schedule it in advance, and do it no matter what result is expected on the exam.

Test-takers should also keep in mind that the basics are some of the most important things, even beyond anti-anxiety techniques and studying. Never neglect the basic social, emotional and biological needs, in order to try to absorb information. In order to best achieve, these three factors must be held as just as important as the studying itself.

## Study Steps

Remember the following important steps for studying:

Maintain healthy nutrition and exercise habits. Continue both your recreational activities and social pass times. These both contribute to your physical and emotional well being.
Be certain to get a good amount of sleep, especially the night before the test, because when you're overtired you are not able to perform to the best of your best ability.
Keep the studying pace to a moderate level by taking breaks when they are needed, and varying the work whenever possible, to keep the mind fresh instead of getting bored. When enough studying has been done that all the material that can be learned has been learned, and the test taker is prepared for the test, stop studying and do something relaxing such as listening to music, watching a movie, or taking a warm bubble bath.

There are also many other techniques to minimize the uneasiness or apprehension that is experienced along with test anxiety before, during, or even after the examination. In fact, there are a great deal of things that can be done to stop anxiety from interfering with lifestyle and performance. Again, remember that anxiety will not be eliminated entirely, and it shouldn't be. Otherwise that "up" feeling for exams would not exist, and most of us depend on that sensation to perform better than usual. However, this anxiety has to be at a level that is manageable.

Of course, as we have just discussed, being prepared for the exam is half the battle right away. Attending all classes, finding out what knowledge will be expected on the exam, and knowing the exam schedules are easy steps to lowering anxiety. Keeping up with work will remove the need to cram, and efficient study habits will eliminate wasted time. Studying should be done in an ideal location for concentration, so that it is simple to become interested in the material and give it complete attention. A method such as SQ3R (Survey, Question, Read, Recite, Review) is a wonderful key to follow to make sure that the study habits are as effective as possible, especially in the case of learning from a textbook. Flashcards are great techniques for memorization. Learning to take good notes will mean that notes will be full of useful information, so that less sifting will need to be done to seek out what is pertinent for studying. Reviewing notes after class and then again on occasion will keep the information fresh in the mind. From notes that have been taken summary sheets and outlines can be made for simpler reviewing.

A study group can also be a very motivational and helpful place to study, as there will be a sharing of ideas, all of the minds can work together, to make sure that everyone understands, and the studying will be made more interesting because it will be a social occasion.

Basically, though, as long as the test-taker remains organized and self confident, with efficient study habits, less time will need to be spent studying, and higher grades will be achieved.

There are many useful steps to become more self-confident. The first of these is "self talk." It has been shown through extensive research, that self-talk for students who suffer from test anxiety, should be well monitored, in order to make sure that it contributes to self confidence as opposed to sinking the student. Frequently the self talk of test-anxious students is negative or self-defeating, thinking that everyone else is smarter and faster, that they always mess up, and that if they don't do well, they'll fail the entire course. It is important to decreasing anxiety that awareness is made of self talk. Try writing any negative self thoughts and then disputing them with a positive statement instead. Begin self-encouragement as though it was a friend speaking.

Repeat positive statements to help reprogram the mind to believing in successes instead of failures.

## Helpful Techniques

Other extremely helpful techniques include:

- Self-visualization of doing well and reaching goals
- While aiming for an "A" level of understanding, don't try to "overprotect" by setting your expectations lower. This will only convince the mind to stop studying in order to meet the lower expectations.
- Don't make comparisons with the results or habits of other students. These are individual factors, and different things work for different people, causing different results.
- Strive to become an expert in learning what works well, and what can be done in order to improve. Consider collecting this data in a journal.
- Create rewards for after studying instead of doing things before studying that will only turn into avoidance behaviors.
- Make a practice of relaxing - by using methods such as progressive relaxation, self-hypnosis, guided imagery, etc - in order to make relaxation an automatic sensation.
- Work on creating a state of relaxed concentration so that concentrating will take on the focus of the mind, so that none will be wasted on worrying.
- Take good care of the physical self by eating well and getting enough sleep.
- Plan in time for exercise and stick to this plan.

Beyond these techniques, there are other methods to be used before, during and after the test that will help the test-taker perform well in addition to overcoming anxiety.

Before the exam comes the academic preparation. This involves establishing a study schedule and beginning at least one week before the actual date of the test. By doing this, the anxiety of not having enough time to study for the test will be automatically eliminated. Moreover, this will make the studying a much more effective experience, ensuring that the learning will be an easier process. This relieves much undue pressure on the test-taker.

Summary sheets, note cards, and flash cards with the main concepts and examples of these main concepts should be prepared in advance of the actual studying time. A topic should never be eliminated from this process. By omitting a topic because it isn't expected to be on the test is only setting up the test-taker for anxiety should it actually appear on the exam. Utilize the course syllabus for laying out the topics that should be studied. Carefully go over the notes that were made in class, paying special attention to any of the issues that the professor took special care to emphasize while lecturing in class. In the textbooks, use the chapter review, or if possible, the chapter tests, to begin your review.

It may even be possible to ask the instructor what information will be covered on the exam, or what the format of the exam will be (for example, multiple choice, essay, free form, true-false). Additionally, see if it is possible to find out how many questions will be on the test. If a review sheet or sample test has been offered by the professor, make good use of it, above anything else, for the preparation for the test. Another great resource for getting to know the examination is reviewing tests from previous semesters. Use these tests to review, and aim to achieve a 100% score on each of the possible topics. With a few exceptions, the goal that you set for yourself is the highest one that you will reach.

Take all of the questions that were assigned as homework, and rework them to any other possible course material. The more problems reworked, the more skill and confidence will form as a result. When forming the solution to a problem, write out each of the steps. Don't simply do head work. By doing as many steps on paper as possible, much clarification and therefore confidence will be formed. Do this with as many homework problems as possible, before checking the answers. By checking the answer after each problem, a reinforcement will exist, that will not be on the exam.

- 311 -

Study situations should be as exam-like as possible, to prime the test-taker's system for the experience. By waiting to check the answers at the end, a psychological advantage will be formed, to decrease the stress factor.

Another fantastic reason for not cramming is the avoidance of confusion in concepts, especially when it comes to mathematics. 8-10 hours of study will become one hundred percent more effective if it is spread out over a week or at least several days, instead of doing it all in one sitting. Recognize that the human brain requires time in order to assimilate new material, so frequent breaks and a span of study time over several days will be much more beneficial.

Additionally, don't study right up until the point of the exam. Studying should stop a minimum of one hour before the exam begins. This allows the brain to rest and put things in their proper order. This will also provide the time to become as relaxed as possible when going into the examination room. The test-taker will also have time to eat well and eat sensibly. Know that the brain needs food as much as the rest of the body. With enough food and enough sleep, as well as a relaxed attitude, the body and the mind are primed for success.

Avoid any anxious classmates who are talking about the exam. These students only spread anxiety, and are not worth sharing the anxious sentimentalities.

Before the test also involves creating a positive attitude, so mental preparation should also be a point of concentration. There are many keys to creating a positive attitude. Should fears become rushing in, make a visualization of taking the exam, doing well, and seeing an A written on the paper. Write out a list of affirmations that will bring a feeling of confidence, such as "I am doing well in my English class," "I studied well and know my material," "I enjoy this class." Even if the affirmations aren't believed at first, it sends a positive message to the subconscious which will result in an alteration of the overall belief system, which is the system that creates reality.

If a sensation of panic begins, work with the fear and imagine the very worst! Work through the entire scenario of not passing the test, failing the entire course, and dropping out of school, followed by not getting a job, and pushing a shopping cart through the dark alley where you'll live. This will place things into perspective! Then, practice deep breathing and create a visualization of the opposite situation - achieving an "A" on the exam, passing the entire course, receiving the degree at a graduation ceremony.

On the day of the test, there are many things to be done to ensure the best results, as well as the most calm outlook. The following stages are suggested in order to maximize test-taking potential:

Begin the examination day with a moderate breakfast, and avoid any coffee or beverages with caffeine if the test taker is prone to jitters. Even people who are used to managing caffeine can feel jittery or light-headed when it is taken on a test day.

Attempt to do something that is relaxing before the examination begins. As last minute cramming clouds the mastering of overall concepts, it is better to use this time to create a calming outlook.

Be certain to arrive at the test location well in advance, in order to provide time to select a location that is away from doors, windows and other distractions, as well as giving enough time to relax before the test begins.
Keep away from anxiety generating classmates who will upset the sensation of stability and relaxation that is being attempted before the exam.

Should the waiting period before the exam begins cause anxiety, create a self-distraction by reading a light magazine or something else that is relaxing and simple.

During the exam itself, read the entire exam from beginning to end, and find out how much time should be allotted to each individual problem. Once writing the exam, should more time be taken for a problem, it should be abandoned, in order to begin another problem. If there is time at the end, the unfinished problem can always be returned to and completed.

Read the instructions very carefully - twice - so that unpleasant surprises won't follow during or after the exam has ended.

When writing the exam, pretend that the situation is actually simply the completion of homework within a library, or at home. This will assist in forming a relaxed atmosphere, and will allow the brain extra focus for the complex thinking function.

Begin the exam with all of the questions with which the most confidence is felt. This will build the confidence level regarding the entire exam and will begin a quality momentum. This will also create encouragement for trying the problems where uncertainty resides.
Going with the "gut instinct" is always the way to go when solving a problem. Second guessing should be avoided at all costs. Have confidence in the ability to do well.

For essay questions, create an outline in advance that will keep the mind organized and make certain that all of the points are remembered. For multiple choice, read every answer, even if the correct one has been spotted - a better one may exist.

Continue at a pace that is reasonable and not rushed, in order to be able to work carefully. Provide enough time to go over the answers at the end, to check for small errors that can be corrected.

Should a feeling of panic begin, breathe deeply, and think of the feeling of the body releasing sand through its pores. Visualize a calm, peaceful place, and include all of the sights, sounds and sensations of this image. Continue the deep breathing, and take a few minutes to continue this with closed eyes. When all is well again, return to the test.

Remember, one's own reality can be created, so as long as the belief is there, success will follow. And remember: anxiety can happen later, right now, there's an exam to be written!

After the examination is complete, whether there is a feeling for a good grade or a bad grade, don't dwell on the exam, and be certain to follow through on the reward that was promised...and enjoy it! Don't dwell on any mistakes that have been made, as there is nothing that can be done at this point anyway.

Additionally, don't begin to study for the next test right away. Do something relaxing for a while, and let the mind relax and prepare itself to begin absorbing information again.

From the results of the exam - both the grade and the entire experience, be certain to learn from what has gone on. Perfect studying habits and work some more on confidence in order to make the next examination experience even better than the last one.

Learn to avoid places where openings occurred for laziness, procrastination and day dreaming.

Use the time between this exam and the next one to better learn to relax, even learning to relax on cue, so that any anxiety can be controlled during the next exam. Learn how to relax the body. Slouch in your chair if that helps. Tighten and then relax all of the different muscle groups, one group at a time, beginning with the feet and then working all the way up to the neck and face. This will ultimately relax the muscles more than they were to begin with. Learn how to breathe deeply and comfortably, and focus on this breathing going in and out as a relaxing thought. With every exhale, repeat the word "relax."

As common as test anxiety is, it is very possible to overcome it. Make yourself one of the test-takers who overcome this frustrating hindrance.

# Special Report: Retaking the Test: What Are Your Chances at Improving Your Score?

After going through the experience of taking a major test, many test takers feel that once is enough. The test usually comes during a period of transition in the test taker's life, and taking the test is only one of a series of important events. With so many distractions and conflicting recommendations, it may be difficult for a test taker to rationally determine whether or not he should retake the test after viewing his scores.

The importance of the test usually only adds to the burden of the retake decision. However, don't be swayed by emotion. There a few simple questions that you can ask yourself to guide you as you try to determine whether a retake would improve your score:

1. What went wrong? Why wasn't your score what you expected?

Can you point to a single factor or problem that you feel caused the low score? Were you sick on test day? Was there an emotional upheaval in your life that caused a distraction? Were you late for the test or not able to use the full time allotment? If you can point to any of these specific, individual problems, then a retake should definitely be considered.

2. Is there enough time to improve?

Many problems that may show up in your score report may take a lot of time for improvement. A deficiency in a particular math skill may require weeks or months of tutoring and studying to improve. If you have enough time to improve an identified weakness, then a retake should definitely be considered.

3. How will additional scores be used? Will a score average, highest score, or most recent score be used?

Different test scores may be handled completely differently. If you've taken the test multiple times, sometimes your highest score is used, sometimes your average score is computed and used, and sometimes your most recent score is used. Make sure you understand what method will be used to evaluate your scores, and use that to help you determine whether a retake should be considered.

4. Are my practice test scores significantly higher than my actual test score?

If you have taken a lot of practice tests and are consistently scoring at a much higher level than your actual test score, then you should consider a retake. However, if you've taken five practice tests and only one of your scores was higher than your actual test score, or if your practice test scores were only slightly higher than your actual test score, then it is unlikely that you will significantly increase your score.

5. Do I need perfect scores or will I be able to live with this score? Will this score still allow me to follow my dreams?

What kind of score is acceptable to you? Is your current score "good enough?" Do you have to have a certain score in order to pursue the future of your dreams? If you won't be happy with your current score, and there's no way that you could live with it, then you should consider a retake. However, don't get your hopes up. If you are looking for significant improvement, that may or may not be possible. But if you won't be happy otherwise, it is at least worth the effort.

Remember that there are other considerations. To achieve your dream, it is likely that your grades may also be taken into account. A great test score is usually not the only thing necessary to succeed. Make sure that you aren't overemphasizing the importance of a high test score.

Furthermore, a retake does not always result in a higher score. Some test takers will score lower on a retake, rather than higher. One study shows that one-fourth of test takers will achieve a significant improvement in test score, while one-sixth of test takers will actually show a decrease. While this shows that most test takers will improve, the majority will only improve their scores a little and a retake may not be worth the test taker's effort.

Finally, if a test is taken only once and is considered in the added context of good grades on the part of a test taker, the person reviewing the grades and scores may be tempted to assume that the test taker just had a bad day while taking the test, and may discount the low test score in favor of the high grades. But if the test is retaken and the scores are approximately the same, then the validity of the low scores are only confirmed. Therefore, a retake could actually hurt a test taker by definitely bracketing a test taker's score ability to a limited range.

# Special Report: Additional Bonus Material

Due to our efforts to try to keep this book to a manageable length, we've created a link that will give you access to all of your additional bonus material.

Please visit http://www.mometrix.com/bonus948/gmat to access the information.